Reading
Mavis Gallant

STUDIES IN CANADIAN LITERATURE

Series Editor: Richard Teleky

ADELE WISEMAN

*Memoirs of a Book Molesting Childhood
and Other Essays*

LINDA HUTCHEON

*The Canadian Postmodern:
A Study of Contemporary English-Canadian Fiction*

ROBERT KROETSCH

*The Lovely Treachery of Words:
Essays Selected and New*

JANICE KULYK KEEFER

Reading Mavis Gallant

Reading
Mavis Gallant

JANICE KULYK KEEFER

Toronto   New York   Oxford
OXFORD UNIVERSITY PRESS
1989

For Robert Weaver

Oxford University Press, 70 Wynford Drive, Don Mills, Ontario, M3C 1J9

Toronto Oxford New York Delhi Bombay Calcutta Madras Karachi
Petaling Jaya Singapore Hong Kong Tokyo Nairobi Dar es Salaam
Cape Town Melbourne Auckland

and associated companies in
Berlin Ibadan

CANADIAN CATALOGUING IN PUBLICATION DATA

Keefer, Janice Kulyk, 1953–
Reading Mavis Gallant

(Studies in Canadian literature)
Includes bibliographical references and index.
ISBN 0-19-540687-7

1. Gallant, Mavis, 1922– – Criticism and
interpretation. I. Title. II. Series: Studies in
Canadian literature (Don Mills, Ont.).

PS8513.A44Z74 1989   C813'.54   C88-095287-3
PR9199.3.G348Z74 1989

Contents

Preface

Mavis Gallant is one of the finest contemporary writers in the English language. Her body of work is prodigious: not only short fiction and novels and a play, but also journalism, essays, and review articles, all of a characteristically outstanding quality. Gallant was born in Montreal and spent most of her childhood, that formative period of a writer's imaginative development, in Canada. Since the age of twenty-eight, however, she has lived and written in Europe, dealing in her fiction with Canadians, Americans, Australians, Eastern and Western Europeans, and their distinctive social and cultural milieux. Gallant is obviously a 'citizen of the world', yet she has deliberately retained her Canadian citizenship, prizing it, perhaps, for the detached and disinterested vantage point it gives her from which to observe other, more historically complicated nations and cultures—the German, for example, or the French and English. By treating Gallant as a Canadian writer I do not mean to delimit her work, privileging those narratives with Canadian settings or characters. Nor, it need hardly be said, do I intend any diminishment of her achievement or curtailing of her importance. But 'Canadian' is more than a label: it tells us much about the social and cultural context that has formed a writer's vision and that continues to influence her, whatever her country of residence might be.

Yet if Gallant is one of our finest writers, she is also one of the most problematic. Her readership is comparatively small, and though she is well-known to readers of *The New Yorker*, such contemporaries as Mary McCarthy, Nadine Gordimer, Muriel Spark, and Alice Munro spring more readily to mind in any discussion of the development of post-war fiction in the English-speaking world. Only a portion of Gallant's prose has been collected in book form, and a portion of that is out of print; there is a pressing need for a collected edition of her works as well as full-scale critical enquiry into her art. The present study is intended as a comprehensive, and thus necessarily glancing, look at Gallant's work, and as a preliminary identification of the rewards and challenges that her writing poses to readers. For if Gallant's very situation as a writer is decidedly anomalous—a Canadian living in France and in French, writing primarily for an American English-language publication—her fiction itself is remarkable for the ambivalent responses it has elicited.

Gallant is a writer who dazzles us with her command of the language, her innovative use of narrative forms, the acuity of her intelligence, and the incisiveness of her wit. Yet she also disconcerts us with her insistence on the constrictions and limitations that dominate human experience. She is a writer who must be savoured in small doses: reading the entirety of her fiction can be like downing a bottle of the finest vinegar. Gallant does not merely observe, she judges as well, and the very obliqueness of her assessments make us all the more wary—is she judging only her characters and the world they have made for themselves, or is she judging her readers as well? It is for this reason, perhaps, as well as her refusal to become a 'media personality', that Gallant is not as well-known, particularly in Canada, as a writer of her calibre deserves to be. Where many of our important writers—Robertson Davies and Margaret Atwood, for example—possess 'high-profile' personalities (which, of course, have little to do with the intrinsic qualities of their fiction), Gallant seems sworn to a cult of impersonality: where superb writers such as Alice Munro and, particularly, the late Margaret Laurence can be described as 'well-loved', in the sense that their fictions create a trusting intimacy between narrator and reader, Gallant is respected and relished, but from a considerable distance.

The purpose of this study is not to destroy that distance, which is, after all, one of the signal achievements of Gallant's writing, but rather to analyze it, to explore how and why it works. One of the chief difficulties critics encounter in writing on Gallant is to get beyond the stage of simply extolling the excellence of her prose. In this study I will attempt to proceed as a critic, not a hagiographer: one of the aspects of her work with which I shall attempt to come to terms is the 'silencing effect' of her authoritative tone and incisive diction, which can turn every narrative statement into a pronouncement *ex cathedra*. Part of the delight in and engagement with any text worth reading is the quarrel one inevitably picks with the text's authorization of its *données*, its insistence that this is the way life is, as far as the writer can see. The more masterful and suasive the narrative, the more the reader may be prompted to resist it. D.H. Lawrence maintained that the novel could contain no 'didactic absolute'; that readers must spend their time evading the laws the text lays down for us.[1] This is no less true when the laws according to which the writer structures her vision of human possibility are presented in elliptical and oblique guise: in such instances it behoves the reader to be on a perpetual *qui vive*.

Mavis Gallant is an important writer because she writes superbly, creating fictive worlds in which politics, history, personal relations, and sexual difference coalesce to create a fabric of reality that compels as much as it repels. As I intend to show, she is not an epigone of modernism, continually controlling chaos within the polished walls of language and structure: such texts as *A Fairly Good Time* and *The Pegnitz Junction* are disrupted narratives in which gaps, chasms, jokes, and pastiche constantly interrupt the 'story-line', frustrating with rare art any expectations of a securely sited story. Even in such marvellously controlled pieces as 'Bernadette' or 'Acceptance of Their Ways' the consolations of form do not compensate us for the disturbances Gallant creates in our fields of response: she means to discomfort us, and she succeeds brilliantly.

'The task of the artist', Lucian Freud reminds us, 'is to make the human being uncomfortable, and yet we are drawn to a great work by involuntary chemistry, like a hound getting a scent; the dog isn't free, it can't do otherwise, it gets the scent and instinct does the rest.'[2] The task of this critical study of Mavis Gallant's work is to explore the parts played by the writer's art and by readerly instinct in creating that uncomfortable yet 'involuntary chemistry' without which books would never be read or written in the first place.

The first chapter deals with the essential literary aspects of Gallant's life, and attempts to sketch out the distinctive concerns of her fiction. Since she is in the process of writing her own memoirs, it would be redundant as well as impertinent to speculate about Gallant's private affairs, or to tease out obscure autobiographical elements in her fictions. Chapter 2 looks at critical and readerly responses to her work in order to effectively analyze the 'problematic' quality of her fiction. In the following chapter I concentrate on interrelated aspects of language, style, and narrative authority by examining representative fictions from different periods of Gallant's writing life. Chapters 4 and 5 concern themselves with two fundamental areas of her fiction: respectively, children and childhood, and the world of women. In Chapter 6 I examine that engagement with history which informs some of Gallant's most significant and rewarding writing. Finally, Chapter 7 looks at her non-fiction, both the journalism with which she began her writing career and the longer 'social narratives' republished in *Paris Notebooks*, in order to establish the fact that Gallant is as significant a writer of non-fiction as she is of short stories and novels.

Praising a biography of Elizabeth Bowen, Gallant remarks with relief that Bowen's writing 'has not been strung up on the gibbet of methodology, or otherwise tortured, and that the language of the biography is free from critical jargon and cant'.[3] While I make use of certain insights afforded by poststructuralist literary theory, I have intended this book to be both informative and accessible to the general reader. Throughout, I make detailed reference to the numerous and accomplished fictions Gallant has published in magazine but not in book form, and to certain of her 'non-fiction' pieces that were not included in *Paris Notebooks*. My prime purpose has been to acquaint readers with the impressive range and scope, and the unsettling force, of Gallant's work, so that they might seek out her writing for themselves,[4] or review what they know of it with more knowledgeable eyes.

*

I would like to acknowledge the generosity of the Social Sciences and Humanities Research Council of Canada, which has greatly facilitated the writing of this study. I'd also like to thank Richard Teleky of Oxford University Press for his interest in and encouragement of this project, Ken Puley at the CBC Program Archives for his ready help in getting me access to recordings of interviews with Mavis Gallant, and the librarians of the National Library in Ottawa, who were tireless in digging out microfilms of Gallant's journalistic pieces for the *Montreal Standard*. As usual, I owe an immeasurable debt to Michael Keefer for his critical acumen and practical help in the writing of this book.

Notes

[1] D.H. Lawrence, 'The Novel', *A Selection From Phoenix*, ed. A.A.H. Inglis (Harmondsworth, Middlesex, England: Penguin: 1979), p. 166.

[2] Quoted by Robert Hughes in 'On Lucian Freud', *New York Review of Books* 34: 13 (13 Aug. 1987), p. 57.

[3] 'Elizabeth Bowen by Victoria Glendinning', in *Paris Notebooks: Essays and Reviews* (Toronto: Macmillan, 1986), p. 233.

[4] Readers wishing to obtain a complete list of Gallant's publications up to 30 June 1982 are advised to consult the entry on Mavis Gallant compiled by Judith Skelton Grant and Douglas Malcolm in the *Annotated Bibliography of Major Canadian Writers*, ed. Robert Lecker and Jack David (Downsview, Ont.: ECW Press, 1984), vol. 5, pp. 179-230.

I Books cited

The Other Paris (OP) 1956; rpt Toronto: Macmillan, 1986.

My Heart Is Broken (MHB) 1957; rpt Toronto: General Publishing, 1982. (Also published as *An Unmarried Man's Summer*, London: Heinemann, 1965.)

Green Water, Green Sky (GWGS) 1959; rpt Toronto: Macmillan, 1983.

A Fairly Good Time (AFGT) 1970; rpt Toronto: Macmillan, 1983.

The Pegnitz Junction (PJ) 1973; rpt Toronto: Macmillan, 1982.

The End of the World and Other Stories (EW) Toronto: McClelland and Stewart, 1974.

From the Fifteenth District (FFD) Toronto: Macmillan, 1979.

Home Truths (HT) Toronto: Macmillan, 1981.

What Is To Be Done? (WTD) Dunvegan, Ont.: Quadrant, 1983.

Overhead in a Balloon: Stories of Paris (OB) Toronto: Macmillan, 1985.

Paris Notebooks: Essays and Reviews (PN) Toronto: Macmillan, 1986.

In Transit (IT) Markham, Ont: Viking-Penguin, 1988.

II Stories cited from periodicals

'The Burgundy Weekend', *Tamarack Review* 76 (Winter 1979), pp. 3-39.

'The Chosen Husband', *New Yorker* 15 April 1985, pp. 40-9.

'Florida', *New Yorker* 26 Aug. 1985, pp. 24-7.

'The Flowers of Spring', *Northern Review* 3:5 (June-July 1950), pp. 31-9.

'From Cloud to Cloud', *New Yorker* 8 July 1985, pp. 22-5.

'Good Morning and Goodbye', *Preview* 22 (Dec. 1944), pp. 1-3.

'Kingdom Come', *New Yorker* 8 Sept. 1986, pp. 32-5.

'Madeline's Birthday', *New Yorker* 1 Sept. 1951, pp. 20-4.

'Night and Day', *New Yorker* 17 March 1962, pp. 48-50.
'The Old Place', *Texas Quarterly* 1:2 (Spring 1958), pp. 66-80.
'Paola and Renata', *Southern Review* 1 (Winter 1965), pp. 199-209.
'The Rejection', *New Yorker* 12 April 1969, pp. 42-4.
'Rose', *New Yorker* 17 Dec. 1960, pp. 34-7.
'Thieves and Rascals', *Esquire* 46:1 (July 1956), pp. 82, 85-6.
'Three Brick Walls', *Preview* 22 (Dec. 1944), pp. 4-6.

III Interviews cited

Beattie, Earl (iEB): 'Interview with Mavis Gallant', CBC *Anthology*, 24 May 1969.

Engel, Howard (iHE): 'Interview with Mavis Gallant', CBC *Anthology*, 9 Jan. 1982.

Gabriel, Barbara (iBG): 'Fairly Good Times: An Interview with Mavis Gallant', *Canadian Forum* 66:766 (Feb. 1987), pp. 23-7.

Gibson, Graeme (iGG): 'Interview with Mavis Gallant', CBC *Anthology*, 31 Aug. 1974.

Hancock, Geoff (iGH): 'An Interview with Mavis Gallant', *Canadian Fiction Magazine* 28: (*Special Issue on Mavis Gallant*, Nov. 1978), pp. 19-67. (Reprinted in Hancock's *Canadian Writers at Work* [Toronto: Oxford University Press, 1987].)

Keefer, Janice Kulyk (iJKK): Interview with Mavis Gallant, Paris: June 1987.

Lawrence, Karen (iKL): 'An Interview with Mavis Gallant', *Branching Out* Feb./March 1976, pp. 18-19.

Markle, Fletcher (iFM): 'Interview with Mavis Gallant', CBC-TV *Telescope*, 22 and 29 Jan. 1965.

McLean, Stuart (iSM): 'Interview with Mavis Gallant', CBC *Sunday Morning*, 19 April 1981.

IV Translations

(The following schedule was supplied by Mavis Gallant in a letter of 7 March 1988.)

Rue de Lille (*Overhead in a Balloon*). Tr. Pierre-Edmond Robert. Paris: Tiersé, 1988 (May.) Tiers also intends to publish, as a *plaquette* or pamphlet, the May 1968 journal from *Paris Notebooks*.

From the Fifteenth District (French title undecided). Paris: Fayard, 1989

L'été d'un célibataire (*An Unmarried Man's Summer*). Paris: Fayard, 1990

Home Truths has been in the process of being translated since 1982, to be published by Boreal Express of Montreal.

Chapter 1

A Literary Life

> A writer's life stands in relation to his work as a house does to a garden, related but distinct. It is the business of critical biography to make the two overlap—to bring some of the furniture out to the garden as it were, and spread flowers all over the house. (PN 234)

Gallant's comments on critical biography, made à propos of Victoria Glendinning's study of Elizabeth Bowen, are curiously revealing. The analogies Gallant seems to be drawing are the reverse of what would commonly be expected: surely the ordered structures of fiction are much more like a house, and the irrepressible growth of a garden—which surely must contain weeds as well as flowers—is much closer to one's idea of what human life is like than the life: house, work: garden equations she has set up. Yet Gallant is a writer who preserves a near-inviolable discretion and decorum about her private life; the manner in which she has arranged her life so as to be entirely free to write fiction seems, in fact, to answer to architectural rather than emotional or social imperatives. She has quite deliberately chosen to have neither husband nor children, those two great deterrents to any woman's attempt to live by and for writing. Moreover, Gallant's work is as abundant as one could wish any garden: eight collections of short fiction, two novels, a play, a book of essays and reviews, and a wealth of as yet uncollected stories, social satires, book reviews, not to mention over a hundred pieces penned for the *Montreal Standard* at the very beginning of her writing life.

Before I set about mingling selected flowers and furniture, however, one preliminary question should be dealt with: Is Gallant a Canadian writer at all? Is the question a valid, or even an interesting, one to pose? Only a vulgar nationalist would accuse Gallant of opportunism or disloyalty in having made her writing life in Europe, and in having published almost all of her work in *The New Yorker* rather than *Saturday Night* or *Canadian Forum*. And could any but the most obtuse literary nationalist believe there is a determinable quality of Canadianness, to be measured like degrees of mercury in a thermometer, according to preordained notions of setting, theme, style, or vision? Gallant, at any rate, considers herself a Canadian despite her protracted residence abroad (HT xii-xv); if one compares her career to that of a John Kenneth Galbraith, for example, one can easily see how strong and persistent her identification with Canada has proved. One should not, however, entertain confident expectations that she, like Mordecai Richler and Norman Levine before her, will one day come 'home'. Gallant has said that if she could no longer live in Paris, she would settle for Manhattan, her second-favourite city (iFM).

It might be more legitimate to inquire about Gallant's particular sense of relation to the country of her birth and childhood, and about her attraction to other cultures, with the aim simply of arriving at a more comprehensive and illuminating portrait of this artist. First of all, Gallant regards herself not as an English-Canadian, but simply as a Canadian: her remark on the Anglo-Irish writer Elizabeth Bowen is illuminating in this regard: 'to be a hyphenated writer is no joke; identity swings like a metronome. The writer is not two things at once, but one thing slightly modified' (PN 232). While declaring herself Canadian, however, Gallant has made clear her absolute detestation and rejection of nationalism and patriotism, which she distinguishes from a 'national sense of self' (HT xv); she has also stressed that, as far as their work is concerned, artists owe 'no more and no less to [their] compatriots than to people at large'(HT xiii). One can interpret this as meaning that artists may choose their subjects from any locale, and may travel to or reside in any country under the sun in order to develop and sustain their art: in this context Henry James, Joseph Conrad, Katherine Mansfield, and Malcolm Lowry come irresistibly to mind.

Gallant's words also have a more practical application: she has always depended on the American market in order to survive as a writer, having had no interest in supporting herself by teaching creative writing or by culling grants when these two means of eking out a living became available to Canadian writers. She possesses a marked bias against British and towards American social and cultural forms. She has confessed herself unable to understand why Canadians are so antipathetic to Americans (iFM): she considers Canadians, in fact, to be 'a species of American' (iEB). Gallant has been quoted as offering the following précis of

Canada's position between the two imperial stools: 'I have this image of the monarchy holding Canada back. It's like a political cartoon. The mother, marked "Queen", is dragging a child named Canada away from the other children in the playground marked USA. Canada points back to where all the other kids are playing and says, "Mother, that's where all the exciting things are being done."[1] That, however, was in 1977—the view some ten years later might be different, particularly since Gallant has recently expressed her disappointment with the current 'homogenized' school of American writing, the results of the institutionalized creative-writing programs that hold sway over the imagination in contemporary America (iJKK). Still, one might take issue with another of her quoted confessions:

> Had I remained in Canada, I would have become one of those frustrated housewives who would like to write and wouldn't. I would read books and listen to music and take night school courses and say to other sensitive housewives who would like to write books and don't, 'Have you read the latest Muriel Spark?'[2]

One thinks immediately, in this context, of just such a frustrated housewife who wanted to write and did—and ended up being published in *The New Yorker* as well. In fact, Gallant's comments can most profitably be read as a reminder of the extraordinary limitations of the literary scene in Canada, especially for women, in the nineteen-forties and -fifties, and also as an indication of just how swiftly conditions can change —as they did for Alice Munro. Gallant, like Margaret Laurence and Elizabeth Smart, needed to move away from Canada in order to write in any serious and sustained way. Laurence returned at a point when it was economically feasible and personally desirable for her to do so; Gallant did not, although she has visited Canada numerous times since her departure in 1950. Canadian characters continue to crop up in her latest work—Lydia Cruche in 'Speck's Idea' and the diplomat-narrator of her new novel, an instalment of which has recently appeared in *The New Yorker*.[3] Whether they are representative Canadians is scarcely the issue—as Gallant has insisted, a story is art, not 'the photography of life'(iEB). These characters are creatures compounded of observation and imagination: their Canadianness is no more or less important than the peculiarly French situations in which Gallant places them. In an intriguing comment upon which she was not asked to enlarge, Gallant named Canada as the country in which people fabricate backgrounds and histories that do not have to fit their actual circumstances; in which the 'invention of reality', and the shock that occurs when reality and dream don't fit, most comprehensively define experience (iEB).

Asked whether she would call herself a 'Canadian' or an 'international' writer, Gallant has replied: 'I'm a writer in the English language. Was Katherine Mansfield a New Zealand writer to you? . . . I *am* a Canadian *and* a writer *and* a woman. If the basic facts of my existence created problems for me, I would not be myself but a character in someone else's fiction' (iGH 61, 62). And here the matter would seem to rest. Given the fact that there now seems to be no incompatibility between being Canadian and possessing international standing—I'm thinking of Margaret Atwood, Alice Munro, Robertson Davies, Timothy Findley—there should be no great difficulty in being an internationally recognized Canadian writer living abroad. Mavis Gallant's position on the subject of the great Canadian identity-or-lack-of-one can, in fact, be seen as deconstructionist. For her the 'national sense of self' is not an affair of essences, but rather of difference: she is Canadian because she is not British or American, or any other nationality. And this is not a mere matter of empty negatives. One could argue that Gallant's characteristic authorial neutrality, the distanced and disinterested tone of her fiction, is integrally related to her sense of herself as a Canadian in Europe, a representative neither of the expired British nor of the declining American empire, but of a country perched precariously between them. Perhaps this is why she can deploy such devastating ironies in portraying Americans or the English abroad—Carol in 'The Other Paris', Bob Harris and Bonnie in *Green Water, Green Sky*, Walter in 'An Unmarried Man's Summer', or the Webbs in 'The Remission'. All these characters bring a set of distinctive social and cultural assumptions to bear on their situations: their historical and political niches are as fundamental a part of their stories as are their love and financial affairs. Gallant's Canadian characters also bear the imprint of the country that made them, but they are remarkably varied: the repressed and bewildered Agnes Brusen of 'The Ice Wagon Going Down the Street' is continents away from the erratic, impulsive Shirley Perrigny of *A Fairly Good Time*, just as Shirley could not be more different from the perfectly disciplined, beautifully free-floating Linnet Muir of 'In Youth Is Pleasure'.

Let us hope that Canadian readers and critics have reached a stage of cultural confidence and awareness, however precarious, in which the desire for a standard make of Canadian writer—whether myth-monger, fabulist, or magic realist—has been succeeded by a recognition of the variety of ways in which Canadians can be excellent writers. In this chapter I'd like to outline one of those ways, a *modus vivendi* chosen by Mavis Gallant nearly forty years ago, and maintained by her today. What follows, then, will be a brief sketch of Gallant's 'writer's progress', drawn from statements she has made in interviews or in prefaces to her work.

*

A writer's visible life and the root of imagination do not connect above ground. (PN 245)

The most succinct statement of Gallant's 'life-project' is to be found in the interview she gave to *Canadian Fiction Magazine* in 1978: 'I've arranged matters so that I would be free to write. It's what I like doing' (iGH 63). Encapsulated therein are the fundamental choices and sacrifices she has made since professing her vocation—to live entirely on her own, avoiding 'the low fever of domesticity' (a quote, from Robert Graves, of which she is especially fond [iEB]); to eschew the financial security that comes with having a steady salary, owning a house, and belonging to a public health-care system. As compressed and illuminating a guide to Gallant's very way of life is to be found in the introduction to *Home Truths*. The most significant phrase in this prefatory text may well be the quotation from Pasternak that she uses as an epigraph: 'Only personal independence matters'(HT xi). In an interview with Howard Engel she supplied the preceding phrases of the quotation: 'Do not organize. Organization is the end of art' (iHE). For Pasternak personal independence was both an impossibility and a necessity in a country that gave its legitimate writers the choice of writing propaganda or of keeping silence—often, by being silenced. For Gallant personal independence was both a personal and a public matter, if not an affair of her very life and death. She did not have the KGB or Zhdanov to contend with, but she did have a family—an utterly 'unmaternal' yet possessive mother and a stepfather she strongly disliked (iBG 26)—in which she felt not so much situated as incarcerated. As soon as she could, Gallant left her mother's home in New York and went back to the city of her childhood, Montreal, where she fended entirely for herself and eventually got a job as a reporter on the *Montreal Standard*. She spent the war years in Montreal, covering a fascinating variety of journalistic beats; yet while happy with her occupation and the mobility it allowed her, she was aware of the ways in which she was being exploited by what might as well be called the patriarchal system. At the age of twenty-three, when she began work for the *Standard*, she quickly realized 'that a male co-worker with less responsibility and doing less work than I, was making eighteen dollars a week more, and at that time eighteen dollars was a lot of money' (iKL 18). On demanding an equivalent raise of salary, Gallant—who was at the time supporting her husband, a student—was told that a man ought to make more than a woman, since he would have a family to support. She has related an anecdote concerning the reassertion of the patriarchal status quo by the men who returned from war to the jobs and women they had left behind them. She was 'reassured' by her male colleagues that the formation of the Montreal Press Club (for men only) was not intended as an affront to female reporters, but as a device to discourage the irritating presence of wives. This explanation, Gallant makes clear, had an 'enormous effect' on her (iKL 19).

Accordingly, she took her life in her hands by quitting Montreal and the now-constricted world of journalism (in which she had also felt that she was beginning to repeat herself) as she had previously quit her familial prison in New York. She had already published fiction in Canadian literary reviews, and decided to submit her work to one of North America's best magazines: *The New Yorker*. Her first submissions were rejected on the grounds that they were too Canadian: then 'Madeline's Birthday', set in Connecticut, was accepted and, on the basis of the $600 cheque that soon arrived, Gallant had the means to put her project into action—the project of giving herself two years to travel in Europe and make her living writing fiction. It was a risky undertaking for a twenty-eight-year-old single woman (she and her husband had divorced by this time) with no private source of income. Gallant was prudent enough to leave open the possibility of returning to journalism in Montreal, should she fail as a fiction writer; she was also single-minded enough to decide she would not be a Sunday writer—if she could not support herself by writing excellent fiction, she would not write fiction at all. She has always been aware of the differences that gender creates in the career of writing: 'A woman has to make choices in a way that a man doesn't. A male writer has someone to protect him from the outside world, to do his typing, to take care of all those little things that can distract . . .' (iBG 27). Her choice was to remain single and independent, to free herself entirely for the pursuit of her vocation.

To write and to live in Europe, about which her reading had led her to form certain high-flown illusions (iHE): these two objectives were inextricably meshed in Gallant's scheme. Having spent most of her childhood in some seventeen different schools (starting, at the age of four, in a Jansenist convent) Gallant has declared: 'There's no milieu I don't feel comfortable in, that I don't immediately understand' (iGH 23). There is, of course, a danger in this instant comprehension: devotees of Alice Munro, for example, might object that Gallant is so quick to slot any given character or experience into her own known schema that she precludes alternative possibilities—those mysterious regions of light and space one glimpses, for example, in such Munro stories as 'Dance of the Happy Shades' or 'Thanks for the Ride'.

Gallant's comfortableness with things foreign or different, the familiarity that has enabled her to write of Europeans or the British as one of them, and not just as a perpetual, observant outsider, goes hand in hand with another condition of the writing life: feeling different, foreign, even on one's own home ground. As Gallant says in her introduction to *Home Truths*: 'Feeling at odds is to be expected: no writer calls a truce. If he did, he would probably stop writing' (HT xiv). The writer's loyalty extends beyond family and nation, she implies, to the truths of imagination (HT xiii). Gallant herself bore this maxim out by turning her attention, in her first published stories, to the Canadian experiences of exiles from Hitler's Europe; fascinated by these war refugees, she 'used to try to write from their point of view; that is, seeing something familiar to [her] the way someone from an entirely different culture might see it'(iGH 31).

This consciousness of extended loyalties and the practice of transforming the familiar into the foreign led Gallant, once she had arrived in Europe, to embark on a different kind of life, and to mix with a different kind of people than did such compatriots as Mordecai Richler and Norman Levine. Fluency in French, which she has described as the European *lingua franca* of the fifties (HT xvii), allowed her to avoid settling in London, which she found neither 'welcoming [n]or open' but 'ugly, heavy, very remote' (iGH 29) from her book-fed expectations. Instead, she established Paris as a base and set out on her travels—to southern France, Italy, Austria, and Spain. She spent the best part of two years in the latter country, to which she was attracted both by its extraordinarily low cost of living and by the mythic status it had acquired for her because of the Civil War. While in Spain she associated with Spaniards as hard up as she: elsewhere she avoided the expatriate Anglo-American set, making friends instead with refugees, whom she has described as 'charmed, incredible people who came to me out of this extraordinary world that was a literary world, really. I was imposing literature on life' (iBG 23). As importantly, however, she was making literature out of the life she was discovering; a great deal of her fiction explores the consciousness and experience of displaced persons: victims, agents, survivors, of World War II, or of the Algerian or the Cold War. What she does not write about, except peripherally, in the Spanish story 'When We Were Nearly Young', is the experience of a young single woman eking out a living as a writer in Europe. Unlike Levine and Richler, she rejected any form of autobiographical fiction: except for the Linnet Muir sequence collected in the last third of *Home Truths*—a sequence whose heroine she describes as 'not an exact reflection' of herself, but as 'quite another person' (HT xxii)—Gallant has generally tried to get inside the skins of characters manifestly different from herself: miserably married women, aging, inept bachelors, Medusa mothers, servant girls, and adolescent prisoners-of-war. Those qualities of abstractness and detachment that characterize her narratives are, in fact, due largely to her fascination with imaginatively taking on the consciousness and experience of people in whom it would seem impossible to take a sympathetic interest. Her story 'Ernst in Civilian Clothes' is a good example of this detachment at work: 'I'm anti-military to the bottom of my heart,' Gallant has confessed, 'but I thought [the disbanded legionnaires] had been treated so shabbily.' (iEB) And so, in a radical extension of understanding, which does not absolve or sentimentalize the luckless Ernst, Gallant creates for us an entrée into his utterly dissociated, frighteningly timeless world of nightmare and subsistence.

If Gallant's writing life, and even her interest in refugees, began well before her flight from Canada, it was in Europe that she wrestled with that most pernicious of the writer's demons: the fear that one may have elected writing as one's vocation without possessing the talents necessary to be the only kind of writer that counts—a superb one. Gallant's own father, she reveals, was 'a virtually untalented painter who passionately lived for this thing for which he had no gift' (iJKK). While living in Madrid she knew not only extreme poverty—not having enough to eat, or warm enough clothes to wear—but something far more devastating: total despair over what appeared to be her failure to write anything worth publishing. Her agent, to whom she had sent a dozen stories, told her that none of them had sold. As she later, quite fortuitously, discovered, the agent was crooked—he had sold all the fiction she had sent him and kept the proceeds for himself, telling the magazines concerned that Gallant was incommunicado. The relief she felt at learning the truth had relatively little to do with her finances: what exhilarated her was this confirmation, however tardy, of her abilities as a writer, of the success of her two years' trial, and of the possibility that she might indeed make writing her profession and Europe her home (iJKK).

Gallant has described herself as possessing an 'urban personality' and as being best suited to 'moving around' (iHE). She has lived for more than thirty years in Paris, declaring that it was the one great European city in which, as a single woman, she could live a more than marginal life, becoming a part of the social class with which she feels most comfortable, though not uncritically so: the bourgeoisie. Knowing that she would never marry again, and understanding that in an Anglo-Saxon society a single woman cannot live her own life, she chose to live in a Latin culture, in which, she insists, she maintains both independence and an agreeable social status (iGG). It would seem that it was not simply her fluency in French that made her settle in Paris: she was very drawn to Rome, she has confessed, but felt that her existence there, as a single woman and a writer, would have had too peripheral a quality. What attracted her to France seems, above all, to have been the esteem and affection with which the French regard writers, and their refusal, as she points out in her essay on Paul Léautaud, to accept poverty as a sign of failure in an artist (PN 143, 180).

Gallant's knowledge of French culture, society, and politics is as impressive as her fluency in the French language. She has written a number of articles dealing with writers as diverse as Colette and Céline, Léautaud and Yourcenar: she has published the journal she kept during the student revolts in May 1968, and a lengthy essay establishing the full context for the 'case' of Gabrielle Russier, the young lycée teacher who was hounded to her death after an affair with one of her students. Gallant is currently at work on a lengthy book dealing with the Dreyfus affair, a project she undertook at the request of Random House, and which, she reports, has been fully researched and now remains only to be written out. Yet alongside this plunge into the private and national life of the Third Republic, Gallant has maintained a passionate interest in contemporary affairs. Her stories of East European and German refugees, to be found in such works as *The Pegnitz Junction* and *From the Fifteenth District*, have been followed by fictions in which the social and political climate created by the New Right plays a significant part, fictions of the kind collected in *Overhead in a Balloon*.

As Gallant's writing makes clear, her experience of Europe has been as much a political as a personal one. During the war she had been an 'intensely left-wing political romantic . . . passionately anti-fascist, [believing] that a new kind of civilization was going to grow out of the ruins of the war' (iGH 39). Once in Europe, however, she found herself living in Spain, under that Franco who had not been deposed or even disgraced after the fall of Mussolini and Hitler. As she reminds us, there was 'a great sense of disappointment. It was only after the war that one felt let down. . . . Over and over, they kept saying, "As soon as the war is finished, we'll get rid of Franco." And people said it and believed it. And Franco died—twenty-five years later—a natural death' (iBG 23). Reminders of World War II, that 'enormous upheaval—not just in history, but in one's life'—surface persistently in Gallant's fiction, forcing us to remember that '[t]he world today as we know it came from that' (iBG 23), but she also insists that we recognize the degree to which the post-war world has vulgarized and turned into kitsch, erotic fantasy, or just plain 'good television' the reality of that 'enormous upheaval'.

Gallant, we may conclude, is European by adoption, Canadian by right of 'citizenship, with its statutory and emotional ties' (HT xii-xiii) and also, we may infer, by imagination, since her childhood was spent here. To quote Margaret Laurence, quoting Graham Greene: 'The creative writer perceives his world once and for all in childhood and adolescence, and his whole career is an effort to illustrate his private world in terms of the great public

world we all share.'[4] But Gallant's personal imaginative world—
the world that informs stories like 'Voices Lost in Snow' or 'The
Doctor' and, in fact, all of her fiction concerned with dislocated
lives—has been profoundly extended and intersected by her experience of and imaginative engagement with some of the most
devastating historical moments of 'the great public world'. It is
this collision of the personal and the public, the North American
and the European, that makes of Gallant such a unique writer: she
may indeed be compared to Henry James, in having voluntarily
quit the country of her birth and youth to establish herself as a
European writer: a writer able to write as a European and not
merely as a foreigner exiled to the social and cultural margins. But
Gallant is not Henry James: her fiction is of her own time and
place—postmodernist and female, if not strictly feminist. And the
major achievement of her work lies in the distinctive way it has
brought together what were previously two mutually exclusive
worlds: the 'woman's world' of personal relationships and the
traditionally 'masculine' world of history and politics. It is with
the interpenetration of these worlds in Gallant's writing that
much of this study will deal.

*

In the preceding paragraphs I have attempted to identify the most
important features of Gallant's writing life: her determined pur-
suit of personal independence, her single-minded application to
fulfilling her vocation as a writer, her comfortableness on what
one would assume to be foreign ground, and her corresponding
interest in otherness and difference, in history's or society's dupes
and victims. In the remainder of this chapter I would like to offer
a composite map of Gallant's fictional world, the primary features
of this writer's imaginative terrain, so as to lay a foundation for a
considerably more detailed look at her writing.

In constructing an overview of Gallant's work, its general lines
of development, several factors must be taken into account. First,
Gallant herself has drawn attention to the often lengthy delays between a story's actual composition and its eventual publication:
thus a story published in the seventies might have been written
one, five, or even ten years before it actually appears. Second, she
is not the kind of writer who is obsessed with one particular idea
or situation, worrying it as a terrier does a bone, until only

splinters are left. She comes back to certain concerns or situations again and again, but from new spatial and temporal perspectives. And these situations are also interdependent, so that a volume of stories one might characterize as predominantly historical—*From the Fifteenth District*, for example—will be grounded in the complexity of interpersonal and impersonally social relationships that distinguishes a collection such as *My Heart Is Broken*. Third, Gallant is that rare kind of writer whose distinctive tone, style, mood, and skills were set almost from the moment she began publishing her work: she doesn't get better and better as she goes along—she was preternaturally good to begin with. This is not to say that all of her writing is of the same superb calibre, that her work does not contain its share of bagatelles, perfectly written but perhaps predictable or even precious. I mean, rather, that it is extremely difficult to take one of her best stories from the fifties, 'The Picnic', for example, and set it beside a recent work like 'Lena' to demonstrate how her technical capacities, her characteristic tone, and the nature of her vision have undergone radical transformations in her development as a writer. As a later chapter will show, Gallant writes many different kinds of narrative: tightly constructed social satires such as 'Acceptance of Their Ways' and 'Grippes and Poche', headlong comic rushes—*A Fairly Good Time*—puzzlingly elliptical and opaque fictions such as 'Bonaventure' and 'The Burgundy Weekend', and more open, many-sided texts: 'The Moabitess' or 'The Four Seasons', and that extraordinarily fragmented, discontinuous novella, 'The Pegnitz Junction'. Yet one can't say that any one kind of narrative is more mature or 'Gallantesque' than any other, though one may prefer, for example, 'The Four Seasons' to 'The Burgundy Weekend'. As we shall see, one's aesthetic response to Gallant's fiction is inevitably a lively and contentious one, since it necessarily involves us in 'epistemological, ethical and moral concerns'.[5]

With these reservations in mind, we can make certain sweeping generalizations regarding the 'situational' pattern of this writer's work as it has emerged over the past thirty-five years. In her fiction of the nineteen-fifties and -sixties, Gallant seems preoccupied with the relations between parents and children, siblings, lovers, husbands, and wives. These relations, unsatisfactory or actively pernicious, are doubly revelatory because they unfold on what the characters perceive as foreign territory—immediately post-war Europe. The paradigmatic text here is *Green Water, Green Sky*, that brief novel whose subtitle could be 'Sanity, Madness, and the Family'. In 1970 Gallant published her other novel, *A Fairly Good Time*, which could be described as a deliberately chaotic revisioning of the principle elements of the earlier novel. The Perrignys' disintegrating marriage and the exceedingly odd relations between mother and daughter, husband and wife, are, however, intersected by a bizarre friendship between the novel's heroine, Shirley (who is crazy but not mad) and an excessively sullen and exploitative Parisienne, Claudie. *A Fairly Good Time* can be considered a kind of runaway, comic swan song to Gallant's extended treatment of predominantly domestic, interpersonal situations in her writing.

The fiction of the nineteen-seventies, in contrast, is pervaded by a preoccupation with the lived 'civilian' experience of European history and politics. *The Pegnitz Junction* (1973) and *From the Fifteenth District* (1979) open the doors to a world of émigrés, exiles, and refugees, the luckless survivors and respectable perpetrators of war and genocide. This is not orthodox historical or political fiction—Gallant declares that she has never been able to take seriously the question of whether she is a tragic writer, and has said: 'I can't imagine writing anything that doesn't have humour. Every situation has an element of farce' (iGH 49; iBG 24). It is for this reason that readers confronting the title novella from *The Pegnitz Junction* or a story like 'Baum, Gabriel 1935- (   )' may be disconcerted and dissatisfied. Gallant does not attempt 'Holocaust' fiction, nor does she write novels-of-ideas that speculate on man-and-history. Rather, she takes the situations that most North Americans would conceive as foreign—war on one's own home ground; the human and material devastation it creates there—and makes them seem disturbingly familiar, located somewhere between the normal and the surreal.

In an interview conducted in 1987 Gallant referred to this period of her fiction: 'I was fascinated by Germany, but the funny thing is that when I finished all those stories . . . I lost interest— not in history or anything, but that overwhelming curiosity I had—just deflated' (iJKK). Once she had answered, in her own terms and to her own satisfaction, the obsessive question of why the Germans had been capable of Nazism, and the origin of those 'small possibilities' for fascism in ordinary people (iGH 41), she was able to turn her attention both to the past—as in the Linnet Muir stories contained in *Home Truths* —and to the present—the stories published in *Overhead in a Balloon*. What distinguishes the latter is the overtly satiric or farcical tone that overrides the subtler ironies of previous fictions. Here we have portraits of the 'post-' generation—grandchildren of those who survived the war, children of the revolutionaries of 1968, indifferent to or ignorant of the catastrophic past. One group of stories—those featuring the *femme fatale* Lena and her erstwhile husband Edouard, the narrator of the sequence—comments on how the elderly survivors of the Second World War arouse derision and even hostility in the young. And yet the protagonists of the Lena stories[6] do not promulgate any heroic version of the past; on the contrary, they controvert the notions we have formed, through narratives and films and photographs, of what World War II was like for those who lived or died through it. Gallant, it would seem, has never tired of deflating our illusions, jostling our expectations, and delighting us with the precision and elegance with which she evokes the most oblique and complex of situations.

If this is the general 'lay of the land', what are the main landmarks of the fictive world created by Mavis Gallant? Chief among them are memory and language, and both derive their primacy from their close connection with childhood (a period of life as important in Gallant's scheme of things as it was for Margaret Laurence). Yet memory, like childhood itself—like so many 'givens' in Gallant's fictive world—is Janus-faced, a double dealer: 'Memory can spell a name wrong and still convey the truth' (HT xxii). It is, however, an utterly malleable substance: what Gallant's fiction shows us, over and over again, is that memory is at the mercy of desire, and can be used to provide 'a coherent picture, accurate but untrue' (EW 33) of that past which is our only means of understanding the present. Perhaps this is how Gallant's own fiction works—conveying uncomfortable or disruptive truths despite or perhaps through her characters' most accomplished efforts to forget or rewrite such truths. In the peculiarly haunting fiction 'Night and Day' (1962), Gallant allows her protagonist, the victim of a car crash, to entertain an alternative to memory: *la belle indifférence*. Utterly indifferent to his fate and future, the accident victim feels 'joyous and pure, as a saint might feel. I have no past and no memories. . . . This is what it means to be free.' Yet this state, 'uncaring, impartial', is recognized for what it is, 'a state of privileged happiness reserved for criminals and the totally insane' (NY 49). Memory, as much as mortality, is the state into which we are born.

Furthermore, in her introduction to *Home Truths* Gallant argues that while one's first years of schooling provide the 'seed of our sense of culture', a more profound culture is contained in memory: 'Memory', she insists, 'is something that cannot be subsidized or ordained. It can, however, be destroyed; and it is inseparable from language' (HT xv). In one of her stories, 'Orphan's Progress' (1965), this symbiosis of language and memory is poignantly demonstrated. Two young sisters are abruptly taken away from their slatternly, manifestly unfit French-Canadian mother, 'whom they loved without knowing what the word implied' (HT 56), and sent to live with their father's mother in Ontario until she dies, a year later. They remain with her long enough to begin to 'speak in the Ontario way'—they had spoken both French and English with their mother—and then are shipped back to relatives in Québec, who refuse to acknowledge, never mind listen to, anything they say unless they speak French. 'Language was black, until they forgot their English' (HT 60). The one word the youngest child does not forget is 'Mummy': she ceases to remember it, however, from the day she is punished for having mentioned it at all. The sisters are separated when the youngest is adopted by a distant relative: made to meet later on in their lives, they 'did not know what to say' to one another. Their memories of childhood—the apartment over the garage in which they had lived with their mother, the bed they had shared with her, and then with each other—are not so much distorted as destroyed by their loss of language. As Gallant develops the issue in this story, language is a more complex and emotional affair than the political question of French versus English. The sisters originally speak a flexible blend of the two tongues: it is only when they are put into environments that demand an either/or response to these languages—one and not so much a hint of the other—that their memories become confused and then finally erased altogether. What the girls have lost, it is clear, is a language of the heart: the mother tongue they possessed without knowing they had it. Physical, linguistic, and emotional dislocation become hopelessly knotted, and this, Gallant implies, is one of the most disabling of all conditions.

Gallant is, in fact, adamant about the need for 'a strong, complete language, fully understood, to anchor one's understanding' (HT xvii). She points to the character Gérard in 'Saturday' (a story 'not about a family or a society in conflict, but about language'), as an example of how a person can become 'intellectually maimed' when deprived of his mother tongue (HT xviii). Gallant herself has deliberately arranged things so that she will not suffer a form of this deprivation despite the fact of her residence in a non-English-speaking country. She acquired fluency in French at an early age, reading as well as speaking the language, and she has spent more than half her life speaking and listening to French. Yet she continues to 'think, write and dream in English' (HT xvii), determined to 'keep a strong writing wall in place' to prevent not just the words but the psychological and intellectual stuctures of these languages from crossing boundaries:

> I cannot imagine any of my fiction in French, for it seems to me inextricably bound to English syntax, to the sound, resonance and ambiguities of English vocabulary. If I were to write in French, not only would I put things differently, but I would never set out to say the same things. Words have an association that the primary, dictionary definitions cannot provide. . . . The French taste for abstraction sails close to rhetoric and can sound false or insincere to an English-speaking listener, while a conversation in English, with its succession of illustrative anecdotes that take their departure from a point, rather than lead to one, soon bores a mind trained in French. (HT xviii)

The rational, disciplined, and obviously successful decision of the adult writer is one thing—quite another is the free interplay of memory and language in which French and English and all their personal and cultural connotations clash or leak, one into the other, as we see in the anecdote Gallant relates about a 'deadlock . . . between a grown woman and a child over a word and its meaning'. The altercation had to do with a children's book called *The Joyous Travellers*, which Gallant had been permitted to take to her Catholic boarding school:

> The nun who taught English, and who might as well have been speaking Swahili for all I ever understood, held the book up to a class of docile little girls and announced that the title meant *Les Joyeux Travailleurs*, or *The Happy Workers*. My objection was taken to be insolence. Insolence was broken by deprivation of food. It is utterly confusing to a small child to be made to swear that black is white, particularly on a subject so vital as language and meaning. I owned up that 'travellers' somehow meant the same thing as 'workers', and received a dish of bread-and-milk. (HT xvi)

This memory of a childhood humiliation is particularly illuminating, for it points not only to the importance Gallant has,
not surprisingly, always placed on language, but, more importantly, to the power and authority one can wield over others in the use
of language. When she remarks that '[c]hildren have fierce feelings about injustice and that is probably why the incident lodged
in my mind' (HT xvi), we see the mesh of memory and language
emblematic of this writer's fictive world and the imagination that
structures it. Memory for Gallant is often associated with a sudden entry into the world of one's childhood—a world with no sentimental associations of a Golden Age, but rather that period of
one's life when, as Linnet Muir remarks, one has all one's wits
about one (HT 316). A period, too, when one most needs them,
since parenthood for Gallant rarely has anything to do with the
'unconditional love' that is the staple maxim of all child-rearing
manuals. In her portrayal of child-parent relationships, parenthood is associated with the exercise of absolute but arbitrary
authority over the powerless and vulnerable. Yet in childhood one
is able to perceive not only the laws and lies one's parents tell one,
but also inexplicable truths or visions—Agnes Brusen's ice wagon
going down the street, for example, or the fairy-tale that Irmgard
remembers in her dreams, in 'Jorinda and Jorindel'.

In an interview for *Canadian Fiction Magazine* Gallant remarked
on how her childhood was marked by 'often unexpected and
violent' changes. 'From the age of four, I was half in life and half
in books. I got on well with other children, but mistrusted adults.
I was not afraid of them, but had the curious idea that they were
incompetent.' From this rather subversive recollection, she went
on to observe, 'All writers have something of the failed delinquent
about them' (iGH 28). Most adults, as well—or so Gallant's fiction
would attest. There, childhood and adulthood form a kind of
möbius strip: the absolute freedom one longed for as a child is
seen to be utterly contingent: the arbitrariness of parental nay-
saying gives way to the obstacles and restrictions thrown up by
social forms and the brutal occurrences of history itself. 'The Moslem Wife' is a paradigm of this continuity between 'the prison of
childhood' (HT 225) and that of adulthood: the quirkily paradisal
relationship that Netta and Jack sketch out for themselves as
children proves no more substantial a home for their married life
than would a house constructed from a deck of playing cards.
Jack's infidelity and casual abandonment of his wife, the priva-

tions and anxieties Netta suffers under the German occupation, and the extremely pessimistic conditions in which their reunion takes place—an unsolicited reunion that spells the end of Netta's own freedom and independence: all of these are simply adult equivalents of that 'portable-fence arrangement' in which children are 'imprisoned' as babies (FFD 40), so as to assure freedom of movement to their parents—a freedom they are, of course, unable to use with either grace or beneficence.

Childhood, in Gallant's fictions, is double-edged: it is that period in which one experiences the only saving truths one will ever be vouchsafed, and yet it is something, too, from which one needs to be saved. So many of the children in Gallant's stories seem to be kidnap victims, waiting out the period of their vulnerability and powerlessness until adulthood arrives to rescue them and make them independent of the mysterious rules and restrictions by which their lives have been bound. Much of her fiction portrays the awfulness of children's being subjected to their parents' whims, and this, one conjectures, is imagination's extension of the conditions of Gallant's own childhood. One senses the shock and rage—and relief—with which she came to realize, around the age of fourteen, that it was not on principle, but rather by whim, that her mother sent her to four different schools in one year. As she remarks, there is an inevitable inequity in any parent-child relationship: 'When you're very small you can't be charged with not getting on with someone who is six times your height. You're not equals. You never are. By the time you've grown up, if things have gone really badly you feel helpless and shut out of the house and alternately neglected' (iBG 26). Yet, characteristically, she refuses to dwell on her tortuous relations with her mother: given a situation in which she had the choice of sinking or swimming, she resolved on the more active option and pursued it with what she describes as 'overwhelming singlemindedness'. As a result she was able to achieve her independence and realize her principal aim: to write as 'a way of life' (HT xxii). Yet the painful experience of childhood and the power politics of family life constitute major territories in Gallant's fictive world, as we shall see in a later chapter.

The risky domain of childhood is complemented by another, infinitely more hopeless area—that of the relations between men and women. Gallant is no feminist, although she is in absolute agreement with one of the central demands of feminists: equal pay for work of equal value. But she insists that the problem of the couple cannot 'be solved by legislation. . . . What goes on between men and women goes on between men and women, *et ça, c'est tout'* (iJKK). What goes on, however, is without exception self-deception and betrayal; at best, delusion à deux, such as Peter and Sheilah Frazier know in 'The Ice Wagon Going Down the Street'; at worst, the psychotic unhappiness of the title characters in 'Malcolm and Bea'. As for the Reeves of 'In the Tunnel' or the Plummers of 'New Years' Eve', the best their marriages reveal is a certain tenderness of infelicity, the result of a couple's lifelong knowledge of one another's flaws and pretensions, cruelties or stupidities. Asked by an interviewer whether her absolute devotion to writing had led to the impoverishment of her own emotional life, Gallant retorted: 'Happiness is for pigs and cows.'[7]

In Gallant's work destructive personal relationships and domestic disharmonies become the medium through which the shocks of history and politics are registered. These constitute that other great domain of her fictive world. She has described her writing as 'permeated with politics' (iGH 33); it is permeated as well with historical experience, whether it be that of Nazi Germany, Mussolini's Italy, *l'Algérie française*, post-uprising Hungary, or the Paris of *la nouvelle droite*. Of all Canadian fiction writers Gallant has shown herself to have the most sophisticated perception of and the most insistent engagement with European politics and history. Moreover, this engagement predated, however much it also impelled, her decision to live in Europe. One can imagine that having achieved at such an early age a remarkable degree of personal freedom and independence, Gallant should, in a generous extension of sympathies, wish these conditions on humanity itself. She became, in fact, the kind of left-wing idealist she so ironically, and yet almost indulgently, depicts via Molly and Jenny in the play *What Is To Be Done?* The tone of that play—which can best be described as satiric disenchantment—was the tone of Gallant's own political awakening after the war. She has described the shock of seeing the first photographs of concentration camps: the devastating impact of this utterly new, unimaginable reality on her faith in culture, on her political ideals, and on her very conception of human possibility (iGH 39). The event was traumatic, she says, in ways that no one of a younger generation can comprehend. For us, Nazi death camps are a part of our common culture, our sense of history—for those of her own generation they were unimaginable, unbelievable: the cancellation of all previous conceptions or assumptions about the progress of history.

Matching this trauma was the 'enormous shock' (iGH 36) of discovering, when she first came to Europe, how politically naïve her ideas about occupied Paris and the war overseas had been. 'I had imagined nearly everyone in the Resistance. The Resistance turned out to be a few thousand out of a population of nearly fifty million' (iGH 36). Gallant had, therefore, to ground herself in the political and historical reality of post-war Europe; it would be no exaggeration to say that her fiction depends on this ground for its very meaning and power. Rather than expanding on ideological issues and political movements, her stories deal with how people provide interior room for these things to develop. The way Gallant writes and the people and situations she chooses to write about show us that we learn no lessons from history, that the world does not become a better, more free and peaceful place after a war to end all wars. Our human refusal or inability to accommodate and be changed by the knowledge history has forced on us is one of her principal texts. But she preaches no sermon rebuking us for having forgotten Auschwitz, Stalin, Algeria: she simply and devastatingly shows how we cannot make ourselves remember, and how succeeding generations cannot perceive the reality of the past.

What Gallant's fiction shows, over and over, is that things are not as we would like to find them—they are what we have made them, and we must acknowledge, even if we don't accept responsibility for, the twisted and broken shape of what remains of our illusions. 'Up close, her moralist's eye selected whatever was bound to disappoint: a stone beach skirted with sewage, a promenade that was really a through speedway, an eerie bar' (EW 142). What is true of the character Sarah ('In the Tunnel') is in many ways true of the writer who created her. As her work reveals, Gallant is a peculiar kind of moralist who sets herself the task not of discriminating between vice and virtue, but of disabusing us of our illusions, particularly those that help us to victimize or abuse others.

Think of the great parade, in her fiction, of divorcée mothers trying to get marital mileage out of the bewildered children they drag across strange continents; or the men who abandon their wives and children for new wives and children, to be abandoned and replaced in their turn; all the husbands and lovers who make themselves believe that no one ever really needs them, that no promises have to be kept—even those made to one's children. One of Gallant's most recent characters, Edouard in 'The Colonel's Child', tears up his novel because he 'can't wrench life around to make it fit some fantasy. Because [he doesn't] know how to make life sound worse or better, or how to make it sound true' (OB 174). Conversely, what Gallant does brilliantly is show us how people wrench life round to fit their dearest or most necessary fantasy. But her fiction pronounces no universal truths—it works by ironic indirection, by oblique angles of vision, and by the presentation of images in clouded mirrors. What she does reveal are the ways we evade knowing ourselves and taking responsibility for our actions. As for the troubling element of opacity one finds in some of Gallant's texts, the sense that one can't quite put one's finger on what this or that story 'means' or 'does', one must concede that it can frustrate and bewilder even the best of readers. These problems will be duly considered; for the moment, however, one might put them into context by recalling an anecdote Gallant related in her interview for *Canadian Fiction Magazine*. She explains how she was given the task, while a journalist on the *Montreal Standard*, of putting captions under the first pictures that paper printed of the Nazi extermination camps. She found the task impossible, for all her skills as a reporter and her gifts as a writer. Some things, she realized, must be left to speak for themselves; it is not the artist's task to write the explanation of things she doesn't understand (iGH 39).

*

What does Gallant understand of the way we live now? That 'we are all travelling. At the end of every day we're one step closer to dying' (iEB). That 'most people feel abandoned—they just think they don't' (iGG). That children are seldom tractable or adults intelligent, generous, or free. That selfish, shallow, silly people are everywhere to be found: the admirable and strong, almost never. That in the 'fight for life' very few of us are capable of action; most of us are simply trapped in 'situations' by our egocentricity, and our lack of vitality and candour (iGG). That cruelty and deception in the name of self-protection are our most common attributes, and that bewilderment, loss, confusion, and dislocation are our most common conditions. That communication, even between people who love one another, is largely 'an uninterrupted dialogue of the deaf' (AFGT 45). That those who are wise will 'not . . . expect too much' (EW 87) from life, and will not give anything away in love. That Paris in the springtime is cold and rainy and stinks of urinals. And worst of all, that what we suffer from is not even the loss but the lack of significance—that meaning itself was never there to be lost.

The metaphysic that informs Gallant's vision of reality is as pessimistic as anything to be found in Joseph Conrad. In a 1974 interview with Graeme Gibson Gallant confessed that as she gets older the idea of God becomes more and more important to her: 'I think I'm going to end up with Luther on one side and Calvin on the other' (iGG). When, on the other hand, Geoff Hancock asked her in 1978 whether she was a practising Anglican, she replied firmly in the negative: though she couldn't 'take seriously a philosophy that excludes the possibility of Divine Intervention', she found it 'hard to believe we're in a world where God walked'. 'Do you think God Incarnate walked here and left us?' she taxed Hancock. 'Look at us. Awful. Dreadful. Get in the Métro and look at people' (iGH 35). She has Molly in *What Is To Be Done?* compare God to a 'cunning old peasant who owns all the land in sight. We meet at fairs and make deals. I promise him this, and he lets me have that. He usually wins' (WTD 58). 'People really must be made in [God's] image,' she has a character remark in 'Overhead in a Balloon', 'for their true face was just as concealed and their true whereabouts as obscure' (OB 58). Later in the same story she has the meditative Walter reflect: 'God is in art . . . then, God *is* art. Today he understood: art is God's enemy. God hates art, the trifling rival creation' (OB 60). So much for the consolations of form, the artist's role as priest of the imagination, and the proposition that art can somehow order and make meaningful the chaos of experience. Gallant's way of seeing is at the furthest possible remove from that of the visionary. She has been accused by some critics of having small eyes, however intent and piercing: of always putting her characters in seats with a restricted view. Nor, one might add, are her readers given ringside seats; her narrators divulge few secrets. Most often we are made to share the same perspective as the character Elizabeth in 'Poor Franzi' (1954): 'she looked around the country, at the hazy summer mountains. . . . Behind the solid peaks were softer shapes, shifting and elusive: she could not have said if they were clouds or mountains. But then, she thought, no one can, unless they have better eyes than mine, and know the country very well' (OP 68).

The question, as we shall see in succeeding chapters, is whether or not we concede that Gallant does, in fact, possess such eyes, whether her knowledge of the country, as set down in her creation of fictive worlds, holds its own against our experience and desire of the extra-literary world we share with her. For this is one of the most problematic yet rewarding aspects of reading Gallant's fiction: we are attracted—through her mastery of language, her narrative authority—to a view of ourselves and our world from which we cannot help but recoil. To read her fiction is constantly to test the imaginative expression of her beliefs—'Most people feel abandoned. They just think they don't'; 'Happiness is for pigs and cows'—against a desire that cannot help but inform our reading: the desire that our lives should admit authentic possibilities of freedom and joy. As we shall see, it is that 'shock' we feel when reality and our dreams don't fit, or when our inventions of reality collide with one another to expose repellent truths, that distinguishes our reading of the fine and discomforting fictions of Mavis Gallant.

Notes

[1] Quoted by Geoff Hancock in 'Mavis Gallant: Counterweight in Europe', *Canadian Fiction Magazine* 28 (*Special Issue on Mavis Gallant*, 1978), p. 5.

[2] Ibid., p. 7.

[3] 'Let It Pass', *The New Yorker* 18 May 1987, pp. 38-64.

[4] 'A Place to Stand On', *Heart of a Stranger* (Toronto: McClelland & Stewart, 1976), p. 13.

[5] Annete Kolodny, 'Dancing Through the Minefield: Some Observations on the Theory, Practice and Politics of a Feminist Literary Criticism' in *The New Feminist Criticism*, ed. Elaine Showalter (New York: Pantheon, 1985), p. 158.

[6] By 'Lena' stories I mean the following: 'A Recollection', 'Rue de Lille', 'The Colonel's Child', 'Lena', published together in *Overhead in a Balloon*.

[7] Dusty Vineburg, 'Mavis Gallant's New Novel Has Quebec Setting', *Montreal Star*, 9 Nov. 1963, p. 12.

Chapter 2

Writer, Critics, Readers

> Don't forget me, Grippes silently prayed, standing . . . in La Hune,
> the Left Bank bookstore, looking for his own name in those quarter-
> lies no one ever takes home. Don't praise me. Praise is weak stuff.
> Praise me after I'm dead. (OB 141)

Gallant's position in the literary world is an anomalous one. She
is a self-exiled Canadian who lives in French, writes in English,
and makes her living by literature. As *Paris Notebooks* reveals,
Gallant has enormous reservations about the practice of literary
translation (the first of her works to appear in French translation
is *Overhead in a Balloon*; plans have been made to bring out *From
the Fifteenth District* and *My Heart Is Broken* over the next two
years). Thus, although she counts writers among her friends and
acquaintances in Paris, Mavis Gallant occupies no conspicuous
place on that city's literary scene: in fact, not until she began hunt-
ing round for precise information on the Gabrielle Russier affair—
about which she was writing a lengthy essay—did the nature of
her professional life become known to her friends, a situation that
gave her 'the most marvellous peace and quiet' (iGH 59). She insists that writers in Paris are not part of any group: 'That . . . existed when there was a café life. And a café life for writers existed
when there was no place to live and houses weren't heated and
people needed to keep warm. Now people are at home with their
television . . . and their place in the country' (iJKK). She is adamant
that 'flocking together is the last thing writers should do—it's different with painters; they have to go to each other's studios to look
at the work [each is doing]. But I don't think writers have any particular conversation. Particularly nowadays when they talk about
publishers and grants' (iJKK).

Nowhere, in fact, does Gallant show herself more resistant and
deflationary towards the mystique of the writer than in the satiric
'Grippes' sequence in *Overhead in a Balloon* ('A Painful Affair', 'A

Flying Start', 'Grippes and Poche'). The pettiness, pomposity, backbiting, financial insecurity, consequent greed and exploitativeness of those who pursue fame in the literary life are chronicled in this sequence, which describes the war of words between that eminent novelist of the Fifth Republic, Henri Grippes, and his English arch-rival, Victor Prism, for recognition by the literary establishment. In the process Gallant portrays the beautifully bizarre relations between Grippes and his tyrannical patroness Mary Margaret Pugh (who 'did not believe in art, only in artists' [OB 109]), and the ludicrous exchanges between Grippes and the taxman Poche, with his 'base' but original idea that all writers kick back a percentage of their income, paying 'publishers to publish, printers to print, and booksellers to sell' their own work (OB 141). At times one expects Gallant's tongue to burst through her cheek: certainly the 'Grippes' sequence establishes the irreverence with which she views that peculiarly self-important, increasingly marginal topography we grace by the name of 'the literary scene'.

Gallant's presence in the extra-literary world of English-language writers, the world of literary associations and mega-conferences and magazine covers, has been minimal by choice. While not reclusive—she has, over the years, given several readings in Canada, and has served as writer-in-residence at the University of Toronto—she prefers to put her writing, not her personality, on public view. She has no academic ties—indeed, she did not even attend university; she belongs to no literary coteries and seems not to be affiliated with any political or social groups. Though utterly refusing the traditional choices and limitations associated with female experience, Gallant cannot be described as a feminist. She has not, to my knowledge, spoken out or written on such issues as censorship or the fate of writers who also happen to be political prisoners. What she does have to say about social justice or change goes into her fiction or essays, not into a microphone.

Mavis Gallant seems to have been born a 'language animal': bilingual at an early age, able to read at four years old, she has been 'half in life and half in books' seemingly forever (iGH 28). Her own literary tastes are, not surprisingly, cosmopolitan: the Russians, the French, individual American, English, and German writers—for example, Edith Wharton and Eudora Welty, Elizabeth Bowen, Günter Grass, and Siegfried Lenz (iGH 21). The English-language writer to whom one wants to compare Gallant is Henry James, and yet she would seem to have no more than a desultory interest in his career and no more than a partial acquaintance with his work (iJKK). The parallels are obvious: James and Gallant both needed not only to travel but to live in Europe in order to write: both deal equally well in their fiction with the 'international theme'—brash and innocent North America meets the Avenging Angel of Europe—and with European life and manners from within an entirely European perspective. Both are masters of the language and prefer obliquity, implication, and indirection to more overt and direct narrative strategies and styles. Smaller points of comparison can be drawn: both writers are particularly adept at giving their characters names that fall just within the bounds of possibility while arching toward symbolism or absurdity: Gallant's Cat Castle, Miss Mewling, and Wishart put us in mind of James's Henrietta Stackpole, Fleda Vetch, and Basil Ransom. Both writers are particularly good at depicting how vulnerable children can be when suffering from the neglect and sometimes the special interest of their parents and protectors. Finally, Gallant gives every sign of being as prolific as her American precursor in the realm of short fiction—her 'Collected Stories' may well run to as many volumes as Henry James's.

The writer whom Gallant has described as a profound and early influence is, however, Chekhov (iGH 31). Indeed, the air of perplexity and bewilderment, stasis and circuitousness so characteristic of the Russian master's writing is breathed, *mutatis mutandis*, by Gallant's characters. *What Is To Be Done?* may well be a 'political romp' and cabaret comedy, as Gallant has described it,[1] but in many ways it resembles *Three Sisters* as well. For at the end of Gallant's burlesque analysis of women and war, Molly and Jenny are no closer to the conditions of '*Vie, Victoire, Vérité*' emblazoned on Jenny's wall than Chekhov's Masha, Irina, and Olga are to that Moscow in which their lives are supposed to begin. Molly has thrown over the uplifting visions of the 'Internationale' for the practical benefits to be obtained by looking like a *Vogue* model: the irrepressibly idealistic Jenny, who imagines that the first thing 'the men' will do, now that the war is over, is get rid of Franco—promises, in her next-to-last words to her newspaperman boss, to be 'a good girl' (WTD 109) so that she can rise to the top of her field—the giddy heights of being an assistant-to-the-editor.

If Gallant's characters are as psychologically paralyzed and physically stranded as Chekhov's, she does not often bathe them in the gentle Scotch mist of melancholy that is the predominant Chekhovian mood: there is a dryness, an ironic scorch to the fabric of her fictions, by which those who cultivate both selfishness and helplessness and those who evade their responsibilities are exposed to a relentless, if obliquely trained, light. In the context of Russian writing one recalls the interview in which Gallant reiterated the maxim that all writers can be characterized as belonging either to the camp of Tolstoy or to that of Dostoevski. Not surprisingly, she declared her own partiality to Tolstoy(iEB). There are no Natashas in Gallant's fiction, and Shirley Perrigny (of *A Fairly Good Time*) makes an exceedingly odd Anna Karenina, but one understands that Gallant's preoccupation with social and historical rather than metaphysical or psychological experience places her closer to Tolstoy than to his equally great contemporary.

Proust, however, is Gallant's favourite writer, with Camus a close second in the French canon (iFM). She has called *Remembrance of Things Past* 'the greatest novel ever written about anything'(iGH 33), and it is certain that Proust's obsession with the processes of memory and time, and his equally powerful fascination with the deceptive surfaces of certain classes of society, have influenced the way Gallant structures and peoples her own fictive worlds. A story like 'Good Deeds', with its delicious portrayal of a rapacious Riviera *grande dame*, and a sequence such as the Linnet Muir stories of *Home Truths*, in which memory functions as a subterranean river, washing up a whole underworld of images and associations, show the distinctive imprint of Proust the way a page of fine notepaper subtly displays its watermark.

As the essays reprinted in *Paris Notebooks* reveal, Gallant is familiar with the work of such well-known writers as Colette and Céline, Nabokov and de Beauvoir, but she is also intrigued by writers who to most English readers would seem marginal or distinctly odd. She admires the inimitable 'dragonfly prose' (PN 196) of Jean Giraudoux and the paradoxical nature of Paul Léautaud, 'an instinctive writer who lacked imagination (he could not write about anything except his father, his mother and himself) . . . a narrow Parisian who never traveled and still knew that "one's country is one's language", and that "the only country that matters is life itself"' (PN 145). Gallant is clearly fascinated by Léautaud's bizarre relations with his disastrous parents, and even more so by that loyalty to language, that sense of one's writing as the prime constituent of identity, which her own writing life has shown her to share.

Yet the contemporary writer she most admires is another expatriate: Marguerite Yourcenar, on whom Gallant has written a long and wonderfully perceptive essay. The epithet she finds for Yourcenar, 'limpid pessimist', could serve just as appropriately for Gallant. Indeed, the account she gives of Yourcenar's work is fascinating for the reflections it casts on her own way of seeing and writing. I do not mean to suggest that Gallant has gone to school to Yourcenar, appropriating her substance or style, but rather that she has discovered in the Frenchwoman's work a correspondance to her own. (Gallant herself prefers to use the term 'acquisition' rather than 'influence' when talking of how reading the work of other writers affects her own writing. One's own distinctive, inimitable style, she suggests, is 'the distillation of a lifetime of reading and listening, of selection and rejection' [PN 179]).

If one were to take the autobiographical approach, one might conjecture that Gallant's fascination with Yourcenar stems partly from domestic and familial similarities. Gallant's relations with her decidedly unmaternal mother were abysmal; Yourcenar, we learn, never knew her mother, and was thirty-five before she asked even to see a photo of her. Gallant draws our attention to the way in which Yourcenar gives 'the back of her hand' to all her close relatives (PN 182), and to the French writer's 'telling remark' that 'family ties have no meaning if they are not strengthened by affection' (PN 183). What seems most important in this context, however, is Gallant's clear admiration for someone who elected writing as a way of life (and emotional independence from family, at least, as the condition for and guarantee of that life). Then too, there is an obvious parallel between the physical and linguistic displacement both writers have undergone, in reverse, as it were: the European to North America, the North American to Europe. It is with considerable sympathetic experience that Gallant observes: 'Writers who choose domicile in a foreign place, for whatever reason, usually treat their native language like a delicate timepiece, making certain it runs exactly, and that no dust gets inside. Mme Yourcenar's distinctive and unplaceable voice carries the precise movement of her finest prose, the well-tended watch' (PN 189).

As far as that finest prose is concerned, Gallant's delineation of its distinctive characteristics is perhaps most illuminating for the

similarities revealed between Gallant's own art and that of Yourcenar. This is particularly evident in her description of the 'cool'
to 'freezing' temperature of Yourcenar's work and her appreciation of 'the calm and dispassionate approach' that results from
such narrative chill (PN 181). That 'marble corridor' ending in a
'wall of ice' (PN 187) to which she likens Yourcenar's fictive worlds
seems in many ways to be an icier version of the worlds portrayed
in Gallant's own fiction. 'She believes that authors who write
directly about "the mystery and reality of sex" show bad manners,' Gallant discloses, going on to observe that this is 'an unex-
pectedly pinch-mouthed observation from someone so supremely
gifted at conveying the mystery and reality of erotic tensions' (PN
186). It is a surprising criticism for Gallant to make, since she herself writes only rarely and briefly about sexual experience, and
since she relies on indirection and obliquity to create erotic tension
in such stories as 'The Other Paris' and 'The Cost of Living'.

And finally, Gallant's comments on Yourcenar's view of
women are of special interest for the light they shed on Gallant's
own narrative practices. She describes the various mysogynists
Yourcenar writes about, and 'the dismal ranks of scolds, harpies,
frigid spouses, sluts, slatterns, humorless fanatics, and avaricious
know-nothings who people her work, and who seem to have been
created for no other reason than to drive any sane man into close
male company' (PN 187). Gallant's own female characters in their
'kitchen in a slum' (GWGS 114) are certainly less repellent: certain
of them, like Flor in *Green Water, Green Sky*, have a pathetic
fragility and a stubborn integrity that distinguish them from the
true harpies and leeches. The sisters in the 'Carette' stories[2] are
shown to be delightfully superior to the lumpen men in their lives,
and the exemplary character in all of Gallant's fiction is, of course,
Linnet Muir, who seems to occupy a higher, finer ground than do
most of the men and women she encounters. Yet if in Yourcenar's
fiction '[w]omen transmit death, the void, until they set the final
example by dying' (PN 187), while in Gallant's they merely flutter
and rattle round a pre-established void, Gallant's readers, inhabit-
ing as they do a world profoundly altered by the advent of
feminism, may find themselves vigorously dissenting from the
restricted possibilities she offers her female characters, the limited
strengths and abundant weaknesses with which she hampers
them.

Yourcenar's 'strong and original literary intellect' (PN 180) is one, Gallant suggests, steeped in the seventeenth century: by reason of the limpid, disciplined nature of her style, and the cast of her mind—'the quirks and prejudices that enliven her conclusive opinions, the sense of caste that lends her fiction its stern framework, her respect for usages and precedents' (PN 181)—she belongs to the vanished world of Poussin and Racine. No more than Gallant herself is Yourcenar an experimental or visionary writer; she does not fabulate but narrate, and what she tells us is not consolatory:

> How the body betrays us. Why we destroy faith and one another. That we can produce art and remain petty. What we can and cannot have entirely. Jealousy, but not envy, is allowed free entry. Reciprocated love is never mentioned and probably does not exist. The high plateau of existence, the relatively few years when our decisions are driven by belief in happiness or an overwhelming sense of purpose are observed, finally, to be 'useless chaos'. (PN 181)

'That useless chaos', remarks Gallant, 'is what fiction is about' (PN 181). Certainly the project of Yourcenar's fiction, as Gallant describes it above, is strikingly similar to Gallant's own, as if the Canadian writer had been reading the French through the screen of her own 'conclusive opinions', usages, and precedents. Again, when Gallant describes how, despite the derivation of Yourcenar's pessimism 'from a French tradition of right-wing literature', Yourcenar's own 'life has been a reflective alliance with the rejected and put-upon, and she never misses a chance in an interview to overhaul racists and bigots of every stripe' (PN 181), one cannot help thinking of Gallant. Though her own pessimism may have its roots in her disillusionment with the liberation ideology of the pre-war Left, and though her affiliations are obviously with 'old-fashioned, liberal and humanist' beliefs (HT xiii) rather than with those of the New Right, one need only read Gallant's journal of the events in Paris in May 1968, her account of the Gabrielle Russier affair, her writings on contemporary Parisian life, and such stories as 'The Four Seasons' to observe just such a 'reflective alliance' with the poor, oppressed, and exploited on her own part.

At the heart of Yourcenar's vision, Gallant tells us, is this desire: to face failure, betrayal, death with open eyes. 'Wrenched out of the heart of her work, with the possibility of love, is any hope of redemption.' 'Violence and cruelty are played out against a world that seems immobile, like . . . a stage set' (PN 184). The mirror image of Gallant's own vision, it would seem. And yet Gallant, by her own admission, cannot take anything—even this appalling metaphysics—seriously: 'I can't imagine writing anything that doesn't have humour. Every situation has an element of farce. . . . Look at the fits of laughter that you get at a funeral, at a wake. It's emotion, and in a way it's relief that you're alive' (iBG 24). One grabs, at first, at the terms 'tragic' and 'comic' to distinguish between Yourcenar's and Gallant's fictive articulations of this vision. But the more appropriate terms for these late-twentieth-century writers would seem to be, respectively, stoic and ironic: the displaced, the only possible present forms of the classical genres.

*

In her essay on Marguerite Yourcenar Gallant warns us against identifying the beliefs and sentiments of any given character within a fiction with those held by the author of that fiction. As *Paris Notebooks* makes clear, Gallant's sympathies and loyalties, her beliefs and ideas are infinitely broader, deeper, more generous and humane than those she allows any but an exceedingly slim 'saving remnant' of her characters to hold. But then the question poses itself: Why write so insistently about characters whose experience and actions—or rather, lack of them—confirm an overwhelmingly pessimistic notion of human possibility? Like Yourcenar, she would have us face this world with open eyes; lucid pessimism would seem to be the writer's only truthful response to the world as it is for most of its inhabitants; the wry, even grotesque humour that accompanies an ironic perspective would seem to be the redeeming feature of observing and recording such a dismal world. She has defined happiness—for herself— as knowing how one wants to live, achieving that way of life, and having the health to enjoy and continue it: making one's living by doing the only thing one is interested in is, she declares, 'sublime' (iFM). That so few people are able to realize this kind of happiness, and that—as her fiction shows—most conceptions of human happiness are hopelessly delusive and unrealizable, seems, however, to belie Gallant's contention that her characters are not portrayed in a pessimistic or hopeless manner. 'They have as much chance as anybody', she says, to free themselves from the situations in which they are entangled (iGG). Yet anyone who reads Gallant's work cannot help but come to the conclusion that for her there are two kinds of people: the free and the trapped. The free are rare birds indeed: by extraordinary acts of single-mindedness (Linnet Muir, Magdalena in the Lena stories) they establish their independence or float over a variety of minefields. The trapped are of two sorts: those helplessly imprisoned by circumstance (children, servants, the victims of history) for whom she has compassion; and those walled-in by their stupid and selfish desire for the kind of happiness connected with romantic love and social status, for whom she demonstrates a kind of regulated contempt.

If, according to Gallant's vision of reality, human beings possess drastically limited possibilities, what is her notion of reality itself? The little she has revealed about the art and practice of her fiction is helpful in this context. What any given author says in his work is 'that something is taking place and that nothing lasts' (PN 177): flux, impermanence, is the condition in which narrative is created, to which it must submit, and by which it is inevitably swallowed. 'Against the sustained tick of a watch, fiction takes the measure of a life, a season, a look exchanged, the turning point, desire as brief as a dream, the grief and terror that after childhood we cease to express' (PN 177). Perhaps this recognition of the radically insubstantial nature of reality is what impels Gallant's perfectly precise use of language, and her development of a position of detachment and disinterestedness within her work itself. For the ultimate irony would seem to be that the writer of fiction only claims to make something lasting and solid out of transitory phantoms: the assurance and authority that stem from mastery of language become sophisticated forms of whistling in the dark.

Language, not plot or characterization, is for Gallant the *nec plus ultra* of fiction. 'A loose, a wavering, a slipshod, an affected, a false way of transmitting even a fragment' of these phantoms makes the reader 'suspicious: What is this too elaborate or too simple language hiding? What is the author trying to disguise? Probably he doesn't know. He has shown the works of the watch instead of its message' (PN 177). In her fondness for the watch metaphor, used twice in the essay 'What Is Style?' and resurfacing in her article on Yourcenar, Gallant betrays a surprisingly straightforward conception of fiction and language: 'living prose' contains an 'inborn tension and vitality'. When used with skill and style, such prose can directly convey meaning—fiction does indeed possess and express a 'message'. And, most importantly, 'content, meaning, intention and form must make up a whole, and must above all have a reason to be' (PN 177). All this is somewhat disconcerting, since these are precepts with which any nineteenth-century writer or reader would be comfortable, but from which many contemporary writers, radically distrusting language and espousing the faith that 'reality' (a term intelligible only within quotation marks) is inexpressibly other than anything we might conceptualize, would dissent. It is doubly astonishing to read an essay such as 'What Is Style?' and try to attach these conventional concepts of the reliability of language and the primacy of meaning over process to some of the decidedly baffling and disconsolate fictions that Gallant has created.

In 'What Is Style?' Gallant declares her desire for invisibility, both in her fictions themselves and in her manner of writing them (PN 176). Consequently, she is cagey about the method and meaning of her work—the one subject of analysis closed to her, she insists, is that of her own writing (PN 177). Her 'prose rhythm' is 'near to the way [she] think[s] and speak[s]'; her manner of writing has become 'instinctive' (PN 176), and towards her finished work she displays a decided disengagement: 'Once too close, the stories are already too distant' (PN 176).

A marginally more rewarding account of her practice of writing surfaces in the interview conducted by Geoff Hancock for *Canadian Fiction Magazine*. It is no surprise to learn there that Gallant has no patience with theory, that she does not start with a governing idea or pattern and write to conform to it. 'There's no mystery and there's no pattern [in my work] that I'm aware of' (iGH 45). It is her habit to keep journals and notebooks, although she does not consult them when she is writing, preferring to let 'memory and imagination do the work'. Unlike Joyce with *Ulysses*, she refuses to tamper with the deformations of memory, to check the accuracy of how and what she has remembered (iGH 31). 'Once something is written, I forget its source. Once you have put reality through the filter and turned it into that other reality called fiction, the original ingredient ceases to exist. Ceases to exist in memory, that is' (iGH 28). If the actual writing of a story induces a kind of amnesia in the writer, the appearance of the work in print produces something 'physically unpleasant', like nausea: 'I think it is because I read so much while I'm writing it. . . . Page by page to the point of obsession. . . . But when it's finished, it is finished forever. I don't want to hear about it anymore'(iGH 48).

There is a final point to be considered in any discussion of Gallant's mode and nature of writing, and that is the influence of *The New Yorker*. She has vigorously and persistently denied contentions that she is a '*New Yorker* writer', insisting that, on the contrary, the magazine has been exemplary in its editing, so that the work she submits always remains her own (iGH 33).³ Yet it can be argued that her alliance with *The New Yorker* has led her to Americanize more than her spelling. Perhaps some instinctive sympathy for the 'American way' underlies her knuckle-rapping of Simone de Beauvoir's 'personal and political' dislike of America, a 'deep resentment' based on 'fatal inaccuracies' (PN 210), none of which Gallant specifies, though she gives examples of the other gaffes committed in de Beauvoir's *All Said and Done*. One may also wonder whether the 'deflationary mode' Gallant favours in writing about Europeans and the English, her insistent skewering of our expectations that anything European must be superior, in terms of culture or civility, to its North American equivalent, has been influenced by her sense of what Americans wish to hear about themselves. A story such as 'Vacances Pax', a trenchant demystification of the 'One Europe' ideal, would certainly have been gratifying to an American reader in the 1960s, since it shows that Europeans can be as vulgar, pretentious, stupid, and barbarous as the economically ascendant Americans were commonly held to be. At the same time, however, Gallant can be seen to be poking fun at the insistently romantic and naïve vision of Europe to which North Americans seem indissolubly joined: consider this description in 'Speck's Idea' of a Paris street, 'resembl[ing] a set in a French film designed for export, what with the policemen's white capes aesthetically gleaming and the lights of the bookstore, the restaurant, and the gallery reflected, quivering, in European-looking puddles' (OB 5).

As far as style and vision are concerned, Gallant's unique way of seeing the world, her notion of what is there to be seen, and the manner in which it can be most convincingly transcribed, the influence of *The New Yorker* becomes the reddest of herrings. Obviously Gallant did not set out to write stories that would be clones of what *The New Yorker* was publishing in the late forties and early fifties. Just as obviously, the magazine accepted and has continued to publish her work because of its quality and not its content or idiom. The reasons Gallant has given for her loyalty to this particular magazine are convincing: the patience and encouragement of William Maxwell; the fact that he did not 'put a . . . hand' on her work, editing it in such a way that her writing would have 'cease[d] to be [her own]' (iGH 33); the magazine's good offices in helping her to get free of a crooked agent at a particularly difficult financial period in her writing life (iJKK). Nevertheless, certain critics persist in accusing Gallant of writing to order for *The New Yorker*, and this would seem to indicate an element of dissatisfaction or dissent in the overall reception of her work. The nature of this problematic reception will be well worth examining.

*

Mavis Gallant is a writer of an unsatisfactorily intelligent kind. Like Mary McCarthy, whom she somewhat resembles, she often seems at the same time admirable and insufficient, and from time to time heartily dislikable. (Robert Taubman, review of *An Unmarried Man's Summer*)[4]

That Mavis Gallant refuses to make . . . connections for us, refuses to speak as a thoughtful omniscience behind her characters, might be admired as indicative of her belief that life's oddities mustn't be ironed out into the orderly understandings of fiction. Yet by cultivating incongruities, juxtaposing voices and memories that fit together in only the craziest way, the author might seem to evade responsibility for saying or caring very much about her characters and their situations. This is the Palace of Art, and Mavis Gallant is perilously close to residing there in a novella which in the long run feels too clever, too oblique, too arty for its own moral and human good. (William Pritchard, review of *The Pegnitz Junction*)[5]

I would shut the book or paper on anyone who uses the word 'arty'. Right then. So that's the end of that. (Mavis Gallant [iGH 60])

Mavis Gallant has always received high praise from reviewers and critics outside Canada: in the last decade or so her work has inspired euphoric commentary—one cannot call it criticism—from the bulk of Canadian book reviewers as well. Where Peter Stevens was forced to lament in 1973 that her fictions were 'more thoroughly ignored than most recent Canadian writing',[6] the vast majority of our current critics acknowledge Gallant's mastery of language and the forms of narrative, the authoritative elegance of her style, the shrewdness of her authorial eye. Since the publication of *Home Truths* and her winning of the Governor General's Award in 1981, graduate students and academic analysts of fiction have corrected the previous dearth of attention paid to Gallant's writing: articles and theses are accumulating and several scholarly books on her work are being readied for publication.

There has been a tendency towards theme-tracking in many studies of her fiction, with critics ignoring Gallant's own insistence that 'content, meaning, intention and form' make up the fictional whole (PN 177). Among the themes run to ground are those of family and marriage, treated à la Austen; of personal relationships, à la Bloomsbury; and of 'inner conflicts' of bewildered, compromised, feckless individuals, à la Chekhov.[7] Gallant is also portrayed as being on the track of that irrepressible theme, the individual's problematic quest for freedom from middle-class conventions and expectations. Others depict her as preoccupied with exile and all its nihilistic or existentialist paraphernalia, so that she can be seen as clinging to the coat-tails of Camus, or as clutching the 'fag-end' of modernism.[8] Conversely, she has been presented as a writer whose concerns are obstinately social and political, rather than metaphysical: 'the grasp of a society, the refusal to treat it as freakishly unrelated to other societies and the rest of life' are what truly distinguish her fiction.[9] More than one critic has stated the case for Gallant's conception of history as being central to the structure and significance of her work.[10] Finally, her obsession with time and memory, which together emerge as the 'principal hero or villain' in her fiction, is declared to be the heart of her matter.[11]

Gallant's fictive world is rich enough to accommodate all these interpretations of the central concerns of her writing. Yet her work is overwhelmingly more than the sum of its 'themes'. Her fictions are masterfully constructed, and critics are correct in drawing our attention, as does George Woodcock, to the intricate texture and surface polish of her narratives.[12] Yet what one queries in this context is the delimiting effect of exclusive emphasis on her undoubted 'acuteness of insight, exactness of detail, radiance of imagery'.[13] Were there nothing else to be found in a work like *From the Fifteenth District* Gallant would still deserve attention as a stylist, a minor master whose talents for ironic understatement, ellipsis, and epigram are nevertheless the literary equivalent of petitpoint, whereas the narrative dynamism, the range and breadth of vision characteristic of a Margaret Laurence or a Robertson Davies are the hallmarks of a major writer.

It is not the breadth but rather the intensity and ruthlessness of her vision that makes Gallant such a disturbing and demanding writer. She resembles that other expatriate in Paris, Samuel Beckett, in the overwhelmingly negative view she has of life on 'this bitch of a planet'. It is interesting to note that what the majority of critics have canonized as profoundly true and moving in Beckett's restricted view of human existence would likely be found merely abrasive and 'bitchy' in Gallant.[14] Perhaps this is because one can classify Beckett's disgust with life as safely metaphysical, his pessimism as cosmic, whereas the sources of Gallant's tunnel vision are visibly social, political, historical—things, in other words, that we are theoretically able to alter. Beckett's fictive world is the literal translation of *reductio ad absurdum*, a limbo created by a minimalist use of language. The fictive worlds Gallant creates through her disciplined use of an abundant, infinitely textured and nuanced language, are, however, the recognizably common world shared by reader and writer: a world of children and adults, husbands and wives, work, love, relationships—which makes it all the more jarring to find that in this world failure and self-deception are the rule.

It is also a fictive world created by a woman and 'placed' by a literary establishment that has always been reluctant to concede major status to women writers. Inadequate response to Gallant's work includes the puzzling attitude that leads a George Woodcock to exclaim that, despite the acute historical sense informing it, her mature work is 'in no way male and ideological'—the product of intellectual deliberation—but rather, 'feminine and intuitive'; or a Robertson Davies to describe 'The Pegnitz Junction'—a novella Gallant herself describes as an attempt to come to conceptual and imaginative grips with the phenomenon of fascism—as a love story.[15] Discomfort with the ironic and disinterested quality of her narrative tone may also stem from expectations and conventions having to do more with gender than with genre. For nowhere in Gallant's work do we find those traditional 'feminine' qualities of tenderness, nurturing, circumspection, and deference belonging to the proper lady and the woman writer.[16] It is interesting, in this context, to note some of the titles under which her works have been reviewed—by men and women: 'Vanishing Creams', 'Love's

Grim Remains', and 'Good Housekeeping'.[17]

While it is true that much of Gallant's early fiction elaborates the layout of that 'kitchen in a slum' (GWGS 114) which, according to one of her characters, comprises the world of women, she has been careful to show how the doors of that kitchen connect to the larger but equally painful, messy, and confined space that has always been the world of men. In works such as *The Pegnitz Junction* and *From the Fifteenth District* she approaches the 'shambles' of history largely from the perspective of female experience—through the eyes of the wives, mothers, mistresses of the men who fought, planned, and profited from the wars. Helena, who has narrowly escaped extermination in a concentration camp, tortures in the 'friendliest' way the middle-aged police commissioner who finds her references to her Jewish background baffling and embarrassing ('The Old Friends'); Bibi and Helga, two German girls whose families and identities have been obliterated by World War II, both defer to and expose the financial-cum-military success of the man who was the one's lover and remains the other's husband ('An Alien Flower'); Carmela, a young Italian servant girl, is exploited by her frightened, déclassé English masters on the Italian Riviera at the outbreak of world war ('The Four Seasons'); Netta, deserted by her charming husband, survives the wartime occupation of the Riviera hotel she owns, and enjoys a brief, precious independence and clarity of mind that were impossible with her husband at her side ('The Moslem Wife'). In the experience of these characters, war between countries, classes and sexes are inextricably entangled. There is no new breadth, nobility, or transcendence in the vision of reality that Gallant offers these women and, through them, the reader. If the world of women is a kitchen in a slum, then the world from which they have been so long excluded is the slum itself—or perhaps only the bombed-out shambles of one. And here is another possible disappointment, for both male and female readers of Gallant's work: the 'man's world' is shown up as the drab, petty, and chaotic place it has always been, yet there is no brave new world to put in its place. A visionary Gallant is not— we are given no panoramic view of the past nor any Handmaid's-eye view of the future, just small patches of the present, patches with innumerable small holes bored through, letting in pinpoints of light.

In subsequent chapters I will develop the argument that the political, historical, and social sense that permeates and shapes

Gallant's best fiction does make her a major and not a marginal writer in the English language. What I would like to press here is the point that, in any adequate treatment of Gallant's work, not just thematic structure or aesthetic surface but, as importantly, vision and narrative tone must be considered, particularly with a writer whose vision is so stringent and pessimistic, and whose tone is so unsettling. The quotations used as epigraphs for this section of the present chapter, quotations drawn from critical reviews stating a definite unease and dissatisfaction with significant aspects of Gallant's fiction, point to the most important element of one's judgement of any writer's work: our response as readers to texts that do not merely charm, but also profoundly challenge us.

Gallant herself has pointed out that positive critical evaluation is not enough to sustain any writer—readership, she argues, is what makes you sink or swim (iJKK). And not the readership one finds via university courses in Canadian writing or modern fiction, but rather the attention of those perhaps rarest of all birds on our present earth, the intelligent common readers who pick up a literary book not because they are taking an exam or submitting an essay or review article on a particular author, but because fiction is for them an indispensable source of delight that also contributes to their experiential knowledge of the world they share with the writer. It is these exemplary common readers who are most likely to be distressed, perhaps even repelled, by the vision and tone that characterize so much of Gallant's writing. Nor is this kind of reader a solitary or isolated species. For from the beginning, despite general recognition of Gallant's technical and stylistic achievements as an artist, there has been a chorus of dissatisfaction and even bewilderment with the very nature of her vision. And this chorus is, I think, much more of an index of the quality, power, and importance of Gallant's writing than is the gush of praise that can be summarized in one reviewer's paean: 'I'm certain there isn't a finer living writer of fiction in the English language. There couldn't be!'[18]

Legitimate dissatisfaction with Gallant's work stems from the reader's recognition that so fine a writer, with such brilliant gifts at her disposal, uses them so relentlessly to box us in, to shave down or pare away what little sense of positive or even new possibilities we believe ourselves to possess. It is interesting to note that from his negative review of *The Pegnitz Junction* William

Pritchard excepts one story, 'An Alien Flower', because he finds it less unrelenting, 'more tolerant toward the possibility of [its] heroines breaking free'. Consequently, he argues, readers are able to enter 'more fully into Mavis Gallant's imagination, artful and moral to the extent that it bears comparison with a Chekhov's or a Katherine Anne Porter's'.[19] One cannot simply 'close the book' on Pritchard's response, even if one disagrees with him about the uniqueness of 'An Alien Flower' in *The Pegnitz Junction*, and certainly not because he uses the term 'arty' in his remarks on the novella called 'The Pegnitz Junction'. He has done so, we now see, in order to draw a legitimate contrast between that pejorative term and the desirable one, 'artful'. Whether or not 'arty' is the most effective term to use in registering resistance to Gallant's techniques, Pritchard's general point is one that deserves discussion, not dismissal.

One significant 'dissenting' response to Gallant's fiction is to be found in Anatole Broyard's review of *From the Fifteenth District*—that collection of stories Anne Tyler has so aptly described as being blessed by 'a sense of limitlessness', openness, and breadth of vision.[20] Nevertheless, Broyard's criticisms are worth examining and testing, for they can be applied to those of Gallant's fictions that appear to enforce closure rather than openness on their characters. Broyard begins with the perceptive remark that much of Gallant's originality consists in her 'refusing to do what the reader wants or expects her to do: that is, to bring her stories to some pleasing form of resolution'. One can take exception, however, with his contention that Gallant never allows us 'to identify or empathize with her characters': while we certainly lose no sleep over the moral sloppiness of Barbara in 'The Remission', we cannot help but be moved by the plight of her young daughter Molly—or, more profoundly, by that of Carmela and Dr Chaffee in 'The Four Seasons'. Moreover, Broyard's deprecating charge that Gallant is a *New Yorker* writer, who therefore slavishly incorporates into her fictions a policy of non-identification between character and reader, is rendered suspect not only by the fact that *The New Yorker* has published such empathetic fictions as 'Going Ashore', 'The Moabitess', and 'The Ice Wagon Going Down the Street'; there is also something suspect about the charged language in which Broyard voices his complaint: 'It is almost as if such sympathy was considered to be vulgar, a naïve instance of uncultivated eagerness, or indiscriminate gregariousness.' Equal-

ly contentious—by virtue of 'gender bias'—is his comparing
Gallant's 'intense[ly] uninteresting' characters to 'a woman who
goes to great expense and trouble to dress very badly, and who
derives a puzzling authority from it'. Yet when Broyard turns his
attention to the troubling opacity of Gallant's fiction, one feels he
is much closer to the mark, if not in relation to the fictions he cites,
then in relation to others—'The Burgundy Weekend', 'The Captive
Niece', or 'Luc and his Father':

> Miss Gallant's stories keep threatening to speak to us, to come to
> terms with our imagination, and then they turn away in impatience
> at our simplicity. These pieces ['The Four Seasons', 'The Moslem
> Wife', 'The Remission'] might be described as a continual, stubborn
> retreat from climax. While her people are allowed to be tragical, or
> even hysterical, it is difficult to find any informing moral in their
> emotions. The stories are like an almost unimaginably sophisti-
> cated foreign tour in which one is taken to see only the digressions
> and parentheses of each culture.

Declaring that, in a 'perversion of Buber's I-Thou', the reader is
made to remain forever outside the lives of Gallant's characters,
Broyard concludes, somewhat anti-climactically, 'one sometimes
wants to resist her'.[21]

Resistant responses to Gallant's work abound. Robert Taubman
finds that her 'chilly if subtle analysis' submits her characters to
'a demeaning kind of art'.[22] Brigid Elson, in a review of *From the
Fifteenth District*, has commented on the 'chilling' clarity of
Gallant's vision, and the 'unsatisfactorily limited' nature of her
characters, which she relates to Gallant's 'unconvincing cosmic
pessimism', her presupposition that 'we are all doomed players in
the random Existentialist crap game of life'.[23] And Constance
Rooke, in a recent essay on three Canadian women writers, points
to just such a discomforting chill in the tone of that classically Gallantesque novella, *Its Image on the Mirror*, while at the same time
declaring her delight in Gallant's art, the enormous pleasure it affords her.[24] This chill factor is induced not only by Gallant's tendency to present characters who, irremediably trapped in
hopeless situations, are incapable of actions that would free themselves or others, but also by the ironic tone with which she
presents such entrapment, her detachment and disinterestedness
vis à vis the experiences her characters are undergoing, her refusal
to take sides and pronounce judgements. In many ways Gallant's

literary persona, the self-portrait her art produces, recalls the iconoclastic description that Joyce's Stephen Dedalus gives of the artist who, 'like the God of creation, remains within or behind or beyond or above his handiwork, invisible, refined out of existence, indifferent, paring his fingernails'.[25] This impersonality, combined with Gallant's ability to dispassionately enter into the experience of inimical characters, has been praised by some critics as the eschewal of sentimentality,[26] and as laudably accurate to the laws of human relationships. By others it has been condemned as 'emotional anaesthesia' and an 'ostentatious withholding of judgement'.[27]

And here again it is tone that creates this impression of authorial evasion or indifference: that tone which has been variously described as mordant, sardonic, bitchy, and gloating. 'From behind a cool eye she winkles out her perceptions with casual and entrancing cruelty,' concludes an English reviewer.[28] One of the most risky aspects of choosing ironic impersonality to define narrative tone is the insecurity and fear it engenders in the reader. In Alice Munro's fiction we have the consoling sense that the narrators somehow implicate themselves in the judgements they make of those characteristic human traits, smallness and ignorance, and in the common experience of failure, betrayal, loss. Gallant's readers, on the other hand, may often perceive the author's presence over their shoulders as the netted insect perceives the shadow of the collector ready to impale him with a pin. Her use of first-person narrators is particularly revealing in this respect: in the Lena stories in *Overhead in a Balloon*, for example, she prevents our identifying with or even being taken into the confidence of the narrator, by making him such a rebarbative character. Yet by her own disinterested attitude toward Edouard and the characters whose lives are entangled in his, Gallant keeps us puzzling out what our own response to egocentric Edouard, masochistic Juliette, and the morally flighty Lena should be. As one reviewer has phrased it: 'And always, Miss Gallant says: "Look, this is what happened. Oh, you want to know what it means? Well, what do *you* think?"'[29]

It is, of course, Gallant's prerogative to create just such a narrator, and to withhold overt judgement on him, thereby preventing her readers from forming easy, conventional responses to the situations he recollects. It is the reader's prerogative, however, to decide whether such a character is persuasive, and such a narrative technique, satisfying; to ask—as William Pritchard did of *The Pegnitz Junction*—whether a direct rather than an oblique approach might not be more challenging, and whether the limitations Gallant places on herself through her choice of character and situation do not lead her writing to become, in some important respects, predictable. Apologists remark that 'if [Gallant is limited], it is because she limits herself and wrings her wit dry of grotesquerie and exaggeration', yet they do not really defuse the charges that 'Gallant's art is in the service of a narrow view of life—too much is left out of the world of [her] stories'.[30]

Even Gallant's acknowledged strengths have been used against her: critics have found her subtleties too finicky: 'one simply cannot put down a piece before finishing it—for fear of forgetting what it is about'; 'she writes as if to the mannerism born'.[31] One might shrug off these remarks as Philistine; they seem, after all, to be the same kind of pebbles cast at Henry James by his contemporaries. Yet Joseph Conrad, in defending James against similar charges, was quick to insist that '[t]echnical perfection, unless there is some glow from within, must necessarily be cold'. He cites James as an 'idealizer' whose 'heart shows itself in the delicacy of his handling'.[32] However delicate her handling, Gallant is no idealizer: there is considerable question, too, as to whether her work possesses any glow or warmth at all.

Critics—no doubt thinking of such stories as 'Bernadette' and 'The Four Seasons'—have praised Gallant's 'compassionate yet detached understanding' of her characters and the situations in which they find themselves, suggesting that though one might be in great distress in the world she envisions, one is never out of reach of love.[33] Yet when we find a writer like Mark Abley underlining the existence of Gallant's compassion with the observation that, although merciless with the complacent, she is with others, 'especially children bruised by neglect . . . patient and even kind',[34] we may find the quality of mercy to be somewhat strained. A careful reading of her fiction shows Gallant to be ambivalent towards many of these 'bruised children', especially those she presents as being merely adults *manqués*. 'Why aren't [her] stories painfully moving, though the people are so recognizably decent, . . . in their lonely plights so jauntily sad? Because none of them wants to take the risk of getting involved, even the author, really. She is a wonderful observer of the ordinary grotesqueries of human encounters that leave hearts bruised and obscurely aching, but not broken—nothing is really changed by these encounters; nothing is added to the sum of life.'[35] Again, the contrast to Munro seems both obvious and inevitable.

How valid are these rather damning reservations? It is tempting to refute charges of gloating and incompassionate clarity by citing evidence of Gallant's sympathy for the exploited and oppressed. *Paris Notebooks* gives ample evidence of this in, for example, the sympathetic but unsentimental attention she pays to the children of Spanish and Portuguese workers in Paris, or in her rage at the way in which those whose old-age pensions were held up by the post-office strike, or 'cancer patients alone in slum bedrooms' (PN 71), were made to suffer during the events in May 1968. And yet the compassionate clarity that is the hallmark of Gallant's 'social narratives' in *Paris Notebooks* is either conspicuously absent or else curiously displaced in her novels and short stories. Thus William Pritchard, praising the 'sympathetic intelligence and ironic penetration of . . . judgement' evident in Gallant's introduction to a book on the Gabrielle Russier affair, goes on to remark that the bulk of the stories collected in *The Pegnitz Junction* 'do not command full, responsive belief of the sort solicited by her essay'.[36] 'Full, responsive belief', we may counter, is an emotional option that Gallant consistently refuses her readers because of an awareness of how easily and dangerously our feelings can be manipulated, by ourselves and others. In a crucial scene of *What Is To Be Done?* Gallant has the irrepressibly idealistic Jenny reject the truth about her political illusions: 'It doesn't matter. I don't care. What matters is what I felt when I believed. When I thought it was true. I've never been so happy' (WTD 59). For Gallant most notions of human happiness are, we recall, not only illusory but actively pernicious.

A text that illustrates the dangers of foisting one's own interpretation of happiness and freedom on the lives of other people is 'Bernadette', the account of a master-servant relationship whose tensions parallel the conflict of progressivism and traditionalism in Québec society on the eve of the *révolution tranquille*. Because the narration of this story is deliberately dry and distanced, the reader, too, is forbidden 'full, responsive' and fatuous belief; we are made to see Bernadette not as an object of sympathy, but as subject in both senses of the word. Yet while we applaud Gallant for allowing the uneducated, torpid servant girl to be presented squarely in her own terms, to refuse definitions imposed by politically 'correct' and easy sympathy, and while we relish the exquisitely modulated irony with which Gallant draws parallels and contrasts between the lives of masters and servant, we still have to deal with the fact that Bernadette is just as trapped within her ignorance as is Jeannie in 'My Heart Is Broken'. These women are representative of an entire strain of Gallant's characters—those who do not kick against the pricks, but go gently into the dubious night of single parenthood and northern mining towns, of punitive marriage and even more dubious divorce, without so much as a glimpse of alternatives or a hint of protest.

In large part such a dismal fate is enforced by the dictates of context and the operative rules of irony. In those of Gallant's fictions that deal with the brutal closure that history or sexual politics effect on human experience, any celebration of joy, freedom, openness, and love would be as out of place as fireworks at a funeral. Similarly, the intricate, dispassionate kind of irony that Gallant employs in her fictions makes equally intricate demands on the reader. What she writes of Paul Léautaud applies in some ways to her own work: 'Léautaud was an almost exact mixture of breadth and smallness, and we prefer writers to be consistent. Like most people who save face with irony, he expected to be understood even when he was dealing in opposites' (PN 146). The concerns of Gallant's fiction are similarly broad and small, in that she shows us the whole gamut of a decidedly limited kind of experience. Yet her distinctive brand of irony proceeds not by simple opposites, but by creating a puzzling distance between narrator, characters, and readers. One of the principal targets of Gallant's irony is the belief that we can make clear and sweeping judgements of people and situations: she shows us not only that we do not know more about a certain character than that character knows about her or himself, but also that we do not know nearly as much as we think we do about our own responses to others and the desires that provoke those responses. Again, the uncomfortable principle of extension operates here: not only Gallant's characters but also her readers are revealed as self-deceived and imperfectly aware.

This discomfort at being implicated in her irony is matched by an equally unsettling sense of Gallant's 'invisibility' within her fictions (PN 176). Authorial impersonality and the obliqueness it engenders are crucial to the very project of her fiction. In reading her work we are suspended between the fixed plight of the characters and the subtly planned manoeuvres of the narrative, having to work out our salvation as readers for ourselves. With a very few of Gallant's fictions—the Linnet Muir sequence in *Home Truths*, or the deliciously and tenderly comic Carette stories—we are made to feel at one with a narrator whose ironic appreciation of her characters' situations is matched by her obvious empathy with or affection for her heroines. But with other texts—long fictions such as 'Bonaventure', for example—we haven't that privilege. Readers of 'Bonaventure' may well ask themselves why they are being given such a mass of information about such actively unlikeable characters and why they should be asked to care what happens to whom and why. This is not to demand that Gallant write like P.G. Wodehouse or Jane Austen, to demand that her fictions flirt with the satirical or malicious but end by offering us and all the characters involved sufficiently pleasant rewards and consolations. As Frank Kermode argued in *The Sense of an Ending*, books are 'fictive models of the temporal world', and we find them satisfying only 'when there seems to be a degree of real complicity with reality as we . . . imagine it'.[37] Individual works of fiction cannot be too consoling, or they will not satisfy the reader's demand for 'complicity with reality'. Neither, we might add, can they be too harassing. I have deliberately chosen the term 'harassing' instead of 'harrowing', since the effect of Gallant's vision is not tragically cathartic but ironically disturbing, leaving, as one critic has described, 'an unsettling aftertaste'.[38] With remarkable candour, Gallant has confessed that she does not think of herself as possessing a large talent—she is no Dostoevski, she admits (iGG). Yet she is quick to insist she does not feel she has neglected anything in her fiction by leaving taxing situations unexplored or tidying up that 'useless chaos [which] is what fiction is about' (PN 181).

At this point voices may be raised, insisting that Gallant's pessimism has been exaggerated, that her role as a satirist, a comedian of manners, a lampooning wit should be duly recognized. To be sure, Gallant's work is permeated by a distinctive kind of humour; however, her comic gifts are savage compared to the gentle Forsterian comedy of manners, and she has no program of 'less muddle' or 'only connect' to dull the cutting edge of her narratives. Her latest stories are overtly satirical in the majority of cases, *Overhead in a Balloon* offering us clinical revelations of certain social specimens: the right-wing upper class of Paris, the movers and manipulators in the world of High-Cost Art and Trendy Literature, and the patrons and bureaucrats who prey upon them. The kind of humour that derives from Gallant's deftness with language and the assurance of her presentation of character is a humour 'poised between eccentricity and malice'.[39] A ready example can be found in 'The Chosen Husband', with Gallant's description of how, when a luckless suitor stuffs too many caramels down his throat, his hosts 'looked away, so that he could strangle unobserved' (NY 44).

It is her penchant for this kind of humour that makes Gallant 'a bit voyou, a bit rapscallion . . . walking with a foot off the curb' (IGH 28)—a quality she believes most writers share. Her humour is at its most enjoyable and disturbing when it is interwoven into her narratives, springing out at the reader like a succession of sly tigers. Gallant's purely satiric bagatelles—the pieces that have appeared in *The New Yorker* under such titles as 'La Vie Parisienne', 'Treading Water: (More *Sturm und Drang* from Cosima Wagner's Diaries)', and 'A Revised Guide to Paris'—would seem, however, to be verbal equivalents of that magazine's cartoons: Gallant has said she writes them 'just for fun' (IGH 65). Her most impressive vein, as humorist, is a mix of the savage and subtle, as in this account of a dinner-table battle in 'Acceptance of their Ways':

> Mrs Freeport's pebbly stare was focussed on her friend's jar of yoghurt. 'Sugar?' she cried, giving the cracked basin a shove along the table. Mrs Garnett pulled it toward her, defiantly. She spoke in a soft, martyred voice. . . . She said that it was her last evening and it no longer mattered. . . .
>
> 'I look upon you as essentially greedy.' Mrs Freeport leaned forward, enunciating with care. 'You pretend to eat nothing, but I cannot look at a dish after you have served yourself. The *wreck* of the lettuce. The *destruction* of the pudding'. (MHB 9)

This is a subtle version of the Dickensian kind of humour that works by absurdity and exaggeration. Other forms of humour to be found in Gallant's fiction are less innocent--the description, for example, of a character with large white teeth: 'Slumped in the doorway she looked like a cynical horse' ('In Italy') or of the 'tall, fat' Valerie in 'Vacances Pax': 'She had what seemed to his besotted eyes a Tudor bearing, and was majestic in flowered slacks' (IT 191). This is that irresistible practice of 'amusing oneself at the expense of others' against which we have all been warned in childhood, a kind of humour that leaves us feeling slightly guilty as we exercise it. For it is ever so slightly nasty, this little twist of the narratorial knife. Characteristically human: quintessentially Gallant.

Gallant's use of humour increases rather than relieves the disturbances her fictions create in our experiential fields. What, then, do we make of those stories in which only the most desolate ironies are permitted any entrée? As an example of the bleakest, grimmest kind of closure that her fictions enact, and as a means of examining the validity of criticism that takes Gallant to task for her glacial tone and for the overdetermined limitations she applies to human possibility, let us look at a representative fiction from *Home Truths*, 'Saturday' (1968). Gallant herself has described it as a story about language, and indeed for one character, Gérard, the problem of having no mother tongue creates the conditions for his psychic and physical derangement. But the point of view in this story keeps shifting, from Gérard's 'Wild Strawberries' dream, to his 'sacrificial' mother's reflections on her abysmal marriage, to the consciousness of her freakishly intelligent nine-year-old son, Léopold, and finally to the confused but idyllic memories of the senile father. In some ways the story is traditional Québec Gothic, with all the requisite ingredients stirred into the narrative: the convent-girl wife, married off to a man thirty years her senior; the seven children she bears, despite her revulsion at her husband's sexual advances. What Gallant adds to the broth is anti-clericalism—all the children but the last-born speak English in the home, to prevent them from getting sucked into the maw of the Catholic church. Gérard, as a result, 'speaks French as if through a muslin curtain, or as if translating from another language' (HT 39); his sisters marry indistinguishable Anglophones, while only Léopold has learnt a pure, crystalline French at the only secular Francophone school in the province.

The story, in fact, becomes a tug of war between the two decisive and effectual members of the family—the domineering mother and her solipsistic youngest child. And it is in the delineation of these characters that a maximum of writerly disaffection and readerly repulsion is reached. For these are characters hermetically sealed in their repulsiveness. The mother, we are told, 'has led the life of a crown princess, sapped by boredom and pregnancies. She told each of her five daughters as they grew up that they were conceived in horror; that she could have left them in their hospital cots and not looked back, so sickened was she by their limp spines and the autumn smell of their hair, by their froglike movements and their animal wails' (HT 38). The last-born son, Léopold, 'who never touched anyone' (HT 48), is perceived by his siblings as embarrassing 'evidence of an old man's foolishness' (HT 40). Even his mind is a handicap rather than a boon: Léopold's intelligence will always show him the limit of a situation and the last point of possibility where people are concerned; and so, of course, he is bound to be unhappy forever. How will he be able to love?' (HT 39-40). The question—posed by the child's 'large, dull' sisters—seems quite beside the point: in the world of this story, as in so many other of Gallant's fictions, love is neither credible nor possible.

Unlike Léopold's mother, who since she 'likes her stories cruel, so that her children will know more about life than she once did' makes a habit of unhappy endings (HT 43), Gallant brings 'Saturday' to a close by allowing the doddering husband to escape the limits of his unenviable situation by the use of imagination. During his wife's temporary absence from the house, he walks the dog on a city street and conjures up a near-paradisal image of a 'blue and green day' in the country (HT 48). And the last line of this most discomforting story has Léopold waiting on the porch for the old man's return and then 'press[ing] his lips to his father's hand' (HT 48). Léopold's sisters, it turns out, were wrong: it is precisely because Léopold is aware of limits, the finite nature of existence and affection as prefigured in his father's frailty, that he can make this one gesture of what appears to be love, or respect, or simply communication. Yet for the reader, if not for Léopold or his father, unanswered questions seethe. As Gallant remarks elsewhere of one of Nabokov's fictions, 'if love can be the opposite of death sometimes, here it is made to sound like contempt for the living' (PN 201). Do love and pathos, the dream-like lack of gravity, the very beauty of 'Saturday's' last paragraphs, enlarge or deepen a vision of reality that has otherwise been presented as a marvellously articulated, masterfully succinct portrait of domestic hell? Is this portrait complicit with reality as we imagine or experience it—are we sufficiently 'consoled' by the ending for the brutally short, viciously sharp way in which the characters and their experiences have been served up to us? Or does the ironically idyllic ending—the prospect of the moribund father and grotesquely precocious child spending a free and affectionate afternoon in each other's company—constitute no persuasive counter-reality to the pernicious one earlier enforced? Enforcement is the key here—what freedom is the reader given to dissent, to challenge the authority of this narrative, to query the ultimate value and validity of such a fictive model of experience? If the 'only question worth asking about a story . . . is, "Is it dead or alive?"' (PN 177) then what sort of answer do we give regarding 'Saturday', which seems to recount nothing so much as death-in-life, and does so with such a degree of narrative chill that we seem to be reading about and responding to the denizens of a morgue, not the members of a family?

Given Gallant's own use of Lawrencian terminology, one might continue the interrogation by asking whether her art, as evident not only in this consummately repellent story but in quantities of others, is bereft of that crucial element D.H. Lawrence discerned in any fiction worth writing and reading—the narrative's own quarrel with and questioning of its very premisses. One might also ask whether a deadly predictability develops from Gallant's insistence on closure, diminution, and disillusionment, as her fictions show us, over and over again, the small sum not of what is possible, but of what is inevitable.

These fundamental questions are raised by a sustained examination of Gallant's work—not just 'Saturday', and not simply the stories reprinted in various collections, the two novels and the play, but all those fictions still imprisoned within back issues of *The New Yorker* and other magazines. Despite their enchantment with Gallant's extraordinary narrative and descriptive gifts, readers may resist the vision of an intolerably impoverished reality that these gifts so often create. With the rarest of exceptions,[40] Gallant's work refuses us not only any convincing example of human happiness stemming from relations between friends or lovers, masters and servants, parents and children, or siblings, but also the very possibility of happiness under any conditions whatsoever. She is relentless in her deflation of ideals and illusions: her play *What Is To Be Done?* is nothing so much as a set of irony-bound variations on that particular theme. The narrator of 'Its Image on the Mirror', Jean Duncan, is emphatically not Mavis Gallant, yet for all that Gallant excoriates Jean's WASP prudishness and aridity, she confers upon her the narrative authority to enforce a closed, diminished view of life. No viable alternatives are envisioned; all dissenting voices—most notably that of the once free and amorous Isobel—are silenced. We are locked in separate cells of the same prison; as Malcolm discovers in the story 'Malcolm and Bea', we are 'each of us flung separately . . . into a room without windows' (EW 19).

Yet some of Gallant's characters lament this constriction and loss: 'There has been such a waste of everything; such a waste' (PJ 129), laments the otherwise impeccably reserved narrator of 'An Autobiography'. And certain of Gallant's fictions in *The Pegnitz Junction* and *From the Fifteenth District,* as well as in back issues of *The New Yorker,* are distinctly open rather than closed, their ironies lambent rather than caustic. If, as V.S. Pritchett claims of *Fifteenth District,* 'at the core of each story there is a clinching sense of the central moral dilemma in which the characters find themselves',[41] then the tightness of the clinch is loosened, somehow, by the very existence of a moral dimension in which it can be situated. Dr Chaffee's benediction and Carmela's vision of heaven when eating her first dish of ice cream, in 'The Four Seasons', become small chinks in an appallingly oppressive wall. If they do not offer us transcendence of the conditions that Gallant sees as integral to our very humanness, they do offset that enormous pressure of metaphysical or existential closure with which Gallant's other fictions brick us in.

Like Lucian Freud's spectators, we return again and again to Gallant's art—an art that can be defined as the negative of the one practised by the popular novelist Mr Cranefield in 'The Remission'. The 'golden' girl and boy who took the lead in his fictions 'stood for a world of triumphant love, with which his readers felt easy kinship. . . . They raised the level of existence—raised it, and flattened it' (FFD 99). Gallant's fictions make us feel uneasy kinship with a world in which most doors are slammed and rooms sealed off, leaving us little more movement than her imprisoned characters possess. Yet such a world also bespeaks a 'flattened' existence, which could become as predictable as that authored by Mr Cranefield's fictions, were it not for those rare stories in which Gallant leaves the prison doors convincingly ajar, revealing possibilities, however precarious, of perception and knowledge that might open and extend experience.

It is for this reason that anyone wishing to do critical justice to Gallant's fiction must read it *en masse*, and not in small, random doses. For while it is remarkably pleasurable to come across one of her stories in a magazine or anthology—as pleasurable as coming across an elegant and witty acquaintance at a stuffy social gathering—the cumulative effect of reading Gallant is very different. One admires her technique and relishes her style no less, but one becomes both more aware of and more resistant to the pessimism of her vision, and the forms it takes in her fictions. This is not to say that one rejects or slams shut the book, but that one quarrels with it, becoming a resistant reader of a body of work that can exasperate as much as it enchants. 'A shrewd eye, a selective ear, and a spirit of flint'—this description of a character in the story 'Good Deeds' (IT 253) could apply as well to Gallant's literary persona—the writer as our reading permits us to know her. Yet unsentimental compassion, delicacy, even a revivifying warmth are also to be found in Gallant's fictions. In any case, were her writing not so accomplished, her intelligence so acute, her language so irresistible, her work would never possess the authority to engage us, the power to disturb and challenge us, at all.

Though a resistant reader's response to Gallant's writing will be intractably paradoxical, an understanding of how her fiction engages our responses will help us to hold our own against—not dismiss—the vision that informs it. 'All accounts of reality are versions of reality. [W]e have to be constantly alerted to *what* reality is being constructed, and *how* representations are achieving this construction.'[42] To do so we must examine the role of narrative authority in Gallant's fiction, discovering the ways in which this writer's mastery of her medium forces our assent and compels our resistance to her fictive worlds.

Notes

[1]Interview by Peter Gzowski of Mavis Gallant and Urjo Kareda, CBC Radio, *Morningside* 11 Nov. 1982.

[2]A sequence including 'The Chosen Husband', 'From Cloud to Cloud', and 'Florida'.

[3]Gallant's earliest recorded denial of any *New Yorker* influence on her writing is to be found in an interview with Zoe Bieler in the *Montreal Star*, 30 Aug. 1955, p. 26.

[4]Robert Taubman, 'Peace Institute' (review of *An Unmarried Man's Summer*), *New Statesman* 3 Sept. 1965, p. 329.

[5] William H. Pritchard, review of *The Pegnitz Junction*, *New York Times Book Review*, 24 June 1973, p. 4.

[6]Peter Stevens, 'Perils of Compassion', *Canadian Literature* 56 (Spring 1963), p. 61. This neglect may in part be attributed to critics whose highly

selective regard for Gallant's writing is a product of that nationalism which Gallant herself abhors. Anything in her work that smacks of national or regional focus they seize upon; anything tainted with solely European or American content is ignored or slighted as lacking the 'resonance' that her Canadian stories possess. (See Martin Knelman, 'The Article Mavis Gallant Didn't Want Written', *Saturday Night* 93 [Nov. 1978], p. 25.) Yet the point remains that Gallant is concerned to write resonantly not just for Canadian, but also for American and British readers, as well as for those Europeans who can read her fiction. Moreover, she takes as a given that history is as much the province of a Canadian as a European--why shouldn't she write about Germany and the Germans in *The Pegnitz Junction* as well as about Canada and Canadians in *Home Truths*? One can thankfully point to the existence of critics who, like Wayne Grady, insist that *Home Truths* gives us a vision not of Canada, but 'of the world, of life', or who, like John Ayre, deplore the use of criteria based on 'nationalist ideologies' to deny Gallant's 'considerable abilities in creating stories about any social reality' ('The Other Canada', *Books in Canada* 10 Oct. 1981, p. 19; 'The Sophisticated World of Mavis Gallant', *Saturday Night* Sept. 1973, pp. 35-6).

[7]See Robertson Davies, 'The Novels of Mavis Gallant', *Canadian Fiction Magazine* 28 (Special Issue on Mavis Gallant, 1978); Stevens, 'Perils of Compassion' and Knelman, 'The Article Mavis Gallant Didn't Want Written'. See also Elizabeth Jennings, 'New Novels', *The Listener* 18 Aug. 1960, p. 273, and Rose Feld, *Saturday Review*, 25 Feb. 1956, pp. 17-18.

[8]See G.D. Killam, 'A Thinking Stone', *Canadian Forum* 60 (June-July 1980), pp. 30-1; R.P. Bilan, review of *From the Fifteenth District*, *University of Toronto Quarterly* 49 (Summer 1980), p. 326.

[9]Pritchard, review of *Pegnitz Junction*, p. 4

[10]See Ronald Hatch, 'The Three Stages of Mavis Gallant's Short Fiction' in *Canadian Fiction* 28. Hatch's forthcoming book on Gallant emphasizes her preoccupation with the idea and experience of history.

[11]Pritchard, review of *Pegnitz Junction* p. 4.

[12]George Woodcock, 'Memory, Imagination, Artifice: the late short fiction of Mavis Gallant', *Canadian Fiction* 28.

[13]Doris Cowan, *Books in Canada* 13 (Jan. 1984), p. 22.

[14]Robert Weaver, for example, describes Gallant's trademark as 'a kind of itchy impatience' ('Introduction', *The End of the World and Other Stories* [Toronto: McClelland & Stewart, 1974], p. 13); Robert Fulford finds her lack of feeling for her central characters to betray 'a kind of gloating nastiness' ('On Mavis Gallant's Best Fiction Yet: the Memoirs of a WASP in Wartime Montreal,', *Maclean's* 5 Sept. 1964, p. 45). These elements may

well be discerned by readers of certain of Gallant's stories; the point is that they are there to be discerned by readers of *Malone Dies* or *Murphy* as well, though critics never seem to take Beckett to task for his cramped and desolate view of human possibility.

[15]See Woodcock, 'Memory, Imagination, Artifice', p. 81, and Robertson Davies, 'The Novels of Mavis Gallant' *Canadian Fiction* 28. Gallant speaks of the historical and political nature of 'The Pegnitz Junction' in her interview with Geoff Hancock in the same issue of *Canadian Fiction*.

[16]See Mary Poovey's *The Proper Lady and the Woman Writer : Ideology as Style in the Works of Mary Wollstonecraft, Mary Shelley, and Jane Austen* (Chicago: University of Chicago Press, 1984) for a discussion of the traditional strategies open to women writers wishing to bridge 'the gap between the possibilities promoted by the ideology of bourgeois individualism, and the rewards possible in a world where resources are limited and power is unequally held' (p. 241).

[17]Constance Pendergast, 'Love's Grim Remains', review of *Green Water, Green Sky*, *Saturday Review* 17 Oct. 1959, p. 19; Christopher Lehmann-Haupt, 'Vanishing Creams', review of *A Fairly Good Time*, *New York Times Book Review* 5 June 1970, p. 33. Of Eve Auchincloss's review of *My Heart Is Broken*, 'Good Housekeeping' (*New York Review of Books* 25 June 1964), Gallant has remarked: 'There was a review published in a prominent American magazine . . . reviewing my work along with that of Mary McCarthy and another woman with whom I had nothing in common except that we were women. They called it 'Good Housekeeping'. I never bought the magazine again. I mention this in interviews whenever I can' (interview with Karen Lawrence, 'From the Other Paris', *Branching Out*, Feb.-March 1976, p. 19.)

[18]I.M. Owen, *Books in Canada* 8 (Oct. 1979), p. 14.

[19]Pritchard, review of *Pegnitz Junction*, p. 4.

[20]Anne Tyler, 'European Plots and People', review of *From the Fifteenth District*, *New York Times Book Review* 16 Sept. 1979, p. 13.

[21]Anatole Broyard, review of *From the Fifteenth District*, *New York Times Book Review* 2 Oct. 1979, p. 9.

[22]Taubman, review of *An Unmarried Man's Summer*, p. 329.

[23]Brigid Elson, review of *From the Fifteenth District*, *Queen's Quarterly* 87 (Spring 1980), p. 161.

[24]Fear of the Open Heart', *A Mazing Space: Writing Canadian Women Writing*, ed. Shirley Neuman and Smaro Kamboureli (Edmonton: Longspoon/NeWest, 1986), pp. 256-69.

[25]James Joyce, *A Portrait of the Artist as a Young Man* (Harmondsworth, Middlesex, England: Penguin, 1972), p. 215. Compare Dedalus's notion

of the artist with Gallant's comment, à propos of her manner of writing: 'I would like to be invisible' ('What Is Style?' [PN 176]).

[26]See Mark Abley, 'Home is Where Complacency Is', *Maclean's* 94 (9 Nov. 1981), p. 78.

[27]Helen Hoy, review of *Home Truths*, *University of Toronto Quarterly* 51: 4 (Summer 1982), p. 323; Auchincloss, 'Good Housekeeping', 18.

[28]See Montague Haltrecht, 'The Condition of Women', *The Scotsman* (Edinburgh) Sept. 1965, p. 3; Killam, 'A Thinking Stone', p. 31; W.H. New, 'The Art of Haunting Ghosts', Canadian Literature 85 (Summer 1980), p. 154; Robert Weaver, Introduction to The End of the World and Other Stories (Toronto: McClelland & Stewart, 1974), p. 13; Fulford, 'Best Fiction Yet'.

[29]Elizabeth Janeway, 'We Exit Wondering: Review of *My Heart is Broken*', *Saturday Review*, 18 April 1964, p. 46. It is a tactic Gallant also uses to re-establish control of interviews.

[30]Elizabeth Janeway, review of *A Fairly Good Time*, *New York Yimes Book Review* 7 June 1970, p. 34; Bilan, review of *From the Fifteenth District*, p. 327.

[31]Hoy, review of *Home Truths*, p. 322; Elson, review of *Fifteenth District*, p. 160.

[32]Joseph Conrad, 'Henry James: An Appreciation', *Notes on Life and Letters* I (1921; rpt. London: Dent, 1949), pp. 270-1.

[33]Michael Thorpe, 'A National Sense of Self', *Canadian Forum* 61 (Feb. 1982), p. 40; New, 'Haunting Ghosts', p. 155.

[34]Abley, 'Home', p. 78.

[35]Auchincloss, 'Good Housekeeping, p. 18.

[36]Pritchard, review of *Pegnitz Junction*.

[37]Frank Kermode, *The Sense of an Ending* (1981 rpt.; New York: Oxford Univ. Press, 1966), pp. 54, 63.

[38]Jon Kaplan, 'Good Gallant', *Now* (Toronto), 2:8 (Dec. 1982), p. 13.

[39]Elizabeth Berridge, review of *A Fairly Good Time*, The Daily Telegraph (London, England), 16 July 1970, p. 7.

[40]The gentle, reverie-like quality of the Linnet Muir sequence, the graceful nostalgia of the Carette stories, and the bulk of the fictions included in *From the Fifteenth District* are conspicuous exceptions to the grim and gritty rule.

[41]V.S. Pritchett, 'Shredded Novels', *New York Review of Books*, 24 Jan. 1980, p. 32.

[42]Rosalind Coward, 'Are Women's Novels Feminist Novels?' in *The New Feminist Criticism: Essays on Women, Literature, and Theory*, ed. Elaine Showalter (New York: Pantheon, 1985), p. 227.

Chapter 3

Narrative Voice and Structure

> Reading an early poem of Prism's . . . [Miss Pugh] had been stopped by the description of a certain kind of butterfly, 'pale yellow, with a spot like the Eye of God.' She had sent for her copy of the Larousse dictionary, which Rosalia was using in the kitchen as a weight on sliced cucumbers. Turning to a color plate, Miss Pugh had found the butterfly at once. It turned out to be orange rather than yellow, and heavily spotted with black. Moreover, it was not a European butterfly but an Asian moth. The Larousse must be mistaken. She had shut the dictionary with a slap, blaming its editors for carelessness. (OB 109-10)

Gallant is most commonly commended for an uncanny mastery of language and form: in Margaret Atwood's astute words she is 'a terrifyingly good writer'.[1] This chapter will examine the ways in which Gallant's extraordinary art creates a formidable authority within her narratives: the kind of authority that may lead the reader to follow Miss Pugh's example, and slap shut the book of experience in order to submit more completely to the laws and dicta of the fiction at hand.

Language, in fiction, is primarily a matter of narrative voice: the creation, through that voice, of modes of expression—acerbic or consolatory, declarative or interrogative—and, as well, the creation or even control of the reader's reception. The writer's first business is to speak in her own voice: 'If it is not a true voice, it is nothing' (PN 179). She must speak in such a way that she is listened to: a voice that fails to command attention, to compel interest—or, if you prefer a less aggressive approach, to enchant or seduce the reader into listening from beginning to end—might as well never have broken silence in the first place. It seems a stupidly simple point to make, and yet it is a necessary one, given a climate in which most readers of serious imaginative literature (as opposed to those who consume mass-market fluff or dreck) take up a book under some sort of utilitarian compulsion—to write an academic essay or scholarly article on a prescribed text. Ideal readers—that vanishing community of amateurs and connoisseurs to whom life and literature compose a continuum, not a polarity, and who read for the sheer pleasures and challenges of the text—open books with a certain cupping of the ears, the better to catch the tone and mood, the style and the rhetorical flair of the narrative. When the book they happen to pick up is *My Heart Is Broken* or *Home Truths* they will encounter a narrative voice that both delights and dictates; they will experience extraordinary pleasure in the precision, delicacy, subtlety, and assurance with which language is used, and, as we have seen, they may recoil at the vision of reality, the sense of human possibility which that language does not so much express as enforce.

If Gallant's vision of reality is as stark and unaccommodating as Samuel Beckett's, there is a marked difference in the kind of language these writers use—equally effectively—to communicate that vision. Gallant's response to Beckett's writing is characteristic of her unproblematic relation to language: '[English] is an absolutely fabulous language. It's so misused, so underused. For writing there's no comparison between English and French. When Beckett chose French, deliberately, it was because he wanted a tighter, smaller framework. I can't imagine anyone wanting that' (iGH 26). Her love for 'the sound, resonance, and ambiguities of English vocabulary' (HT xviii) is manifest in Gallant's writing: one imagines her fictions flowing effortlessly from her pen, though she insists that two years is 'nothing' for the completion of a story, and six months is 'quite fast' (iEB). Part of the 'obsessional'(iGH 48) quality of the process of writing, for Gallant, would seem to lie in her desire to phrase things perfectly and precisely, to give an air of inevitability both to the situations her writing creates and to the words she uses to inscribe those situations on the reader's consciousness.

The role of language in Gallant's fiction is a matter of structure as well as style: one of the important ways in which her fiction works is by the arrangement and playing out of ironic contrasts, and one of the cardinal contrasts is that between the reduction of character and the closure of experience on the one hand, and on the other the freedom of language either to pin down the most finicky detail of a situation or else to cloud and obscure what seem the simplest and most general precepts. And the contrast in Gallant's fiction between the dazzling and delicious language, the appreciative joy such marvellous fluency produces, and the reductive world this language portrays, is one of the constant shocks her readers encounter.

Yet such shocks seem necessary, even desirable; Gallant's supreme confidence in the English language is something for which readers can be immensely grateful. She does not write fiction about the delights or difficulties of writing fiction; she does not agonize over the ingrained deceitfulness of language, its parade of substance over the chasm of silence, or of mere convention. She does not, like many contemporary women writers, dream of creating a new language, free of all patriarchal taint, expressive of unlimited possibility, either beyond gender or else wholly expressive of the biological rhythms and psychological givens of female existence. Like Virginia Woolf, she has simply claimed the English language as her birthright, proceeded to master it so that she could do whatever she wished with it, and set about using it to create fictions, many of which devastate 'patriarchal' presumptions and expectations concerning women's relation to language. What some critics designate as 'bitchy' in her tone, is, of course, subversive—the fingernail scratch that deflates male pomposity or impairs the male sense of the natural order of things. Gallant, as we know, has made her living from using language; power over words has been the means by which she has secured her independence and very identity, and one gets the impression that she would never jeopardize this by radically questioning the nature and efficacy of what to her is as much a given as the ground under her feet.

Yet this is not to say that Gallant is a dishonest writer, a superficial or facile spinner of verbal webs. What she does face squarely, what she recognizes in the very structure of her fictions, is the insubstantiality not of language, but of human definitions and evasions of time. What fiction says, she has told us, is that 'something is taking place and that nothing lasts' (PN 177). Impermanence, erasure—those disobliging facts of existence are as inimical to narrative as they are to that most central of our narratives: our lives themselves. 'The watch continues to tick where the story stops' (PN 177). In fact, it can be argued that the predominant rigidity of Gallant's vision of reality and the fixed corners of her imagined world reflect her recognition of the inefficacy of our power over time, of our attempts, through memory and fictions, to control the past and direct the future. The home ground of her fiction is the amorphous and exigent present; she chronicles our attempts to close it off, to contain and control it. Even those of her fictions that remember time past—the Linnet Muir sequence, for example—seem a species of narrative magic, transforming memory into present consciousness, making the borders between past and future vanish into an all-inclusive but shifting present.

Gallant's fiction, then, imposes a purely nominal and temporary order on the 'useless chaos' of experience. We have seen that for her this chaos is not teeming with new forms and untried possibilities: it is more like an infinite dead end, the gargantuan smash-up of all illusions and desires against a metaphysical brick wall. There are no brave new worlds awaiting us in our lives, only the eternal return of fixed, unpalatable, and unavoidable truths; that 'grief and terror' which 'after childhood, we cease to express' (PN 177) would seem to have to do with our early recognition of this state of affairs. It is a recognition brought home to us by our experience of utter vulnerability in the 'prison of childhood' where we spend those few years in which we have 'all [our] wits about [us]' (HT 316).

Gallant does not use language to evade or rage against the fact that human life is at the same time an experience of time—the watch that ticks on and on—and an expression of closure—the inevitable point at which our individual 'story' runs down while the clock ticks on. Rather, she admits this state of affairs and asserts it through the very shape and style of her fiction. If Beckett makes his own appalling metaphysics the focus of his fiction, Gallant is more interested in the situations and effects created by the inescapable order of things. Her perfectly assured and authoritative narrative voice does not coerce so much as marshal us into acquiescence with her version of how things are. Take the opening paragraph of the story 'Bonaventure':

> He was besieged, he was invaded, by his mother's account of the day he was conceived; and his father confirmed her version of history, telling him *why*. He had never been able to fling in their faces 'Why did you have me?' for they told him before he could reason, before he was ready to think. He was their marvel. Not only had he kept them together, he was a musical genius, the most gifted child any two people ever had, the most deserving of love. He began to doubt their legend when he discovered the casualness of sex, and understood that anyone who was not detached (which he

believed his own talent would oblige him to be) could easily turn into parent and slave. He was not like his own father, who, as a parent, seemed a man who had been dying and all at once found himself in possession of a total life. His father never said this or anything like it, though he once committed himself dangerously in a letter. The father was more reticent than the mother; perhaps more Canadian. He could say what he thought, but not always what he felt. His memories, like the mother's, were silent, flickering areas of light, surrounded by buildings that no longer exist. (HT 135)

That initial onrush of narrative energy—'He was besieged, he was invaded'—pulls us into the vortex of this character's consciousness: the seductive image of memory as vanished structures, tenuous light, confirms the centrality and significance of the as yet unnamed hero's perceptions. We accept his obsession with self from the moment the story begins, and even when his reactions to other characters reveal the perfect selfishness, manipulativeness, and cruelty his policy of 'total detachment' entails, we stick with Douglas Ramsay, to the end. The main reason for this is the absolute assurance of the narrative that details Ramsay's experience at the villa of the man who was to have been his mentor, Adrien Moser, and the inescapable fact that there is no other character in this story to whom the reader can transfer imaginative loyalty. The people Ramsay is made to meet are equally egotistical and manipulative, when they are not the stupid or helpless victims of other people's whims and conveniences.

The opening of 'Bonaventure', structured as it is on an example of the revising of story to uncover the truth of personal history, prefigures the central paradigm of the piece: the ironic revelation that Katherine Moser, far from nurturing and extending the career of her composer-husband by whisking him off into Swiss bucolic bliss, drastically shortened and saddened the life of this genius who detested nature and felt alive only in cities. Thus the notion of imprisonment within one's parents' fictions of meaning, which the story's first lines sketch out, prepares us for and confirms the story's presentation of marriage, or any emotional relationship in or outside the family, as a fatal trap of dissimulations, cross-purposes, and graduated tortures. True, we are given this revelation through the agency of a 'vivisectionist' (HT 163) hero who has all the charm and warmth of a fish on a marble slab; the counter-view, however, is presented by the consummately self-deceiving Katherine Moser, with her disastrous passion for flowers and fields, her faith in married love, her ineptitude with a daughter whose principal pastime seems to be the merciless twitting of a piggish, priggish friend from school—a young girl to whom the moribund composer once made sexual advances. Curiouser and curiouser: nastier and nastier. We may interrupt our reading to protest that these are strange and horrid characters indeed, that their perceptions offer us a pathology rather than a morphology of experience, only to have the whipcrack narrative draw us back into a text whose exuberant precision and energy assert not just that one particular set of lives has taken this peculiar configuration, but that the configuration is expressive of life itself.

Gallant's very method of characterization[2] presses home this assertion, for she does not develop or even portray characters, in this story, so much as line them up for summary execution. Ramsay's mother is treated accordingly: 'Some women took their husbands home and lay like corpses so the husbands could see for themselves the marriage was over, but [she] wouldn't have that. She was fiercely honest and saw nothing the matter with manslaughter' (HT 149). So is 'Peggy Boon, fourteen, too plump and too boring to be a friend for Anne. . . . She was an English rose, she feared silence, and pronounced her own name "Piggy"' (HT 142). Caricature, we might observe, not character. One might protest that Peggy is a minor character, a figure of fun, yet Gallant uses her to underscore the emotional exploitation that characterizes the Moser ménage: instead of introducing an element of pathos, however, 'poor Peggy' merely draws our attention to the bloodlessness even of purely erotic relations at Katherine Moser's. Here is Douglas Ramsay spying on the sleeping Peggy and Moser's daughter, Anne:

> Ramsay . . . saw Peggy hunched, sheet up to her forehead, tufts of coarse hair showing like bristles. . . . Anne lay with a leg and an arm and a small breast outside the blanket . . . Watching the sleeping girl, he knew what he could be capable of, provided she loathed him, or was frightened of him. Better fear than hate. When he touched Anne her breathing changed; he thought he saw a gleam between her lashes. Watching, she made no move. . . . Peggy awoke, and with a rapidity he would never have thought possible in the dull girl, sat up and looked. There they were, Anne cold and ex-

cited, her heart like a machine under his hand, and Ramsay the vivisectionist, and poor Peggy, who had been in love. (HT 162-3)

All the characters in 'Bonaventure'—Ramsay, 'piggy Peggy', the aloof Anne, the formidably destructive, life-worshipping Katherine, the tormented but caricatured political radical, Nanette—are cut off from one another, set out in glass boxes. Not only are they innoculated against any kind of generous response to one another, but the reader is not allowed to form any kind of relationship with them—the narrative voice whips us behind the chosen line: better fear than hate. This is how they are; this is how life is for them; all one can do is observe and articulate what is there to be seen. Does the authority with which Gallant pronounces her observations, or snaps her verbal fingers to sum up the possibilities of any given character, derive from the fact that her truths are meant to be topical rather than wide-reaching, significant within only an exceedingly narrow social range? If so, this would imply crushing limitations to her work. Surely 'Bonaventure' does not so much posit as incise connections between the way life is lived at the Moser villa and the way we live now. Again, one's resistance to the story stems not from some fatuous desire to have only warm-and-loving characters in fiction, but rather from a recognition that Gallant in 'Bonaventure' has precluded even the possibility—however unrealizable—of alternatives to hate and fear and exploitation. In a way, her authoritative vision of how and what we are can breed a species of contentment in the reader—*j'accepte* rather than *j'accuse*. But such satisfaction affords a false security—how valid, even persuasive, are the elegance, succinctness, and precision that make a narrative like 'Bonaventure' a classic example of the kind of art that attracts even as it repels?

To attempt an answer we can consider another aspect of narrative voice. For Gallant, '[v]oices are important. The language, the tone, the pitch, even the accent' (iGH 50). And it is certainly true that she is good at doing different voices —a fearful spinster or a feckless bachelor, a bratty child, a tyrannical husband, a waspish or charmingly faithless wife. Yet so strong is the reader's sense of the omniscient narrator's manipulation and control of the various voices within the text that any convincing discourse of opposition to the narrative line is exceedingly difficult to hear. Gallant's omniscient narrative voice reminds one of how a tiger's stripes both camouflage and distinguish that creature—she rarely comments on or supplements what her characters and their situations 'say', yet her own narratorial accent is so precise and distinguished, so unmistakably Gallant, that one cannot read more than a few of her sentences without adding to the fiction's list of characters an addditional one: the superbly articulate author who situates and directs all.[3]

Yet when Gallant uses first-person narrators, which she does in perhaps a third of her fictions, a curious awkwardness is sometimes evident—not in the writing of the texts, but in our 'overhearing' of them.[4] Authorial detachment and disengagement do not always suit first-person narrators. With the important exception of the Linnet Muir stories and the odd piece such as 'Wing's Chips', this reader, at least, has trouble in accepting the very premise of the first-person narrator in fictions such as 'April Fish', 'Autumn Day', and even 'Its Image on the Mirror' or 'The Cost of Living'. One's reading of these texts is vexed by a question that points to the unpersuasiveness of Gallant's choice of narrative mode: *why* is this person telling us his or her story in the first place?

In many of Gallant's first-person narratives the tellers themselves are passive recorders of already-dealt hands. Those who seem most passionately in need of making confessions, unmasking themselves to themselves and not just to the readers, can never really bring themselves to do so. With these narrators 'fear of the open heart' (IT 50) is a congenital disease. Consider 'Its Image on the Mirror', with its prim, prissy heroine, Jean Duncan, forever pitting her memories/fictions of the past against what her mother's ethos dictates the past was or should have been. Before the story even begins, she would appear to have come to the devastating knowledge that she is dead in life; it is obvious that neither this recognition nor her telling of her story has had any cathartic effect: a passively ironic recognition would seem to be the only response this revelation of her profound disaffection from love and from life has engendered in her. Curiously, Jean's 'confidences' are broached to no one; there is no imagined character to whom she is speaking, and the reader certainly never feels like a confidante; Jean's unflinching revelation of self does not ultimately engage our compassion or admiration. The whole tenor of this story insists on narrative detachment and isolation: Jean is locked inside her head, talking to the self she never acknowledges, and who does not seem to be listening in any way that will affect the speaking self. This isolation and detachment prevent us from caring very much about Jean, or Isa, or anyone else in the fiction, so that a second question crops up: not only why is this character telling her story, but why should we care? Even she doesn't seem to.

Of course, the whole point of the story is that Jean's inherited contempt for intimacy and confession, her congenital inability to let anything show, dooms her to the lovelessness and loneliness her matronly manner so carefully conceals. Her recital is so tortuous precisely because her need to shout love, to be listened to and answered, is perfectly checked by her fear and suspicion of need itself. She hasn't the right kind of voice, and she certainly lacks any language to make herself heard. All she can do is talk to herself, but even as she does so she prevents herself from hearing and acting on anything she discloses about herself. Fear of the open heart may be one subtext of this fiction: fear of the open ear is certainly another. Jean is irrevocably cast as narrator, not character, within her own story, and she is bound by the same laws of detachment and disinterest that bind all of Gallant's narrators, third- or first-person: her telling of her own tale becomes a monologue of the deaf.

'Its Image on the Mirror' is a wonderfully incisive account of the deathly nexus of family life, and of the inability of people to leave one another alone. A fascinating reworking of the polarities between siblings with which fairy-tales make us familiar (two sisters, completely unalike—one free, the other imprisoned; one pretty, one plain; one who loves, one who remains respectable), it is also a disturbing exposure of conventional notions of happiness and union. Yet this fiction works almost despite itself. Gallant herself has declared that the 'failing' of the story lies in the fact that Jean 'knows too much about herself'(iEB) and thus presumably alienates rather than engages her 'listeners'.

With the kind of first-person narrator one encounters in the Lena stories the problem of the articulate but deaf narrator becomes particularly acute. For the man who is made to speak to us is the kind of man who would never be guilty of so grave a lapse as confession. One might argue that he is not confessing but simply narrating, and that the irony of the narrative device lies in the fact that Edouard seems totally unaware that his chronicle of the two women in his life is a self-indictment of monstrous egoism, indifference, and moral stupidity, made all the more damning by the very urbanity with which he speaks. But then Gallant's first-person narrators never learn anything about themselves, never share with us any convincing moments of self-revelation or discovery. It is as though Gallant has had them paint a 'self-portrait with blindfold'. What moves us so profoundly in Rembrandt's self-portraits is the dramatic interplay that reveals itself in the 'telling' quality of the painter's eyes: our apprehension of the fact that the artist is not only recording his appearance but also judging himself. With the narrator of the Lena stories what seems entirely lacking is any sense of the toll that is being taken by what should be an act of self-revelation. What Gallant's first-person narrators tell us is that even when we want to tell the truth about and to ourselves, we cannot—or that if we inadvertently do so, we survive the error, masking it as Jean Duncan does:

> We woke from dreams of love remembered, a house recovered and lost, a climate imagined, a journey never made; we woke dreaming our mothers had died in childbirth and heard ourselves saying, 'Then there is no one left but me!' We would wake thinking the earth must stop, now, so that we could be shed from it like snow. I knew, that night, we would not be shed, but would remain, because that was the way it was. We would survive, and waking—because there was no help for it—forget our dreams and return to life. (MHB 155)

'Its Image' is a profoundly disturbing story not only because it is so disheartening in what it tell us about 'the way it was' and is, but also because it pronounces this judgement in such marvellously compelling language—the images of slipping into winter, the whole dream-memory-snow configuration, and the way in which words are made to mime the very slowness and stillness of falling snow. Language as masterful as Gallant's exerts a commanding authority over the reader; one cannot dispute the summations of her narrators without suspecting onself to be as self-deceived, as enmeshed in confused desire, as her characters are. Such language compensates if it does not console the reader for the bleakness of the vision it articulates: if our lives are shabby, spiteful, barren, and dull, the artist's 'living prose' crackles with an 'inborn vitality and tension' (PN 177). In fact, so powerful a force is language in Gallant's fiction that it comes to play a central role in the very structuring of the stories themselves.

*

> A story usually begins, for me, with people seen in a situation, like
> that. (*Locks fingers together.*) The knot either relaxes or becomes
> locked in another way. Why that should be I couldn't tell you. . . .
> The situation has a beginning and as much ending as any situation
> has in life. (iGH 45)

Gallant's narrative authority is directed not only outwards, to
guiding and controlling her readers' responses, but also inwards,
to the shaping of the fiction itself. For above all it is her superb
deployment of language that holds together those fragments of
experience from which her fiction is constructed. Gallant has
protested that short stories should not be 'just something snatched
out of a larger fiction, or something you don't know what to do
with, that you turn into a story because it's not good for anything
else' (iGH 48). Her own fiction can be divided into three kinds:
short, 'perfect' stories such as 'Acceptance of Their Ways', 'Good
Deed', or 'Bernadette', which delight by the succinctness of their
observations and the compression of their wit; longer, 'opaque' or
discontinuous narratives such as 'The Burgundy Weekend' or
'The Captive Niece'; and, finally, fictions such as 'Going Ashore'
and 'The Remission', 'The Four Seasons' or 'The Latehomecomer'—texts in which wit opens rather than tightens the situation observed, and obliquity, not opacity, determines the
'message' the fiction encodes. I will deal at a later point with this
last, most rewarding group of stories; what I would like to examine now is the second, more problematic group.

They can, of course, be easily distinguished from those brief,
flawless fictions that show Gallant's art at its most instantly attractive, and that make the act of reading rather like attending a display of fire-works when one knows that none will be a dud, that
the effect of the whole will be a marvellous bouquet of light. In
these stories Gallant makes frequent use of summary yet 'packed'
first paragraphs that open out in the ensuing narrative like those
Japanese paper pellets that unfold into flowers under water. Consider, for example, the opening of 'The Statues Taken Down'
(1965): 'Crawley turned his two children loose day after day in the
Palais-Royal gardens, because he thought it would keep them
amused, but they were not brought up to spend a whole afternoon
sitting on iron chairs'(IT 161) or of 'Paola and Renata' (1965):
'During the weeks that preceded the engagement, Paola and

Renata discovered new ways of combing their hair' (SR 199). Such openings can be described as 'prehensile' in their ability to seize and direct the reader's attention; this is certainly the case with the story 'Good Deed' (1969): 'Houses on the French Riviera have in common the outsize pattern of flowers on the chintzes; there is too much furniture everywhere, most of it larger than life' (IT 247). This utterly authoritative statement—declaration rather than observation—compels assent. What, after all, do most of us know about styles of furnishing on the French Riviera? We may know quite a deal about greed and cruelty, about the various ways in which people abuse or betray one another, but not as much, and not as incisively, as does the author of 'Good Deed'. The impression of effortless acuity produced by the opening lines of Gallant's prose can induce a kind of delicious passivity in the reader, a willing deference to the story-teller's point of view. What the first line of this story promises, the rest of the fiction delivers: astute observation of one of the more gratifyingly grotesque examples of a certain kind and class of woman: a wonderfully entertaining account of how she authors her own come-uppance at the hands of one of her victims. Throughout this story we know where we are, with whom, and why. So consummately is the whole thing done that it might be described as an expense of language in a wealth of wit: as Woolf's Mrs Ramsay would say, 'It is enough!'

In Gallant's longer fictions, the ones that I have characterized as problematically discontinuous or opaque, characters drift in and out of chance groupings, embrace haphazard experiences that turn out to be dead ends or wrong turnings, and finish in either the same situations in which they start out or ones that are different but equally imprisoning. Were it not for the sharpness and rightness of the language these narratives might collapse at their joints, work themselves loose, and rattle away from both characters and readers. They tend to be filled with unexpected, unconnected observations and incidents: the narratives sometimes resemble odd bits of string dextrously knotted into one peculiar line. An example of this disconnected or disjointed longer fiction is 'The Burgundy Weekend' (1979), published not in *The New Yorker* but in *Tamarack Review*. In its entirety it resembles those pieces of paper torn into bits by one of its principal characters, the mad Jérôme. The lives of Jérôme, his wife Lucie, their hostess Madame Arrieu, and her granddaughter Nadine remain parallel—there is no chance of intersecting lines, of extended relationships as opposed to encounters bizarre as they are brief.

Jérôme and Lucie are not just any couple from Québec, holiday-ing in France. Jérôme has taken university degrees in France but has never done anything much with them—he met Lucie, a nurse, in the psychiatric hospital he had made his home. As the story opens they are about to be driven from Paris to a country house in Burgundy by Lucie's cousin, the egregious Gilles, 'one of the world's top dermatologists' (TR 13), a man 'on the side of life, not of failure', despite the fact that he lives in a state of virtual separa-tion from the 'obtuse', 'opaque' wife he so admires. Jérôme, of course, is on the side of disorder, eccentricity, random destructive-ness, and equally random desire. And he finds a perfect manifes-tation of such things in the country house of Madame Henriette Arrieu, whose weekend guests he and Lucie appear to be.

Lucie, we are told,

> could not grasp the meaning of this house, which was neither farm nor mansion; did not see why a scythed field required a fence and a wall around it; did not understand the running, breathless, scowling girl with her long cotton frock, bare arms, bare feet, flying hair; even less the plodding old woman who had a white mous-tache. The heels of Lucie's shoes sank into the loose gravel of the drive. Her ankles would not hold her. She felt herself clutching her white handbag. The dog had got out and was digging at the lawn: she saw that in white, as under lightning. (TR 14-15)

This clutch at particulars only underscores the utter absence of meaning, if meaning is associated with pattern, coherence, order, convention. The response of Lucie to Madame Arrieu's house is very much the reader's response to 'The Burgundy Weekend', that narrative structure of peculiar messages continuously trans-mitted, but only intermittently registered. In short, we never know quite what is going on: the narrator provides no floodlights, or even a search beam, but rather, 'a minute ray of light in a dark curtain', exactly like 'the pin-point concentration' of Jérôme's thoughts (TR 4). That small ray of light can be immediate and direct, as in the answer given to a spoiled young woman's com-plaint that washing machines have ruined that joyous sociability of collective action to be derived from laundering clothes at the public wash-house: 'Our hands used to be chapped and covered with blood. . . . We had to leave off rinsing so as not to bloody the clothes' (TR 29). Or it can be more profoundly illuminating, as in

Jérôme's recollection of a protest march held in 1950s Paris by former concentration-camp inmates:

> That day he had seen for the first time in his life how the police destroyed a crowd. They carved the whole into fragments and ground the fragments to crumbs. In those days the police carried capes with lumps of lead sewn in the hems. They rolled up the capes as if they were carpets and swung out. The men wearing the striped costumes tripped and fell and folded their arms for shelter. A head hitting a curb made one sound, a stick on the head made another. In those days you still remembered the brain beneath the bone: no one ever thought of that now. There were no crash helmets for protection, only hands and arms. Even Jérôme ran, though he still believed then that you could not have police running after you unless you deserved it. (TR 19)

Henriette Arrieu is a woman whose husband had played an important role in the Resistance and been betrayed by his most trusted friend. Jérôme had met her years earlier, while a student in Paris; coming to her country house for a weekend seminar on 'Socialism and the French-Speaking Union', talking alone with her late at night, he had glimpsed the possibility of becoming transformed into another person altogether by her—but nothing, of course, came of this (TR 22). Now, years later, nothing comes of his chance encounters with Madame Arrieu's granddaughter—the running, breathless, scowling girl in the cotton frock whose presence so mystifies Lucie.

Randomly connected 'pin-point' illuminations played off against a strange obstacle-strewn darkness—this is the stuff of 'The Burgundy Weekend'. It seems to resemble, in many ways, the entries in Flor's notebook in the novel *Green Water, Green Sky*: 'None of these fragments led back or forward to anything and many called up no precise image at all' (GWGS 71). The point of 'The Burgundy Weekend' is there being no point at all, just the unsettling effect of these collisions of light and darkness, meaning and muddle. In effect, nothing 'happens'—Jérôme literally plays with matches, but never succeeds in burning any houses down; the graceless, neglected Lucie gets through the weekend as best she can; Madame Arrieu is absent for most of her guests' visit, and Nadine, who has overheard a quarrel between Jérôme and Lucie during which Lucie recalls the various forms his madness has taken, comes to the conclusion that Lucie, not Jérôme, is the mad one of the couple. The story ends with the pompous Gilles ('In youth Gilles had looked like Julius Caesar, but now that he had grown thickly into his forties, he reminded people of Mussolini') driving an exhausted Lucie and a temporarily pacified Jérôme back to Paris. The three converse about fascism, and the sauerkraut and *soufflé Hiroshima* Gilles has consumed at a banquet in that gourmet's paradise, Dijon. It has been a nightmare of a weekend; it is a nightmare of a story, one with which the reader can do little except cling—as to the handstraps in a jolting subway car—to the elegance and precision with which such oddly knotted situations are narrated.

The deliberate opacity at the heart of 'The Burgundy Weekend' is quite different from that quality of obliqueness whereby Gallant teases extraordinary nuances and subtleties from what seem to be the most clichéd of characters and straightforward of situations— the rape of a provocative young woman in a northern mining camp in 'My Heart Is Broken', the eking-out-a-half-life by a timid and impoverished spinster in 'The Moabitess'. 'Nobody knows that I know,' Lucie cryptically concludes at the end of 'The Burgundy Weekend', after assuring Gilles that Jérôme really is 'all right': the trouble is that 'nobody' continues to include the reader. Gilles reflects that 'nothing less than a murder could round off the Burgundy weekend' (TR 39) and in the sense that a murder would at least be a concrete situation, a definitive act or response, he may be right. What has happened? 'Language' is the safest answer one can venture. Readers of this fiction may find themselves recalling William Pritchard's reservations about Gallant's refusal 'to make connections for us, . . . to speak as a thoughtful omniscience behind her characters' and her evasion of authorial responsibility in 'cultivating incongruities, juxtaposing voices and memories that fit together in only the craziest way'. The kind of omnipresent opacity one finds in 'The Burgundy Weekend' may reduce all but the most slavish of Gallant's readers to that state of perplexity experienced by a character in the story 'Sunday Afternoon'—'not certain what she meant, and not sure that it was true' (MHB 205).

*

Gallant knows she has finished a story when she feels 'not that the story seems all right, but that it seems inevitable' (iGH 55)—that inevitability, it would seem, is another term for a kind of closure characteristic of her fiction. I am not referring, in this context, to formal closure, for as we have seen with 'The Burgundy Weekend', Gallant's creation of opaque or discontinuous narratives can leave us without any sense of structures and borders at all. Rather, I mean a species of psychological or even ontological closure, an *a priori* closing-off or denial of possibilities to her characters, a tendency to imprison them within situations rather than to permit them the freedom of action. In Gallant's finest stories, however, the 'boxing-in' effect of this latter kind of closure is offset by the text's spiralling or 'helical'[5] structure: 'the story builds around its centre, rather like a snail' (iGH 45). Yet another counter to closure is to be found in the many gaps and unreadable traces that haunt the finished narrative. This effect of ellipsis works quite differently from the opacity we have seen in 'The Burgundy Weekend': in 'The Wedding Ring', 'Malcolm and Bea', and 'Jorinda and Jorindel' the conspicuous absence of connections between incidents and emotions points to their presence offstage, as it were: poignantly inaccessible to the characters. Gallant has said that she often begins a story with a scene in mind—a scene that may well be discarded by the time the story has reached its inevitable form (iGH 47). And within the finished text allusions are often made to incidents, images, structures of meaning that are never elucidated, remaining baffling gaps in the narrative line. The emotional givens in 'The Cost of Living', for example, seem written in a cipher for which we are given no code. Like the narrator, we are left out in the cold and the dark about essentials—Louise's feelings for Collie, the husband she lost after only weeks of marriage, and for the sluttish, greedy Sylvie, are knots too tightly tied for anyone to unpick. Even the distinctive objects that Gallant uses like hooks on which to drape the drifting fabric of her fictions are not so much symbols as signifiers that have only tenuous connections to their signifieds. This is true of the enormously expensive necklace with the 'rough, careless', warm appearance that, in a masochistic fit of generosity, Louise buys to give to Sylvie, and that Puss, who has coveted it all along, takes back from Sylvie once Louise has fled Paris for the arid safety of Australia.

Gallant's earliest published fictions reveal her fascination with and her precocious skill at combining lacunae and cross-hatching in her narratives, her creation of opaque patches with glints of light at their edges. 'Goodmorning and Goodbye', published by

Preview in 1944, has as its only character or centre of consciousness a Jewish refugee living with a Canadian family. His own German name and the 'Canadian' name he now goes by have split him into two persons: 'one here, and one almost lost, on the other side of the ocean' (P 1). This fiction is one that pits polarities against one another—the 'well of silence' that has become Paul's mode of being, (P 2) against 'the rattle of voices' and 'waste of words'(P 3) around him. Language, its absence and presence, and the contexts of physical and psychological displacement that govern these are the principal concerns of this story.

The title of any story is its envelope, Gallant has remarked (iGH 64). The title and opening sentences of 'Goodmorning and Goodbye' are characteristically Gallant; in them are coded the disaffection and contingency of being that are the laws of Paul's behaviour. The play of light and shadow through the leaves that he observes as the story begins seems appropriately unrelated to his mood or actions—this deployment of 'unrelated' observation is a staple with Gallant, a technique she uses to disorient the reader's expectations not so much of pathetic fallacy as of a reliable code whereby impenetrable states of mind can be translated into immediately apprehensible physical manifestations. Perhaps the clearest signal this story gives is that of the character's and reader's imprisonment, or at least detention, within a sealed structure. For though polarities are everywhere suggested—silence and speech, imprisonment and release—and though the action anticipated is one of potential freedom—the train journey to effect an escape from family—what predominates is 'the sense of ending, and the slipping into the vacuum that lies between the patterns in a life' (P 2). This peculiar sense of closure is ironically underlined by the text's final repetition of its elliptical title.

'Three Brick Walls', also published in *Preview* in 1944, is a rather less interesting continuation of Paul's story. As the title suggests, the refugee has achieved a problematic independence through his flight from the family that had been sheltering him. He is now on his own, searching for the freedom that comes of losing oneself in a crowd, as opposed to the imprisonment of being singled out as solitary and handicapped—not being able to say what one means. Yet 'Three Brick Walls' is noteworthy for the eruption, in its deliberately drab, drifting narrative, of two characteristics that are recognizably Gallantesque. There is one sentence in which we distinguish an authoritative narrative voice, using figurative language to interpret and assess: 'The people who poked repetitive keys into the doorways and climbed the stairs inside were those who have nothing of themselves outside lying around loose' (P 4). And a trace of Gallant's idiosyncratic, slightly malicious delight in the grotesque appears in a description of the man at the soda fountain, his two little tufts of black hair 'like rosettes behind the ears' (P 4).

With 'The Flowers of Spring' (1950), however, we are into fictive territory that is vintage Gallant, possessing a depth and resonance understandably lacking in her first publications. Whereas in 'Bonaventure' she will, in the margins of her text, give us a sketch of a disastrous wartime marriage, with Ramsay's mother coming to the realization that her marriage is dead at precisely the moment her soldier-husband is returning to her, 'The Flowers of Spring' takes a revealingly sidelong look at a situation that would be hackneyed and melodramatic faced head on: the wreck of a marriage between a thirty-two-year-old woman, Estelle, and the war-crippled, institutionalized husband to whom she is expected to remain loyal and loving. Gallant also introduces an ironic twist into the situation: Estelle is obliged to play the role of mother to her disaffected husband, Malcolm, and of devoted mistress to an indifferent lover, her husband's friend Bill.

What characteristics of this narrative define it as Gallant's work? The ironic title or 'envelope', of course, and the barbed, epigrammatic language Gallant employs, as in the description of Estelle as 'a charming bride . . . but a delinquent wife' (NR 32-3). There is the use of obliquely revelatory detail in, for example, Estelle's perception of Malcolm: 'His face had lost form, the features were blurred. The only sharpness was in the line from that terrible haircut' (NR 32). Characteristic, too, is the fiction's primary symbolic object—the unwanted daffodils Estelle brings Malcolm, and for which there is no container. The daffodils are used more directly and simplistically than their equivalents in Gallant's later fiction, but they play the same part as Emma's ill-fitting bracelet in 'Going Ashore' or the gecko in 'Better Times'. And true to form there is a flash of malicious humour in the passage on the dubious Dr Zatz: 'He was everything Estelle distrusted. He perspired, he was profuse, he was emotional. His wife, it had given Estelle joy to learn, was called Nadra' (NR 36).

In terms of narrative tone 'The Flowers of Spring' gives us full force that detachment and disinterestedness so characteristic of

Gallant's fiction: though Estelle's situation is clearly a poignant one, Gallant refuses us any luxury of engagement or identification with her any more than with the prickly Malcolm or the despicable Bill. Estelle is trapped in a hopeless situation, but then nothing about her suggests qualities that would make her worthy of any great happiness or even a measure of contentment. We watch her flipping through a hospital magazine and coming upon posed pictures of the wives of disabled men: 'she searched their faces for despair and discontent. If the feelings existed they photographed badly' (NR 32). The bitterness of the remark attests to the basic lie that is the premise of the photographs, but there is also a flippancy that points to Estelle's vacuity. She is a woman defined by her relation not to her lover, but to his apartment (she has no place of her own): 'any imprint she made on the rooms left with her each morning. Like water closing over a stone the air took back its own shape' (NR 38). She is the kind of woman one will meet again and again in Gallant's fictions, the sharp-eyed but passive prisoner of the feminine mystique.

'Madeline's Birthday', published a year later as Gallant's début piece in *The New Yorker*, takes us into more complex territory—that of the entangled love and resentment between parents and children, husbands and wives. As I shall show in the following chapter, Gallant writes startlingly and poignantly well about children and childhood: in 'Madeline's Birthday' she gives us a portrait of a psychologically displaced adolescent girl who is taken under the wing of her irresponsible mother's friend, Mrs Tracy. Having found Madeline abandoned in a Manhattan apartment, leading a life of delectable freedom, Mrs Tracy takes charge of the girl out of 'mixed motives of curiosity and kindness' (NY 20). Bringing her back to her Connecticut summer home, she only puts Madeline into full possession of unhappiness: 'She was unmarried and not in love and without a trace of talent in any direction' (NY 21). Madeline catches her benefactor's husband 'looking' at her in a way that is both arousing and insulting; she has no romantic interest whatsoever in the other young house guest, the refugee Paul, who 'seemed to Madeline doomed for life to ask for help and speak with a slight accent' (NY 21). Madeline, like Estelle, is facing a life term in the prison of patriarchy; unlike Estelle, however, she is still a child, and has not yet surrendered her dreams of freedom.

With these first publications—a dizzying leap from *Preview* and *Northern Review* to *The New Yorker*—the characteristic style, techniques, and tone of Gallant's narratives are set. What does vary in her subsequent publications is form: tightly structured, epigrammatic stories such as 'Acceptance of their Ways' and 'The Picnic' alternate with longer, elliptical fictions such as 'An Unmarried Man's Summer' or 'The Cost of Living'. Relatively late in her career, Gallant has begun producing sequential narratives—the Linnet Muir, Lena, and Carette stories, for example—though she continues to produce succinct, satirical, 'tightly fitted' fictions as well. If she began to write longer narratives because the subjects that intrigued her demanded more tenuous and desultory forms than those suited to her sharp, short comedies of manners, then she may have turned to story sequences in order to achieve not openness so much as continuousness, with narratives flowing out of the containers constructed for them and creating new ones in their turn. Because of the way in which it successfully avoids programmatic closure, because it represents that third, most rewarding kind of fiction written by Gallant, and because it is arguably her finest creation, the Linnet Muir sequence deserves to be commented upon here, however summarily.

The distinguishing feature of these stories is a dreamlike treatment of time that perfectly illustrates Gallant's statement: 'the process of time going on is a mystery to me. I have no sense of time—twenty years ago seems five minutes to me' (iHE). The narrator's random circling through the pools of memory gradually creates the self-portrait of a writer, that Linnet Muir who is not Mavis Gallant, we have been warned (HT xxii), but whose life bears some striking resemblances to Gallant's own. 'In Youth Is Pleasure' chronicles Linnet's declaration of personal independence, her freeing herself of her father's ghost and her refusal to accept the constrictions people would place upon her because of her background and gender. Because of the 'evaporation' of her remembered past, Linnet has to 'start from scratch' to establish the reality of her present situation and possibilities (HT 235). 'Between Zero and One' elaborates the limits and terminal points people set on their lives—men as well as women—and establishes Linnet's political awareness—the fact that 'there are two races, those who tread on people's lives, and the others' (HT 244). It ends with a suggestion of the fundamental choice open to Linnet—entrapment or escape. 'The blackest kind of terror', she feels, has 'to do with the men [with whom she works], with squares and walls and limits and numbers.' The story ends, however, with her speculations on movement, development, change: 'How do you stand if you stand upon Zero? What will the passage be like between Zero and One? And what will happen at One?' (HT 260).

The next story, 'Varieties of Exile', does not, of course, do anything so direct and simple as provide the answer. Instead we are given a sketchy portrait of a fledgling writer determined to turn life into literature: 'Anything I could not decipher,' she confesses, 'I turned into fiction, which was my way of untangling knots' (HT 261). In this story, in fact, the narrator defines writing as that state of 'quite right and perfectly natural' exile involved in putting life through a sieve in one's stories and then discarding it (HT 281). At the end of 'Varieties of Exile', however, the now-married Linnet, trapped in Montreal with her husband overseas, is consumed by a ferocious desire to occupy nothing but present time. By burning her manuscripts she attempts to destroy that former self so romantically attracted to refugees and remittance men. That her project ultimately fails, that her discarded experience returns to be rewritten, not analytically but in the spiralling, elliptical idiom of memory, is proved by the very existence of both the story 'Varieties of Exile' and the fiction that follows it in the sequence.

'Voices Lost in Snow' plunges us precisely into that 'dark' world of childhood preceding Linnet's exile in New York and her radical restructuring of memory and reality in Montreal. There is no causal relation between Linnet's progress in the previous three stories and her dreamlike fall into the past, her listening to 'the only authentic voices [she has]', those of the dead (HT 283). The transition is abrupt, unsettling, yet so authoritatively managed with its supremely confident opening that the reader willingly follows wherever the narrator leads. Yet 'Voices Lost in Snow' moves from acerbic recollections of the power of parents to tyrannize over or neglect their children, to a sketching out of the relations between the child Linnet and her dying father. It is all the more poignant for the delicacy with which it is done, as if the child's perception of her father's fatal squandering of strength and stifling of pain, the expression of helplessness on his face, and her own awareness of her love for him, were so tenuous and vulnerable that the utmost circumspection is called for, lest memory itself crumple and vanish. The survival of love is a close call, rather like Linnet's own brush with tuberculosis, a brush made all the more dangerous by the language in which it is expressed and evoked: '"*Votre fille a frôlé la phtisie*"*. . . .* "*Frôler*" was the charmed word in that winter's story; it was a hand brushing the edge of folded silk, a leaf escaping a spider-web. Being caught in the web would have meant staying in bed day and night in a place even worse than a convent school' (HT 289).

The last stories in this sequence move us from the 'distant' past of Linnet's childhood to that intermediate past of young womanhood with which this sequence began. 'The Doctor' begins by presenting Dr Chauchard in terms of his bewildering rejection of the child Linnet, when she runs away to his office from her hateful convent school. It then moves into a bemused attempt to realize Chauchard through the fragments of recollection Linnet can muster—the eccentric behaviour of one of his lovers; Chauchard's obituary, giving the news that the man Linnet had thought of only as a doctor was a poet as well. The impact of this discovery was, as she describes, 'an earthquake, the collapse of the cities we build over the past to cover seams and cracks we cannot account for' (HT 313). Yet this destruction of complacent fictions allows her to hear, through the words of Chauchard's published journals, 'his real voice, the voice that transcends this or that language' (HT 316). This is the voice Linnet has cause to hear in a special way, since she too will become a writer.

The final story, 'With a Capital T', is like a coda—less powerful, less profoundly immersed in a dreamlike past. Indeed, it presupposes the disappearance of that past altogether through the agency of Linnet herself, according to her godmother, Georgie: 'I was the final product, the last living specimen of a strain of people whose imprudence, lack of foresight, and refusal to take anything seriously had left one generation after another unprepared and stranded, obliged to build life from the ground up, fashioning new materials every time' (HT 326).

'With a Capital T' continues from the point at which 'Between Zero and One' left off, with Linnet fighting the conditions of personal impoverishment and professional closure that her time and sex impose. 'I had longed for emancipation and independence,' she relates, 'but I was learning that women's autonomy is like a small inheritance paid out a penny at a time' (HT 318). Into this disheartening quotidian struggle erupts the voice of Georgie, the mysterious 'other' woman whom her father takes her to visit in 'Voices Lost in Snow'. This voice is perceived by Linnet as one of 'the unexpected signatures that underwrite the past: if this much is true, you will tell yourself, then so is all the rest I have remembered' (HT 325). A strange double-take occurs in this fiction, for just as Linnet's memories of her childhood and her father are triggered by Georgie's voice, so her godmother's reappearance in 'With a Capital T' summons up our previous reading of 'Voices Lost in Snow'. Time, place, character, event overlap and blur, one into the other—the reader experiences the same dreamlike super-imposition of past and present as does Linnet herself. We are left with her response to this meeting, which is in itself a variation of that experience of rejection with which 'The Doctor' begins. Su-perficially, at least, Linnet wins out in this encounter—she writes a scathing account of her godmother's so-called war work, so scathing that it causes a complete and final rupture between Lin-net and this one woman who is the only representative of her parent's world left her:

> I did not forget her, but I forgot about her. Her life seemed silent and slow and choked with wrack, while mine moved all in a rush, dislodging every obstacle it encountered. Then mine slowed too; stopped flooding its banks. The noise of it abated and I could hear the past (HT 329).

Hearing the past is the principal action of this sequence of fic-tions in which various strata of memory are revealed, and the idiosyncratic, unhurried flow of recollection moves from story to story, doubling back and leaping forward. It is an outstanding ex-ception to the rule of Gallant's fiction, not only in its form, but also in the engagement and warmth of its tone, so different from the detachment and chill that characterize so many of her narratives. What in other fictions would be a disquieting opacity appears here as an indeterminacy entirely appropriate to the play of memory. Instead of the succinct comic satisfactions afforded by her shorter fictions, the Linnet Muir sequence offers the reader a sense of privileged inclusion, of entering the confidence of a narrator whose unhurried remembrance of time and places past is compell-ing in ways that the narrative manoeuvres of such a fiction as 'Its Image in the Mirror' cannot be.

*

Having briefly looked at the actual genesis of Gallant's works and distinguished the various forms her stories take, I will end this chapter with a consideration of her two attempts at the staple by which most prose writers are inevitably measured—the novel.[6] Her first essay in this genre was *Green Water, Green Sky* (1959), a work comparable to Elizabeth Spencer's *Light in the Piazza*. Gallant's novel is, above all, an exploration of the inseparableness of love and resentment—in this case, between a criminally inept but charming mother and her passively schizzy daughter. Gallant turns the truism about the desirability of closeness between mother and daughter violently around, making her characters discover that 'their closeness had been a trap, and each could now think, If it hadn't been for you, my life would have been different. If only you had gone out of my life at the right time' (GWGS 55).

But *Green Water, Green Sky* is also an examination of the unpredictability and unreliability of memory, of the way it can shade imperceptibly into a kind of fantasy that dissolves the reality and stability of present time. The madness of the central character, Flor, stems from her having abruptly lost both her father and her home, only to be trailed round countless foreign places by her fluttery-helpless mother, Bonnie. Loss of one's native familial ground—of the past itself—is tantamount to loss of any convincing sense of self. Flor's radical insecurity with and in the present, and the 'torment, nostalgia and unbearable pain' (GWGS 55) she feels in trying to reconstruct her own past, drive her to create a fictive golden world; at the point where she is crossing the shore from teetering sanity into fixed psychosis, she loses herself in memories of being her father's adored and perfect little girl, and riding out of an alley of trees into her father's arms. But the memory is a fantasy—for Flor the latter displaces the former: she refuses, for example, her younger cousin's recollection of how wildly she once played with a broken necklace, because the memory does not fit in with the picture of herself she has drawn in order to please her mother. 'We don't remember the same things,' she tells her cousin (GWGS 20); it is this that cuts off the various characters from one another, making it impossible for them to share a life, or a world.

Yet for all that Flor perceives herself as rootless, wavering, she and the other characters in this novel are given a firm social grounding. The Fairlies, Flor's and Bonnie's people, see themselves as genetically confirmed aristocrats; they are 'someone' in terms of breeding as well as money. The grandfather of Flor's husband Bob Harris, on the other hand, was a Jew from a Polish ghetto. A great deal of the highly strung ironic counterpoint in this novel derives from a complex play of cross-purposes: Bonnie's preoccupation with social class and money as determinants of identity, as opposed to Flor's drowning clutch at sexual love and marriage as props on which to arrange some convincing, solid sense of self, as opposed to Bob Harris's attempt at confirming an upwardly mobile self-image by taking on a well-connected, decorative, childlike bride.

Green Water, Green Sky is composed of four self-contained sections linked by an artful fluidity of narrative line. Events in one section are mirrored by or refracted in other sections; images, phrases, observations compose a 'watery world of perceptions, where impulses, doubts, intentions, detached from their roots, rise to the surface and expand' (GWGS 111). This fluid plenum is a structural correlative to Flor's madness, which takes her from 'a narrowing shore' into 'a moving sea' (GWGS 28). The novel's structure is also determined by its perception of that most fluid of all mediums, time. The events of *Green Water, Green Sky* are related in the past tense, though 'past' here is an unfixed quantity. The narrative flows from distant to immediate to intermediate past, with temporal dips and flutters in between. Thus we are shown (i) Flor at fourteen in Venice and at twenty-four as a bride in New York, (ii) Flor as Bob Harris's wife, going quietly mad in Paris, (iii) Flor as a desperately marriageable girl in Cannes, where, to her mother's despair, she takes up with the only moderately eligible Bob Harris, and (iv) Flor absent from any real world, since she is now an inmate of a discreet asylum outside Paris, and only unreliably present in the memories of her husband, mother, and cousin.

Though *Green Water, Green Sky* is forever shifting its point of view—Flor, her mother Bonnie and cousin George, and Bonnie's dubious gentleman friend, Wishart, are all centres of narrative consciousness—what dominates the novel is Flor's madness, a product of the relentless displacement and decentring of her life since her divorced mother's banishment to Europe. Gallant achieves this by design and, surprisingly enough, by narratorial intrusion. Even when we are nominally in George's, Wishart's, or Bonnie's heads, the narrator breaks in to underline the errors and anomalies in their judgements and perceptions, to act as a metacharacter, an amusing but manipulative *raconteur* directing our responses back to Flor. Narratorial discourse plays a not insignificant part in this novel, as, for example, when Gallant interrupts the evocation of a perception to tell us what distinguishes Flor's saving supports—'continuity and the past' (GWGS 111)—from her lover's. (This kind of holding forth, this placing of a character's most significant yet hidden thoughts firmly within the reader's grasp, is a device that will vanish altogether in Gallant's second novel, *A Fairly Good Time*.)

Though individual characters are shown as being hostile to or clueless about Flor, the narrative voice itself is in almost total sympathy with her. Yet there is a curiously desultory quality about the narrative, as the unfolding of Flor's madness is interrupted or sent offstage by forays into the consciousness of that consummate sponger, Wishart, or the plight of that quintessentially abandoned wife, the egregious American Doris, who does not belong to Paris but 'to an unknown cindery city full of used-car lots' (GWGS 56). Perhaps the most disconcerting thing about this novel's structure is the disruption of what one assumes will be its central sequence of events. Flor's final breakdown, climaxing in the hallucinatory visions of a fantasized childhood, occurs at the end of the novel's second section. It is followed by a return to the past—Wishart's arrival in the south of France as Bonnie's guest; Bob Harris's courtship of Flor at Cannes. The last section of the novel lands us abruptly in the present, with cousin George's arrival in Paris and Flor nowhere to be seen. All this time we have been left dangling as to what has happened to Flor. Is she dead? In an institution? Has she somehow recovered and freed herself from the trap of mother and husband? Only after a deluge of peripheral detail do we find out what, after all, is our primary concern—the mental and physical whereabouts of Flor. We are told that she is presently a memoryless inmate of a discreet hospital, given to feeding her husband pellets of bread off her dinner plate. We are not, needless to say, given any entrée into whatever is left of her mind—she is as good or bad as dead to us, existing only in the other characters' limited perceptions and faulty memories of her.

The dinner shared by characters who have previously seemed marginal—Bob Harris, Bonnie, and George—serves to illustrate the utter lack of any collision between delusion and reality that so afflicted Flor. We watch the three survivors walking into the 'foreign' night, Bonnie contradicting herself flagrantly and George not knowing whether to interpret this as intentional or inadvertent. George, we are told, 'lost hold of the real situation. He could see three people walking, stopping for traffic, moving on;

he could hear their voices, but he could not understand any of the things they said' (GWGS 145). His situation is analogous to the reader's own. Yet this last section succeeds brilliantly, for what it underscores is the horrifyingly easy displacement of Flor, the incorrigible, disastrous egotism of her mother's refashioning of reality, and the triumph of all that is indeterminate and ambiguous, as realized in the 'authentic hallucination' with which the novel ends: the 'changeable' figure—'now menacing, now dear'—of a woman who appears to George first as Flor, then as Bonnie, and finally as a perfect stranger (GWGS 154).

If the form and narrative mode of Gallant's first novel reflect in their eddying and shifting the 'watery world' of Flor's unsettled consciousness, then the technique whereby Gallant establishes the borders and foreground of her fictive world is appropriately painterly, in a post-impressionist way. Objects and images have a pervasive presence, if not solidity or wholeness: the garbage in the canals, Flor's illness taking metaphorical shape as a fox with sharp-pointed muzzle imprisoned in her breast, Bonnie under her parasol becoming an arrangement of 'disks in dwindling perspective' (GWGS 2), and such symbolic incidents as Flor's necklace breaking apart or her wild tossing of the glass beads upward into the sun. Throughout we are given impressions of people and their relations with one another, but never any description of the whole: selected objects come into focus but the background into which they should fit, for meaning's sake, is left a menacing blur. This artful selection and presentation of detail gives one the impression of looking not at a whole canvas, but at reproductions of small, obscure details blown up, enlarged in scale. In an interview Gallant has indicated her preference for a single drawing to a panoramic painting: she confesses herself to be 'more interested in a glimpse of something than in the whole thing' (iEB). This selective, discriminating vision perfectly suits Gallant's strategy of indirection in *Green Water, Green Sky*, whereby essential information is slipped into the interstices of dialogue and description—the crucial fact, for example, that Flor is physically 'different' (she cannot have children), or the information—almost casually mentioned during the dinner scene in part IV—that she is now in an asylum.

Yet of this short novel—154 pages—one can say that Gallant's dextrous use of language, her effortless rightness of diction, and the rich wash of images and perceptions she creates draw a disturbing order out of chaos. As though watching two screens simultaneously, the reader registers the stages of Flor's derangement and the blindness—wilful or helpless—of her family. We perceive as well what must be the most unsettling thing of all—that in the deracinated world this novel creates, a world in which delusion and memory are helplessly, tormentingly blurred, Flor's lapse into madness is a consummation as devoutly to be wished for her as is Krug's insanity at the end of Nabokov's *Bend Sinister*.

If Gallant's desire in her first novel is to achieve an ironic and accusatory order out of a veritable flood of memories and incidents, in her second, *A Fairly Good Time* (1970) she devotes her energies to the celebration of chaos. This account of the hopeless smash of a hopeless marriage, the abandonment of the quirkily intelligent, maddeningly feckless Shirley by her stroppy, bourgeois husband, Philippe, is a burlesque of the usual portrait-of-a-marriage. Bizarre characters wander into the narrative like strangers off the street—Shirley picks up acquaintances the way other people throw away candy wrappers. She cares about all those who aren't worth the time of day, and neglects those to whom she should be most firmly linked. She pushes what should be at the centre of her consciousness to the margins, and lavishes care and attention on the most peripheral, coincidental, and gratuitous of people and circumstances. The whole action of the novel is cerebral—except that what goes on in Shirley's scatty, supersaturated head does not, perhaps, deserve the high seriousness of the term 'cerebral'. Confusion, rampaging disorder, comic catastrophe reign supreme, and yet a kind of parity exists between the hapless Shirley, the author of all this entropy, and its helpless recipient, the reader. Shirley's tardy understanding of what her situation is—she realizes that her husband has walked out on her, that she has been booted out of her apartment and has no visible means of support, only when circumstances finally cram it into her consciousness—brings about no decisive response. She remains supremely adaptable, permanently bewildered, amiably and irredeemably self-deceiving.

Reality, in this fifteen-chapter novel, becomes a species of verbal confetti. The narrative is stuffed to the gills with precise but gratuitous details and with digressions featuring a Mad Hatter's Tea Party kind of logic. Consider, for example, this interlude in which Shirley takes the sulky Claudie, a stranger she has literally picked up in a bistro, to meet a couple who could possibly become foster parents to Claudie's illegitimate and most likely incestuous child, Alain:

> Behind the grey façade of an ordinary village house Shirley and Claudie found a courtyard filled with white geraniums. Claudie spent the day with most of her clothes off lolling in the little garden and admiring the studio, which contained Alain's future foster mother's welding equipment. Cats and doves, killers and victims were the pets of the house. Pig iron and used bicycle parts spilled out of the studio to the court. It looked to Shirley like debris after an accident: she thought of hillsides strewn with women's shoes, ripped handbags, combs. 'The kind of unexpected ingredient you find in the soup in Belgium,' said Van Tong genially. He and Honor would be charmed to have Alain at least as a summer guest. They seemed to think he would be no more bother than one of the cats. Claudie put on her clothes unwillingly and embraced her new, intimate friends as if they were her family and she were emigrating. On the way back to Paris she remarked, 'Alain will grow up surrounded by such good taste.' Shirley had not considered that. She imagined Alain carrying his little pot to the garden and vacantly watching cats leap at doves. (AFGT 172)

The adoption plans, not surprisingly, come to nothing. From this interlude we learn nothing about these characters and their situation that we did not know before, or rather, we know as little after it as we did before. Anyone who tries to read *A Fairly Good Time* as a traditional novel, featuring characters with stable, comprehensible personalities, and a plot in which actions occur in some kind of causal sequence, rather than as a result of 'chance and chance encounters' (AFGT 83), will quickly come a cropper. With this text one reads not a book, but language itself—one is simply carried off on a flood tide of verbal invention, and one clutches at whatever flotsam and jetsam of meaning happen to rush by. This eddying, lunatic narrative tacks wildly between a number of concerns: the insanely problematic 'connection between life and pleasure' (AFGT 6), the notion of forswearing any chance of happiness in order to make for oneself 'a comfortable existence, without memory and without remorse' (AFGT 49), the question of how to be 'saved', not defeated or doomed (AFGT 181) by one's unmeaning, fragmented, dislocated state of being—and the dilemma of what one's relations with others should be: fanatically cold and selfish, *à la française*, or wildly generous, that

promiscuous 'caring for strangers' (AFGT 70) which is the disastrous law of Shirley's being.

The comic energy of Gallant's satire infects her usually discreet
style: with the exception of *What Is To Be Done?*, this novel is unique among Gallant's fictions for the slangy, racy form its discourse
takes, and for the direct references to sexual activity it contains.
The reason for this openness in form and speech is, of course, the
character of Shirley. An only child whose parents were elderly
when she was conceived (her mother would have preferred the
embryonic Shirley to have been a tumour), a wife whose husband
is killed in a particularly senseless accident after they have been
married a month, a woman who has a miscarriage immediately
after her second wedding, and whose new husband walks out on
her because he can't stand the mess of their life and her mind—
this is Shirley. Saint or slattern, victim or manipulator, flagrantly
innocent or helplessly guilty, or all of the above? The reader is
given no more help at interpreting her perplexed existence than is
Shirley herself:

> All her private dialogues were furnished with scraps of prose
> recited out of context, like the disparate chairs, carpets and lamps
> adrift in her apartment. She carried her notions of conversation
> into active life and felt as if she had been invited to act in a play
> without having been told the name of it. No one had ever men-
> tioned who the author was or if the action was supposed to be sad
> or hilarious. She came on stage wondering whether the plot was
> gently falling apart or rushing onward toward a solution. Cues
> went unheeded and unrecognized, and she annoyed the other
> players by bringing in lines from any other piece she happened to
> recall. (AFGT 179-80)

One does not get harmony, wholeness, or radiance out of a fiction featuring such a heroine as its crazily spinning centre of consciousness. What one does get is lunatic farce with appalling
realities randomly breaking through, then sinking under:
Shirley's miscarriage, which she describes as death entering, then
leaving her (AFGT 182), the nasty Renata's suicide attempt, the tor-
turing of Algerians, the appalling upbringing of the leech-like
Claudie's son/half-brother. None of these horrors is presented
with any particular change in tone or shift in emphasis: Gallant's
chosen satiric mode deflects any prolonged engagement with
these realities; they are simply part of the narrative's headlong

rush, to be registered along with Philippe's permutations of Goosey Goosey Gander and the fact that in the icon on James's dressing table the Infant Jesus' head is disproportionately small. Throughout, Gallant insists upon the arbitrariness of insight, the impossibility of establishing the validity of any premise: 'A first impression is always wrong: so is the second, third and twentieth' (AFGT 250).

Much of the narrative consists of Shirley's questionable memories, other people's contradictory recollections and dubious confessions, the fictive scenarios Shirley substitutes for acting and experiencing the consequences of her acts (AFGT 152, 170, 186-7, 251-2), and her unconfirmed hunches about what other characters are like or have done. Interspersed are random texts: the letters of Shirley's mother, Mrs Norrington (letters so marvellously bizarre that to call Mrs Norrington eccentric would be a gross understatement); Philippe's hermeneutical raids on English nursery rhymes; passages from *The Peep of Day*, a terroristic tract for children given to Shirley by her mother's friend, Cat Castle, as her only inheritance; Philippe's lacklustre variations on his one journalistic gold-mine, 'The Silent Cry'; paragraphs from a peripheral character's autobiographical novel; extracts from a neighbour's *Roget's Thesaurus*, Shirley's 'notes' to Philippe after she has realized their marriage is over; and the last, disastrous letter she writes to him. Added to these are references to literary texts: Jane Austen's *Persuasion*, Kingsley Amis's *Lucky Jim*, George Eliot's *Middlemarch*, plus the classics of childhood—*Little Women, Pinocchio, Alice in Wonderland*. Yet none of these texts possesses or confers any interpretative authority—they seem to be tidbits thrown in for connoisseurs of chaos.

Despite—or because of—the extraordinary vigour of this narrative, the energy of Gallant's wit and the immensity of her appetite for detailed observation, certain difficulties present themselves when one sits down to read it—the text is one big eddy of effluvia, chaos for chaos' sake: Gallant's joke, perhaps, on the trusting or tradition-bound reader. How, then, should we read this novel—and why? Not because we feel any compulsive affection for Shirley: she chides her 'friend' Claudie for wanting 'an imbecile life, not worth caring about'(AFGT 187) and yet the reader has strong doubts as to whether the life Shirley mucks her way through is any less imbecilic, or any more worthy of our attention. We certainly do not read *A Fairly Good Time* for a romantic account of a Canadian in Paris: though the Canadian reprint edition of this novel has the Eiffel Tower reproduced on its cover, the Paris Gallant gives us is one of urine-smelling staircases, scabrous suburbs, cheap wine, and sleazy brasseries. Nor are there aesthetic satisfactions to be had from form or structure—this text, on the contrary, seems the postmodernist equivalent of those 'loose, baggy monsters' Henry James reproved Tolstoy's novels for being. In some ways reading *A Fairly Good Time* is like being sucked into a vortex, and yet it would be almost impossible to rush through it at a single sitting. We read this text in fits and starts, with a kind of nervous delight at a narrative energy and abandon that can so assault our expectations of novel-writing and -reading.

Not surprisingly, *A Fairly Good Time* has generated critical responses as problematic as the text itself. Writing for *The Hudson Review*, J.M. Morse somewhat staggeringly describes Gallant's second novel as 'a pleasant novel of manners' whose author exhibits the 'virtues of a good, old-fashioned novelist'. Brendan Gill praises this 'merry and sad and robust and lapidary' novel, its 'unflaggingly comic tone', and the 'suave irony' of Gallant's prose, but then comments on the passivity of Shirley who is not 'accident-prone, but accident-supine'—a fact that makes the reader ultimately uninterested in her plight. He implies that the very structure of the novel is seriously lacking—'The novel is to stop not because its action has run its course, but because there is nothing more that [Gallant] wishes to tell us about poor Shirley'—and concludes that *A Fairly Good Time* allows us to reach the 'level of feeling implied by the motto from which the book's title comes'— a motto Gill describes as a 'breezy wisecrack'.[7]

It is not surprising that Gallant did not go on to write other novels: she has recently published a portion of one in *The New Yorker*, but from what has appeared so far it is obvious that the new novel is a much more sober and reined-in affair; as caustic, elliptical, and elegant as anything else she has produced. And perhaps this is just as well. As it stands, *A Fairly Good Time* is a welcome anomaly, a fiction in which Gallant has let her hair down, producing a text that is technically more adventurous and unpredictable than anything else she has written, with the exception of 'The Pegnitz Junction'. The fictions she has gone on to produce since her second novel move, as we shall see, in less digressive, more resonant, and, for this reader at least, distinctly more engaging and rewarding directions.

Notes

[1] See the back-cover blurb for *From the Fifteenth District* (Toronto: Macmillan, 1979).

[2] Gallant also favours a technique of ironic undercutting, as when she describes George in *Green Water, Green Sky* as 'fair-haired, deeply injured, rather fat' (p. 4). For the most part she creates the people in her stories by bold and cutting strokes of language, rather than by setting them in taxing situations and then revealing psychological depths and complexities. Consequently she restricts herself to what E.M. Forster would term flat as opposed to round characters: feckless, dependent men, bewildered, passive women, tyrannical mothers, shiftless fathers, exploited servants, abandoned and disobliging children. Or else her characters are emotional ciphers about whom the narrators can tell us nothing decisive: they elude us, as Isobel eludes Jean in 'Its Image', or Louise, Puss in 'The Cost of Living': like Linnet Muir's father, they are secrets in closed drawers that do not belong to us.

[3] A master of epigrammatic style and pithy phrasing, Gallant comes to seem like the character Mary in 'Careless Talk': 'She was the rock on which weaker natures broke. She saw their hopes and failings turned back like waves. Hard, lucid, tirelessly inquisitive, her eyes looked beyond Iris, measuring Iris. She seemed totally just' (IT 129). Gallant seems totally just, one may argue, first, because she uses such definitive, masterful speech to articulate her assessments of people and places, and second, because she allows us so little time or space to come to divergent conclusions.

[4] First-person narrators are used in 'Wing's Chips', 'When We Were Nearly Young', 'Autumn Day', 'Rose', 'The Sunday after Christmas', 'April Fish', the Linnet Muir sequence, 'Its Image on the Mirror', 'The Cost of Living', the Lena sequence, 'The Prodigal Parent', 'The End of the World', 'The Wedding Ring', 'An Autobiography', 'An Alien Flower', 'O Lasting Peace', 'The Latehomecomer', and 'Let it Pass'.

[5] George Woodcock, 'Memory, Imagination, Artifice: the late short fiction of Mavis Gallant', *Canadian Fiction Magazine* 28, p. 75.

[6] Gallant terms 'Its Image on the Mirror' (first published in the short-story collection *My Heart Is Broken*) a 'short novel', though it is roughly the same length as 'The Pegnitz Junction', which she calls a novella, and *Green Water, Green Sky*, which she published separately as a novel, although parts of it first appeared in instalments in *The New Yorker*. For the purposes of this study I am considering 'Its Image' as a novella, and hence excluding it from examination in the last section of this chapter.

[7] J.M. Morse, review of *A Fairly Good Time*, *Hudson Review* 23: 2 (Summer 1970), p. 37; Brendan Gill, review of *A Fairly Good Time*, *The New Yorker* 19 Sept. 1970, pp. 132-3. There were, of course, entirely laudatory reviews—most notably Judith Rascoe's in *The Christian Science Monitor* 4 June 1970, p. 7.

Chapter 4

The Prison of Childhood

. . . images of Victorian children in repose, between reprimands, safely over whatever they had been deprived of that morning in the way of food or comfort and considering the safest way of avoiding an unknown offense. ('The Statues Taken Down' [IT 162])

Children are regularly abused and ill-treated and some of them die of their wounds. (PN 130)

'The Remission' (1979), a story collected in *From the Fifteenth District*, is one of Gallant's masterpieces—a fiction with all the barbed wit, the satirical eye (this time turned on the Riviera life of British expatriates) and the narratorial detachment so distinctive of Gallant's work, and possessed, as well, of a power to profoundly move us in its dislocation of our assumptions about justice and love. 'The Remission', like so many of the stories in *Fifteenth District*, possesses this power because the vision it articulates deals with a special sort of high ground, one that may well be the only sacred territory—that world of clear-eyed 'grief and terror' that is childhood. 'The Remission' is a paradigm for much that I wish to say about Gallant's perception of childhood, and the significant role this subject plays in her writing: accordingly, it is a fiction worth examining in some detail.

Nominally, 'The Remission' is 'about' Alec Webb, who tears up his life in 'gray, dim' Labour Party Britain in order to die on the sunny Riviera—a flight financed by his impoverished sister and the prosperous but suspicious brothers of his wife, Barbara. In a way, Alec's fatal disease is not whatever illness is devouring him, but his having survived a war that killed off even the semblance of what had sustained the ethos of the middle-class English gentleman, 'courteous by nature, diffident by choice' (FFD 89). Unfortunately for everyone concerned, Alec does not die with the rapidity his English doctor had guaranteed: he lingers in a pale limbo, a situation as tortuous to his children as it is inconvenient

to his wife, who ends by having an affair with a 'stage En-
glishman' who nevertheless has enough wits about him to arrange
for Barbara's welfare after her husband's death. (The perfectly correct Alec, of course, has not had the strength or conviction to try
to make any kind of provision for his family.) There are well-
meaning neighbours and casual friends who act as an ironic
chorus to the scandals at Lou Mas, the damp and crumbling villa
occupied by the Webbs, as well as a doctor who seems truly to care
about the dying man, shielding him from at least the physical indignities his protracted dying creates. Yet the story would be no
more than an elegant vivisection of a certain spectrum of
Britishers abroad, were it not for the unsentimental, unironic, and
compassionate attention it pays to Alec Webb's children.

'It did not occur to him or to anyone else that the removal from
England was an act of unusual force that could rend and lacerate
his children's lives as well as his own. The difference was that their
lives were barely above ground and not yet in flower' (FFD 75).
Strong verbs, those, particularly menacing given the metaphor
Gallant employs: children as tender plants. She gets away with the
hackneyed image here precisely because of the violence with
which she surrounds it. For what we witness in the next thirty-
nine pages is the laceration of young lives: wounds severe enough
to maim, if not quite kill. The half-unwitting, half-complicit victimizers are, not surprisingly, the children's parents—the
moribund, penniless Alec and the spendthrift, silly Barbara, either
of whom would be incapable of competently raising budgerigars,
never mind children. But then one wonders whether, in the whole
of Gallant's work, any exception to the 'prodigal parent' is to be
found: only perfect strangers, it would seem, are capable of wisdom or kindness as far as children are concerned.

Will, Molly, and James—aged ten, eleven, twelve—are at first
left to their own devices: because their residence at Rivabella will
last only as long as their father's rapidly waning life, they are not
to be 'settled in' or sent to school. In a fine example of arbitrary
parental law, they are forbidden to play in the house, though one
of their father's main reasons for coming to the Riviera had been
to have his children with him at the end of his life. Finally some
sensible, experienced, and childless neighbours impress upon the
Webbs that the children must be sent to school, if not in England,
then at least to a reputable lycée in town—otherwise they will become 'unfit for anything save menial work in a foreign language

they could not speak in an educated way' (FFD 93).

In some ways, Gallant uses the children to prick the illusions of their hapless parents, pitting Alec and Barbara's Lawrentian love of the natives of Rivabella—'classless and pagan, poetic and wise, imbued with an instinctive understanding of light, darkness, and immortality' against the children's uneasiness with 'these strange new adults, so squat and ill-favored, so quarrelsome and sly, so destructive of nature and pointlessly cruel to animals' (FFD 81). Certainly the children's quickness in adapting to their peculiar situation and learning the ways of the Rivabella world distinguish them from the luckless compatriots who make up their neighbours, that elderly crew with their 'nursery ailments'. What they really want, the French doctor concludes, is 'to be tucked up next to a nursery fire and fed warm bread-and-milk' (FFD 82) a treatment strenuously denied to the children themselves. Predictably, Will and Molly and James respond just like the characters of cautionary tales for children: 'in the large house they fought for space. They were restless and noisy, untutored and bored' (FFD 91), especially as the whole *raison d'être* for being at Lou Mas—their father's death—refuses to materialize.

Children do not live in a world of their own, Gallant insists (FFD 99)—they live in 'the adult world of muddle' (FFD 93) and, what's worse, they are at a perilous disadvantage there, lacking the knowledge and strength to hold their own against the tyrannical whims, spurious authority, or simple negligence of adults whose size and age permit them to mistreat children in any way they like. Of the three children in 'The Remission' it is Molly who suffers most, and at the hands of both her parents. For Gallant refrains from any sentimental softening in her portrait of the dying father. Alec dies a shabby death, it is true, but there is more bathos than poignancy in his gestures—for example, his doffing of his invalid's pyjamas to struggle into a suit to watch the televised coronation of the Queen. There is also cruelty, as in his response to Molly's persistent tenderness. When, devastated by her father's helplessness, the girl kneels down beside his chair and presses her hand to his face, Alec does not acknowledge her. 'Presently he slipped the hand away to turn a page. . . . What use was his hand to Molly or her anxiety to him now? Why hold her? Why draw her into his pale world? She was a difficult, dull, clumsy child. . .' (FFD 88-9). The suffering that Molly's selfish and shallow mother inflicts on her daughter seems not harsher than that inflicted by the father, but equally intolerable. Gallant never pronounces judgement on Alec and Barbara Webb, but simply gives them rope enough to hang themselves several times over. The fact that the children get caught in the rope makes it all the more painful for the reader—we prefer the wicked and guilty to be punished, to have our faith in human justice restored. But this fiction will not permit us those illusions. Life isn't like that, we hear the narrator say: the self-seeking and self-deceiving sail through—the 'poor, the honest, the conscientious' (and the young) bear the brunt (iGH 36). There is no call, or worse, no use for hair-tearing, breast-beating: things are so, and ever more will be so, as Molly foresees at her father's funeral. The uprooting and ill-treatment of Alec's children can be compared to his death: 'he ceased to be, and it made absolutely no difference after that whether or not he was forgotten' (FFD 116). The double meanings are crucial here—it makes no difference to Alec, and Molly cannot make her own or her mother's life any different because of it.

Yet that zero degree of narratorial disinterestedness to be found in so many of Gallant's fictions does not apply to her portrayal of these children, or to the story of their lives, as opposed to their parents'. Particularly in her treatment of Molly, Gallant introduces an element of patience, almost tenderness—in her characterization of the girl there is none of that 'summary execution' at which she is so adept. Almost to the end of this fiction, she permits Molly to see and interpret and respond to things in a fashion at once naïve and poignantly authentic. Bewildered, the girl begins to menstruate and grows breasts: because of her mother's flightiness and foolish candour, Molly doesn't dare approach her for advice: 'Another thing still troubled Molly, but it was not a matter she could mention: she did not know what to do about her bosom— whether to try to hold it up in some way or, on the contrary, bind it flat. . . . There was no one she could ask. Barbara was too dangerous; the mention of a subject such as this always made her go too far and say things Molly found unpleasant' (FFD 93). The wonderfully comic passage in which Molly wonders whether it is every woman's fate to have her body turn to india-rubber (she has happened to catch a glimpse of a stout, elderly, naked English-woman) is counterbalanced by Gallant's recording of the real distress occasioned by Barbara's 'refusing or neglecting or forgetting to buy [her daughter] the things she needed; a lined raincoat, a jersey the right size' (FFD 96).

Paradoxically, it is Barbara's neglect coupled with her over-solicitousness that brings about the ultimate catastrophe in the children's lives. Having been ceaselessly warned by her mother never to accept a lift from a stranger, Molly allows Eric Wilkinson, a man she has seen once at a neighbour's, to drive her home from school. (The alternative would have been to wait at the bus stop, inadequately dressed, 'wet through, and chilled to the heart' [FFD 96].) Anxious to exculpate herself, Molly insists on bringing Wilkinson into Lou Mas to meet her mother. A few weeks later he is in her mother's bed, or rather, every evening Barbara leaves the bed she insists on sharing with Molly, now that Alec has been removed to the crumbling-villa-cum-hospital, to sneak into Wilkinson's bedroom at Lou Mas. Molly habitually awakes alone and, still consumed by the anxiety that seems her natural element, sends her brother down the hall to pry their mother from her lover's bed.

Gallant registers the effect on Will of this matutinal errand with a powerfully 'telescoped' description. As he makes his way down the hallway to retrieve his mother, Will hears 'Mr Cranefield's peacocks greet[ing] first light by screaming murder. Years from now, Will would hear the first stirrings of dawn and dream of assassinations' (FFD 100). Likewise, she sketches rather than embroiders the children's 'torment' at their mother's behaviour. 'James imagined ways of killing Wilkinson, though he drew the line at killing Barbara. He did not want her dead, but different. The mother he wanted did not stand in public squares pointing crazily up to invisible saints, or begin sleeping in one bed and end up in another' (FFD 101). What is so perfectly realized, so telling-ly accurate, in Gallant's observation of how children respond to this kind of parental betrayal, is the mixture of outraged egotism and desperate cleaving to decorum and convention that anxious children find natural and necessary. Recalling V.S. Pritchett's discovery of a 'central moral dilemma' at the core of each story in *Fifteenth District*, one may connect that dilemma with Gallant's disinterested treatment of Barbara Webb's affair with the far from monstrous Eric Wilkinson. What is truly culpable in Barbara's behaviour, Gallant makes us see, is not her 'immorality' in taking a lover while her husband still clings to some form of life, but rather, her having maintained the tyrannical authority of a parent while abdicating from the responsibilities and decorum such authority entails. Thus we are shown Barbara trying to make her sons treat her as an equal—sitting on their beds, sipping wine, and offering to share her cigarettes, 'though James was still twelve' (FFD 102). Her sons, of course, refuse her overtures—to them she smells like a cat and stinks of folly. 'They stared at her, as if measuring everything she still had to mean in their lives' (FFD 102).

When Alec proves incapable of dying with any reasonable or decent speed, Molly's brothers, who have bought Lou Mas more as an investment than as a haven for a dying man, force Barbara and her children to move into smaller, shabbier quarters in town. 'To replace their lopped English roots [the children] had grown the sensitive antennae essential to wanderers. They could have drawn the social staircase of Rivabella on a blackboard, and knew how low a step, now, had been assigned to them. . . . The boys had stopped quarrelling. They would never argue or ever say much to each other again. Alec's children seemed to have been collected under one roof by chance, like strays, or refugees' (FFD 106). Molly, at fourteen, assumes the role her mother never cared or knew how to play: 'It was Molly who chose what the family would eat, who looked at prices and kept accounts and counted her change' (FFD 106). It is Molly, of course, who is marked out for the luckless fate of being a spendthrift in love, like Alec's sister Diana, who squanders her savings to pay for her brother's death abroad, and who comes all the way from England for his interment. It is not to the dead Alec that the reader extends sympathy, but to his unreasonably selfless sister—were it not for her presence, the vantage point afforded by her stoic suffering ('Her own loss was beyond remedy, and so not worth a mention' [FFD 111]), the reader would only be repelled and not profoundly disquieted by Alec's end—his being hoisted, without service or ceremony, into a cement cell, sealed up, and marked by a misspelled marble plaque. It is, Diana reflects, 'as if Alec had been left, stranded and alone, in a train stalled between stations' (FFD 111).

Diana's presence at Alec's interment is, in fact, a kind of memento mori for her niece. To console the distraught Molly, a neighbour says: 'You will grow up, you know . . . when you grow up you will be free.' Molly, we are told, 'knew better than that now, at fourteen: there was no freedom except to cease to love' (FFD 113). It is a freedom she is incapable of assuming, no matter how many rebuffs she has received. About her unresponsive father Molly worries even beyond his death, obsessed as she is by the need to confess to him that Barbara's affair with Wilkinson is all her fault. His being walled up in concrete and marble makes that impossible: 'You could speak to someone in a normal grave, for earth is porous and seems to be life, of a kind. But how to speak against marble? Even if she were to place her hands flat on the marble slab, it would not absorb a fraction of human warmth' (FFD 114). Perhaps the most profoundly disturbing and moving aspect of 'The Remission' is the glimpse we are given of Molly's future, a life spent vainly trying to 'speak against' marble, to turn it into 'life of a kind'.

Yet though Molly is quite clearly doomed to be one of those who 'bear the brunt' of loving (while her mother gets off scot-free as only the thoughtless can) the reader never feels as though Gallant has simply stacked the cards against her. If love itself is a trap, as the whole of Gallant's fiction attempts to persuade us, then 'The Remission' shows how complex, deep, and utterly necessary a thing a trap can be for a character so constituted as Molly. Gallant employs her narrative art to delineate the plight of Molly and her brothers with delicacy, compassion, and a saving trace of humour: eschewing clichéd situations or easy pathos, sentimentality or indignation, she draws a haunting portrait of children abandoned, betrayed, and saving themselves in the only ways they can. And if Gallant refuses her readers the consolation of a happy, or even tolerable ending—for example, Diana adopting her brother's daughter, or Molly accepting the freedom to cease to love—she compensates us by creating characters with whom we can feel; for whom we can care. It is this, as well as the wonderfully rich and resonant fictive world she creates in Rivabella, that makes 'The Remission' a story to which we can return, again and again.

*

Before appearing in 'The Remission' Molly, James, and Will had played significant roles, in different guises, in other fictions by Gallant. They, or their *semblables*, were the children in 'A Day Like Any Other', 'An Unmarried Man's Summer', and 'The Statues Taken Down'. Molly was, *mutatis mutandis*, Emma in 'Going Ashore' and Flor in *Green Water, Green Sky*—a daughter forced to exchange roles with her feckless and destructive mother. For Gallant, like Henry James, devotes a great deal of her fiction to examining critically the relationships between parents and children, and is supremely gifted at conveying the world from a child's perspective. The narrative of her early story 'Jorinda and Jorindel' (1959), while not restricted to eight-year-old Irmgard's point of view, nevertheless possesses a magically childlike quality: the use of the present tense throughout, the relating of intense perceptions and emotions, the presence of adult meanings only half-deciphered or else helplessly misinterpreted by inexperienced observers, all combine to plunge us into the uncertain, risky world that children share with adults, but on unequal terms. In the Linnet Muir sequence Gallant describes it as 'the prison of childhood itself', its gaolers being 'people who [are] physically larger and legally sovereign' (HT 225).

What strikes one immediately in any of these fictions is the freshness and immediacy of Gallant's evocation of childhood. These qualities, however, have nothing to do with that 'garden of delight' so favoured by anthologists of children's literature, but rather with night terrors and daily battles against the adult authority and hypocrisy that feature in the subversive classics of the genre—fairly tales and such 'nonsense' works as *Alice in Wonderland*.[1] As Gallant interprets them, the terrors of childhood are rooted in the utter vulnerability of a child's position. 'An Autobiography' sums up the helpless dependence of children in a powerful image suggesting both innocence and terror: 'The child is tossed from home to school, or from one acrobat parent to another, and knows where it will land. I am frightened when I imagine the bright arc through space, the trusting flight without wings. Reflect on that slow drop from the cable car down the side of the mountain into the trees. The trees will not necessarily catch you like a net' (PJ 110).

Gallant's compassion or fellow feeling for the plight of those subject to an authority based not on 'principle' but on nothing more than biological accident and whim disguised as principle (iBG 26) is absolute. It achieves its most painful expression in association with the term 'Pichipoi', explained in the story 'Malcolm and Bea' (1968) as the name invented by Jewish children in France for that unknown destination to which they were being deported, by their countrymen, in compliance with Hitler's racial laws. 'Pichipoi' comes to mind again à propos of one of Gallant's essays, published eight years after 'Malcolm and Bea': in this review article on a study of Céline, she makes reference to Paris as 'a city where ghosts of deported children haunt the railway stations' (PN 218), a reference all the more poignant for its obliquity.

Gallant's extraordinary ability to recall what it is like to be a child at the mercy of unenlightened or inept adults does not, however, prevent her from recognizing the common rather than special humanity of children—the fact that they can be selfish, stupid, and cruel, as well as vulnerable and forlorn. In this context one can quote Gallant's remark on Elizabeth Bowen, with whose vision she has obvious affinities: 'The rock-bottom one discovers rereading [Bowen's] work', she suggests, 'is a foundation of tyranny and victimization, with the innocent character quite often an unwitting tyrant' (PN 234).

Certainly in *Green Water, Green Sky* Bonnie believes she is Flor's victim; she excuses her blithely leechlike propensities with the declaration that, from the time her divorce cut her loose from her social and domestic moorings, her daughter has been the only God she has worshipped. Bonnie's worship rings as false as does Lila Ellenger's devotion to her daughter Emma in 'Going Ashore', a text we shall presently examine. Yet however dubious is the quality of a child's innocence in Gallant's fiction, the fundamental inequity of the parent-child relation is beyond doubt: 'when you're very small you can't be charged with not getting on with someone who is six times your height. You're not equals. You never are' (iBG 26). All children can do in the worst of such situations is to adapt and survive, until they reach the majority that technically guarantees independence.

What so many of Gallant's fictions underscore, however, is that the experience of betrayal, loss, and injustice we suffer in childhood, when our sensibilities are keenest, our defences against 'grief and terror' weakest, does maim our adult lives. Perhaps only a truly luckless few of us are like Douglas Ramsay in 'Bonaventure', so repulsed by the fact of our very conception and the power it gives our parents over us, that we can convince ourselves we have 'never had parents; there [is] nothing behind [us], nothing to come' (HT 145). But many of us, like Will in 'The Remission', are haunted in our dreams, pursued by our memories of what we have suffered at the hands of those 'six times [our] height'. Inability to love, a propensity for suffering, emotional rootlessness, and moral blankness—these form our inheritance on our coming of age.

Gallant herself survived a horrendous childhood—she declares herself one of the lucky ones, able to adapt quickly and to be strengthened by the 'often unexpected and violent' changes in her life as a child. Among them was her father's death (she was told only that he had gone away, and she spent painful years waiting for him to come back and rescue her) and forced attendance at some seventeen different schools. She has related that her 'one desire from the age of about ten was to grow up and become independent and not have anyone try and tell [her] what to do' (iGH 28). This is, of course, the desire from which the Linnet Muir fictions unfold.

Gallant has warned that these stories are not autobiographical. For her readers the important consideration about the Linnet sequence is not whether a biographical mirror to Gallant's own experience is to be found therein, but rather, what these stories can tell us about the reality of childhood as this writer envisions it: the devastating effect our relations with adults can have on our lives if we do not work ourselves free of our need for our parents. The fictions dealing with Linnet Muir are remarkable for a tranquillity, almost a softness of mood, that would seem to stem from the personal and temporal freedom enjoyed by the narrator. It is as though the action of memory has veiled a usually piercing gaze, turned it from outward attack and led it circuitously inward. Memory, as we have seen, is one of the constitutive elements of Gallant's fictive world. A Janus-face turned to present and past, it proves an unreliable yet indispensable agency both for retrieving that past in which one's true self lies, and for deceiving oneself as to what one has become. And memory is rooted in childhood, the period of our lives when, as the Linnet Muir sequence makes clear, our experiences are most intense, our powers of observation keenest, our judgement most sound.

The first few of these stories deal with Linnet's achievement of personal independence from parental authority and her defiance of all those social conventions and fiats threatening to counteract her vow 'that I would never be helpless again and that I would not let anyone make a decision on my behalf' (HT 222). We are told that at fifteen Linnet 'lost interest' in the mother who had never taken much interest in her. Linnet is careful to give us a precise account of her emotions, almost as if to negate the importance of her mother's place in her life: 'It was not rejection or anything so violent as dislike but a simple indifference I cannot account for. It was much the way I would be later with men I fell out of love with' (HT 218).

Linnet's independence from her family is economic as well as

emotional: 'I was solely responsible for my economic survival and
... no living person felt any duty toward me' (HT 219). Her father's
death while she was still a child had, she reveals, 'turned my life
into a helpless migration' (HT 219) and she quit New York with the
vow that she would never return: 'there could be no journeying
backward' (HT 221). Ironically, Linnet's return to Montreal, the
city of her childhood, is a journey 'into a new life and a dream
past' (HT 228), brought about as much by the agency of memory
as by the train propelling her into the dark and the future.
Memory, as Gallant presents it, is a species of narrative, as fictive
a construct as the stories Linnet writes. As she tries the reality of
the city against memories bred by 'exile and fidelity' (HT 223) Linnet finds herself deliberately reordering and recomposing what is
there to be remembered: 'The past, the part I would rather not
have lived, became small and remote, a dark pinpoint' (HT 225).

Linnet's personal 'revolution' involves more than a flight from
her mother's roof—she rejects not just her family but, as importantly, the system of 'refined' manners and the mores that under-
pin them. Like Jean Duncan in 'Its Image on the Mirror', Linnet
has been subjected to a 'crisis' upbringing. Unlike Jean, she is
decisive in judging and condemning it. Keeping a stiff upper lip
in public, she declares, 'is murder in everyday life. . . . The dead
of heart and spirit litter the landscape' (HT 228). Linnet is able to
pronounce judgement so quickly and passionately because she is
speaking not as a matron with her own children to tyrannize, but
as someone who will always be a recent escapee from the prison
of childhood, someone whose awareness of the hypocrisy of be-
having impeccably in public and rampaging in private is so strong
that it cannot be weakened or deformed by memory in the service
of adult propriety. What she has retained from childhood is a
fierce sense of justice, an ability to detect and resist hypocrisy—
for example, 'lying, which my mother regularly did but never for-
gave in others' (HT 236).

Linnet's first action on returning to Montreal is to exorcise her
father's ghost, or rather, any ghost of a reason still to need him.
The premier trauma of her childhood, it appears, was to have been
kept in darkness about her father's death: to have been suddenly
banished from everything familiar while all the time waiting for
her father to return from somewhere in England and claim her.
Suspecting that 'death and silence can be one', she provokes an
adult into losing his or her temper and telling her the truth:

What I had not forseen was the verbal violence of the scene or the effect it might have. The storm that seemed to break in my head, my need to maintain the pose of indifference ('What are you telling me that for? What makes you think I care?') were such a strain that I had physical reactions, like stigmata, which doctors would hopelessly treat on and off for years and which vanished when I became independent. (HT 228-9)

On her return to the city in which she last saw her father, Linnet finds only ambiguous traces of his presence. Those 'friends' who refused him emotional support when he most needed it are as ungenerous to his daughter, whom they perceive as dangerously lacking in 'collateral security—fame, an alliance with a powerful family, the power of money itself' (HT 232).

Linnet's rummaging in the drawers of her father's life produces a brief, damning portrait of her mother—'she made herself the central figure in loud, spectacular dramas which she played with the houselights on' (HT 230). Rather like Barbara in Rivabella, Linnet's mother had flagrant love affairs while her husband was dying of tuberculosis of the spine. Yet, like the narrator of 'The Remission', Linnet makes no black and white judgements, nor does she show her father to have been capable of any great tenderness or affection for her. We are given the strong impression that Linnet's parents were as wildly unsuited to one another as they were to the responsibility of raising a child.

Eventually Linnet deals with the various versions of her father's end—he died of TB or committed suicide with a revolver; he perished on the way back to England, or he never left Quebec city—by creating a fiction that satisfies her. He died, she decides, of homesickness for England. To press on with her investigations would be to look into a drawer that does not belong to her, an act as dangerous as it is impertinent. With the 'evaporation' of her dream past she has to 'start from scratch' (HT 235) to construct a liveable reality for her adult life. She does so with great confidence, a confidence bred of having experienced and survived the worst. 'In Youth Is Pleasure' ends with Linnet watching a crocodile of little girls emerging from the same Jansenist convent school into which she was clapped at the age of four. The apparition of the children—'white-faced, black-clad, eyes cast down' inspires in her eighteen-year-old self not pity but gratitude 'that I had been correct about one thing throughout my youth, which I now considered ended: time had been on my side, faithfully, and unless you died you were always bound to esape' (HT 2367). Linnet, we observe, is no Molly, imprisoned by the need to love.

'Between Zero and One' and 'Varieties of Exile' have more to do with the prison of femininity than that of childhood, except in the peculiar involvement Linnet develops with a 'remittance man'—the kind of exiled black sheep she recognizes her own father to have been. Yet what the involvement points to is not that Linnet is doomed to fall in love with a man just like her father, but rather that she is vastly unlike the remittance man and his kind, those 'tamely delinquent children' whose submission to parental authority entails a lifetime of exile and emotional servitude. Where the remittance men suffer 'the incomparable trauma of rejection' by their parents their whole life long, Linnet, by the end of 'Varieties of Exile', is 'still a minor, but emancipated by marriage' (HT 279)—she manages to procure an ambiguously worded but efficacious letter of consent from a friend in New York so that the marriage can take place. The silence that engulfs the marriage throughout these stories speaks volumes: Linnet is nothing if not a free agent, and her principal freedom is achieved not by disentangling herself from her marriage—of that Gallant never writes—but, rather, by deposing the tyrants of her childhood (HT 225).

In 'Voices Lost in Snow' and 'The Doctor' Linnet returns to her childhood in a kind of desultory yet compulsive drift. The first story gives us a child's-eye view of an adult world riddled with negatives and injunctions:

Halfway between our two great wars, parents whose own early years had been shaped with Edwardian grimness were apt to lend a tone of finality to quite simple remarks: 'Because I say so' was their answer to 'Why?', and a child's response to 'What did I just tell you?' could seldom be anything but 'Not to'—not to say, do, touch, remove, go out, argue, reject, eat, pick up, open, shout, appear to sulk, appear to be cross. Dark riddles filled the corners of life because no enlightenment was thought required. Asking questions was 'being tiresome', while persistent curiosity got one nowhere, at least nowhere of interest. How much has changed? Observe the drift of words descending from adult to child—the fall of personal questions, observations, unnecessary instructions. Before long the listener seems blanketed. He must hear the voice as authority muffled, a hum through snow. The tone has changed—it

may be coaxing, even plaintive—but the words have barely altered.
They still claim the ancient right-of-way through a young life. (HT
282)

The story proceeds to illustrate the precepts voiced above with
an anecdote relating how the child Linnet innocently uses a phrase
she has overheard from one of her father's friends. On being
refused any explanation for why she must 'never say that again',
Linnet remembers being told how she 'ran screaming around a
garden, tore the heads off tulips and . . . *ate* them' (HT 283) 'The
only authentic voices I have,' she interjects, 'belong to the dead'
(HT 283): memory itself is muffled, blanketed by being only the
recollection of what someone else has remembered.

Children, this story establishes, have the lowest status of any
class—as Linnet recalls, 'orders to dogs and instructions to
children were given in the same voice'(HT 305). Children are said
to be 'good' when they behave in a way convenient to adults (HT
286), wordlessly enduring the torments inflicted on them by the
ignorance, snobbery, hypocrisy, or sheer carelessness of adults.
The principal action of 'Voices Lost in Snow' has to do with a baffling trial through which Linnet is put—being brought by her
father, Angus Muir, to her godmother's apartment, and failing to
behave in such a way as to provoke from her godmother, Georgie,
the response her father desires. The buried subtext of the story has
to do with Angus's involvement with Georgie, who had been his
wife's best friend: we are given to understand that if Georgie had
shown any kind of affection, or even acceptance of her lover's
(would-be lover's?) child, all their lives might have dramatically
changed. As it is, the story, like Angus Muir's life, ends indeter-
minately. The adult Linnet brushes 'in memory against the
spiderweb' (HT 294), trying to assemble, out of the blank cards of
what she can remember, some sort of interpretative hand. What
she needs no help in remembering or interpreting, however, is the
expression of helplessness on her father's face as they walk away
from Georgie's apartment:

Already mined, colonized by an enemy prepared to destroy what
it fed on, fighting it with every wrong weapon, squandering
strength he should have been storing, stifling pain in silence rather
than speaking up while there might have been time, he gave an impression of sternness that was a shield against suffering. . . . He
seemed to stretch, as if trying to keep every bone in his body from

touching a nerve; a look of helplessness such as I had never seen on a grown person gripped his face. . . . The kind of physical pain that makes one seem rat's prey is summed up in my memory of this. (HT 292-3)

Linnet's fixing on this particular incident is particularly revealing in what it tells us of the rooting of memory in childhood; in the negligible, vulnerable status a child possesses. For the recognition that her father's pain makes him as helpless as she herself creates the bond of compassionate comprehension—not merely being sympathetic to someone but, through imagination, being able to get inside their skin, to know what they feel and to feel it with them. For a moment Linnet and her father are in the same predicament—she perceives him not as an adult in reprehensible authority over her, but as a *semblable*.

'The Doctor' also deals out the cards of memory, making of them a hand incorporating past, present, and future. From a reference to a painting called 'The Doctor', a quasi-allegorical object illustrating the creed 'that existence is insoluble, tragedy static, poverty enduring, and heavenly justice a total mystery' (HT 295), Linnet articulates a web of memory that comprehends both 'the incomparable trauma of rejection' (HT 268) and the mystery of adult behaviour, the glimpse of answers denied children in their ceaseless asking 'Why?' The reproduction of 'The Doctor', we are told, had been a gift made to Linnet by Raoul Chauchard, the doctor who saved her from the bumbling care of a family friend by correctly diagnosing her persistent 'colds' as the beginning of TB. Since Dr Chauchard is the one adult who has treated Linnet as an equal, it is not surprising that when she runs away from convent school she makes him a surprise visit. Her sense of betrayal when he rejects this not altogether ingenuous gesture of friendship is half-ruefully, half-mockingly recalled:

Now, how to account for the changed, stern, disapproving Chauchard who in that same office gave me not a book but a lecture beginning 'Think of your unfortunate parents' and ending 'You owe them everything; it is your duty to love them'. He had just telephoned for my father to come and fetch me. 'How miserable they would be if anything ever happened to you.' He spoke of my *petit Papa* and my *petite Maman* with that fake diminution of authority characteristic of the Latin tongues which never works in English. (HT 301)

'Fake diminution of authority': that acute eye for the hypocritical and frankly phoney is one of the identifying characteristics of
a child's vision. Children are born, Linnet insists, with a 'clair-
voyant immunity to hypocrisy . . . that vanishes just before
puberty' (HT 304). Linnet, it is true, is a precocious child, but we
are not made to feel that she is an adult in child's clothing. Rather,
she is a particularly clear-sighted and cagey child, one who has
had to learn at an extremely early age the most sophisticated survival tactics, defensive and offensive ploys. There is a world of
tempered bitterness in her placing of her age at the time of this
episode with Dr Chauchard: 'I had been around about the length
of your average major war' (HT 296). Bitterness tempered not by
resignation, but by the recognition that whatever rejections she
has suffered at the hands of those she should most have been able
to trust can no longer imprison her. Her method for achieving
eventual independence is implicit in the motto of the bookplate
her father designs for her: 'Time, Time which none can bind/
While flowing fast leaves love behind' (HT 301). Ironic recognition
and the detachment it induces are crucial to the tone of these
stories, so that Linnet's disclosures of her parents' behaviour
should not seem merely a litany of wounds. When she describes
her weekends home from convent school, and how her parents'
delight in seeing her on Friday evening had, by Saturday afternoon, worn down to impatience that it was not yet time to send
her back; or how, in her absence, her parents would casually go
through her treasured possessions and dispose of anything they
happened to be bored with, it is not with any disconsolate or
peevish air. The distress the child felt on those occasions is vivid-
ly perceptible, but put in its place, so to speak, by the fact that this
distress is being remembered—by the triumphant fact that it is an
adult and free Linnet who chooses to recall such griefs.

'The Doctor' travels from Linnet's opening reminiscences of
Chauchard's office, the books and painting he gave her, and his
refusal to receive her as an equal when she comes to call, to her
recollections of how she perceived him from the vantage point of
those of her parents' parties she was permitted to attend. Again,
memory deals a mysterious hand of cards: Linnet remembers her
mother's rival for Dr Chauchard's attentions, a splendid Mrs
Erskine who would 'sway into the room, as graceful as a woman
can be when she is boned from waist to thigh' (HT 303). But it is
not the discovery of Dr Chauchard's love affairs that so surprises

the adult Linnet, but rather the revelation of his private, independent life as the possessor of a voice that 'transcends this or that language' (HT 316). The news that Raoul Chauchard was a poet as well as a physician 'was an earthquake, the collapse of the cities we build over the past to cover seams and cracks we cannot account for'(HT 313). Ironically or not, Linnet's chagrin is reserved for the fact that she never heard his true voice 'at the start, standing on tiptoe to reach the doorbell, calling through the letter box every way I could think of, "I, me". I ought to have heard it when I was still under ten and had all my wits about me' (HT 316). The story comes full circle, then, describing an arc of recollection that begins and ends with Linnet's appeal to the one adult in her life whose affection and respect had seemed assured. As 'The Doctor' ends we are brought deliberately back from those emotional entanglements that might be of primary interest to an adult, to the experience of rejection central to the child: 'When I read the three obituaries it was the brass plate on the door I saw and "Sur Rendez-vous". That means "no dropping in"' (HT 316).

The lightness with which the dereliction of adults and the vulnerability of children are sketched out, the corresponding deftness with which Gallant impales her targets—the 'shabby' dispersal of Linnet's treasures while she is away at boarding school, the bored intolerance of adults for the children they bring into their muddled world—is possible because of the wry detachment the narrator assumes, a detachment necessary if the 'prison of childhood' is to be fictive territory at all. Between the kind of justifiably insane rage Linnet expressed by lopping off and then eating the heads of tulips, and the pathos bred by the 'incomparable trauma of rejection' (HT 268) is the possibility of disinterested, not disaffected, recollection and articulation, a possibility open only to those children who do not die of their wounds, but are strengthened by them.

Gallant has dealt succinctly with her own response to the traumas she suffered as a child—particularly the unmaternal nature of her mother (and seemingly of all the women in her family). 'I had a mother who should not have had children and it's as simple as that' (iBG 26). She insists that for someone who could now be a grandmother to go on and on about her own mother, 'who was born under Queen Victoria, [would be] really ridiculous'. What does incense Gallant, however, is the 'impossibility of even discussing [the fact that] things could be that bad between a mother and child'. The continuance of the *'maman mystique*, especially with men' (iBG 26) is Gallant's prey in her two novels, particularly in *A Fairly Good Time* with its depiction of two appalling *ménages*, the Perrignys' (Philippe's *petite maman* with her ferocious disinfectants and her equally abrasive stranglehold on her children's lives) and the Maurels' (Claudie's *maman*, the criminally submissive *petite femme*) as well as the impossible Mrs Norrington, another 'woman who should not have had children'. But perhaps the most concise, damning, and powerful portrayal of the *maman mystique* at work occurs in a short story, 'Ernst in Civilian Clothes', in which a character is witness to a particularly vicious scene. A woman—overworked, underfed, no doubt—beats her child, whose screams can be heard throughout the shabby apartment building in which they live. 'When his mother beats him, the child calls for help, and calls *"Maman"*. His true mother will surely arrive and take him away from his mother transformed' (PJ 139).

The attitude of disinterestedness that, as we have seen, Linnet Muir cultivated in order to survive her own childhood has been practised by Gallant in examining the plight of mothers as well as children in her fiction. The truly repellent mother we have seen at work in 'Saturday' represents an extreme of observation—more sympathetic portraits are to be found in Grete Toeppler of 'The Latehomecomer' or the eponymous heroine of 'His Mother', and, most sympathetically, the heroine of 'Irina', whose children are 'darling zeros' in the life she reclaims for herself after her patriarchal husband's death (FFD 235). But it is Gallant's unforced, unsentimental connection with the perspective and position of children that is one of the most remarkable qualities of her writing, giving it what Conrad called a 'saving glow' and necessary warmth.

*

Gallant's preoccupation with children and childhood is a distinguishing feature of her non-fiction as well. Her journalistic career at the *Montreal Standard* actually began with a feature on a day in the life of a 'street-wise' city child. With photographer Hy Frankel she followed a certain 'Johnny' round his neighbourhood, discerning the patterns and rituals in his social existence and giving us a child's-eye view of family relations, or the lack of them.[2] In another article she interviews a group of primary-school children to find out their criticisms of their parents' behaviour, a delightful inversion of the usual procedure in which parents 'tell-off' their young.[3] Gallant wrote several articles touching on children—their shyness, fears, psychiatric problems, their experiences in a bilingual library, their life in boarding school, their first attempts at swimming, their Christmas concerts, and a first excursion into the countryside by city-hardened kids. One especially interesting piece is entitled 'Give the Kid a Gory Story: That Seems to Be the Motto of Those Who Turn Out Children's Fairy Tales'.[4] Gallant argues that because children have a fundamental need to be able to distinguish reality from fantasy, truth from lies, fairy tales are more appropriate for adults than for children. She cites the 'Poe-like horror' of 'Jorinda and Jorindel' as an example—that fairy tale whose title she gives to one of her own fictions, and which acts as a haunting 'super-text' for the first experience of betrayal and loss undergone by the eight-year-old heroine, Irmgard.

In several of Gallant's essays on other writers—Simenon, Colette, Léautaud, and Yourcenar—relations between these writers and their parents become a point of acute interest. In writing on Léautaud, for example, Gallant observes: 'Beyond all question it was the absent mother who warped his life. She came to see him for the first time when he was five and cried, "God, what a disagreeable child" (PN 149). What clearly fascinates Gallant about Léautaud is his relation to the 'maman mystique', his depiction of 'the childhood mother [as the] bringer of "fear and anxiety"' (PN 150) rather than unconditional love, and his revelations in Le Petit Ami and In Memoriam 'that one's mother is not untouchable and that parents are not necessarily noble and good' (PN 150).

In her account of 'The Events in May' the effect of dangerous and uncertain political activity on the relations between children and parents has a particular fascination for Gallant. Refreshingly, she gives an example of how the 'best parents [she] know[s]' let their daughter think and make decisions for herself during the 'events'. 'Parents and children again'(PN 56) becomes one of the refrains of 'The Events in May'. Alarmed by the turn things are taking, Gallant reassures herself near the beginning of her journal that 'I'm not French and these aren't my children' (PN 17)—yet a few pages later she confesses, 'I am frightened for these children who would be angry at being called children' (PN 23). Though Gallant recognizes the naïveté and ignorance of the young—the historical illiteracy that allows them to venerate Stalin as a revolutionary hero, or to tell parents who were in the Resistance, *'nous avons besoin des Allemands'*—her primary sympathies are with the idealism and courage of the French 'kids', who before the 'events' had always seemed to her like 'little old men' (PN 59). Her greatest revulsion is reserved for those of the parents' generation who seem to have learned nothing from the experience of the Occupation, or who have jumped on their children's bandwagon in order to cash in on political opportunities, or simply to recapture a sense of youthful romance. When she finally sums up the events of May 1968, she makes a most revealing observation: 'I suppose for the young it had to do with that perfect lucidity I remember at seventeen, seeing (as you never do later) exactly what people are like and deciding to have no part of it' (PN 91).

Even Gallant's essay on the Gabrielle Russier affair contains a 'vindication of the rights' of children as well as women. It is the childlike qualities in Russier that appeal most to Gallant, her passionate idealism, her living in literature rather than life. Yet before describing the appalling treatment that Russier's lover, Christian Rossi, suffered at his parents' hands, Gallant takes care to show how absurdly strict and repressive a parent was Gabrielle Russier. If 'even the most selfless and indulgent parents will seldom grant the right to a private life without a struggle' (PN 105), then Russier, had she not been tormented to suicide, might have proved as disastrous to her own children as were Christian's parents to him. The Rossis, Gallant reveals, forced the notorious 'sleep cure' on their son and incarcerated him in a private psychiatric clinic, all with the full consent of the law and approbation of the land: 'The guardian of a minor has not only the law but the full weight of public opinion behind him' (PN 117). The penultimate part of Gallant's essay shows how totally Christian repudiated his family, and underscores the basic hypocrisy of parent-child relationships. As the boy remarks: 'You don't choose your parents. It seems fine to have parents who say they are on the left, who tell you, " It's the right thing to seize the college, or to occupy the lycée", but when it comes to adapting their ideas to their life or to the life you lead with them, *eh bien, ça ne va plus*' (PN 139).

And finally, in 'Paris: The Taste of a New Age', collected in *Paris Notebooks*, Gallant shows the connection between her concern with children as the lowest, most helpless class on the human scale and her sympathy for their adult counterparts—the immigrant workers who perform the most menial tasks for the meanest of wages. One of the by-products of immigration, she reveals, is the inevitable chasm it creates between parents faithful to the ethos of their country of origin, and children cleaving to the customs of the new country. Of Paris's immigrant workers Gallant observes: 'Mediterranean warmth congeals in the north. The mothers are tired and bewildered, lonely and lost. The maternal hand, raised and threatening, is a gesture against life' (PN 169). She relates how the indigenous French have relaxed their child-rearing methods ('The voice of infant protest has crossed the Atlantic, a few years after the news about women. Children can even be seen sucking their thumbs in public, or clutching a close friend—a diaper or a small pillowcase. Even two years ago it would have been beyond imagining' [PN 169]). Ironically, it is the new wave of immigrants who are intolerably strict: 'Now the children of Paris wear comfortable clothes, and that race of tense, elderly, overdressed young has all but disappeared. It is the children of immigrants who are often set down in the sandpit wearing pale colours, with heavy instructions about keeping them clean' (PN 168).

*

That the experience and perspective of childhood are constant preoccupations for Gallant can be seen by a glance at the course of her fiction. Her early work deals preponderantly with women and children—these groups being alike, in the immediately post-war world Gallant describes, in their helplessness and dependence. 'Madeline's Birthday', 'Jorinda and Jorindel', 'A Day Like Any Other', 'Going Ashore', 'About Geneva', 'Thank You for the Lovely Tea', 'Wing's Chips', all feature children whose parents have more or less abandoned them, or who have only the most tenuous or dubious assurances of their parents' interest and affection. The child in 'Wing's Chips' is portrayed as particularly anxious in this regard, making it her task to remind her father to worry about her. And the child protagonist of 'An Emergency Case' (1957), the unlikeable Oliver, has suffered the worst abandonment of all—his parents' death in an accident.

When Gallant shifts her fictive territory from the arena of women and children to the field of recent European history (*The Pegnitz Junction*, *From the Fifteenth District*) she makes an interesting choice of characters: most often they are adolescents, actual or arrested—people who have grown to adult stature, but whose emotional lives have been cut short by the catastrophe of war. Of one of these characters, the narrator of 'The Latehomecomer', Gallant has remarked: 'Try to put yourself in the place of an adolescent who had sworn personal allegiance to Hitler. The German drama, the drama of that generation, was of inner displacement. You can't tear up your personality and begin again, any more than you can tear up the history of your country. The lucky people are the thoughtless ones. They just slip through' (iGH 51). As she shows in fictions such as 'An Autobiography', 'An Alien Flower', and 'Ernst in Civilian Clothes', it is the misfortune of most adolescents to be thoughtful—only for a few of them does the transition to adult life bring about a selective amnesia or corruption of memory that totally disarms the past. When the protagonists of these dramas of 'inner displacement' liken life to a fairy tale they are remembering stories 'where little children are abandoned in deep woods by parents who can no longer can feed them'; tales of 'dark branches, night, crows spreading their wings, inch-high demons squealing a hideous language' (PJ 184).

In *Overhead in a Balloon*, Mavis Gallant's preoccupation with parents and children is represented by the slight, elliptical 'Larry' and the long story 'Luc and his Father', an exposé of the triviality and stupidity of a set of ultra-right-wing Parisians situated somewhere between the minor aristocracy and the upper bourgeoisie. Roger and Simone Clairevoie are portrayed as infallibly inept in their dealings with their decidedly unclever child, Luc. By opening Luc's mail, snooping and prying into his love affair with Katia, a rather lively girl who seems not to have registered the fact of Luc's deficient intelligence, the parents destroy any chance their son might have had to become something other than a mediocrity. 'Luc and His Father' is the latest variation on one of Gallant's most cherished themes: that the main problem with families lies in their members' inability to leave one another alone, while their every attempt at communication results in a dialogue of the deaf. This absurdity is caustically revealed by the story's last paragraph, in which Roger is trying to give to the son who has disappointed all his parents' hopes and most cherished illusions 'the essence of his own life . . . bottled in words' (OB 100). The words turn out to be 'Whatever happens, don't get your life all mixed up with a dog's'. In 'Luc and His Father' the satiric mode establishes a deliberate distance not only between narrator and characters, but between reader and story. The centre of our attention is not really Luc, but rather Gallant's skewering of the snobberies and stupidities of the Clairevoies. The caricatures that abound in this narrative (and in many of the others included in *Overhead in a Balloon*) keep us at arm's length from the situations in which Luc and his parents are knotted. This story certainly represents one strategy for dealing with 'the prison of childhood'; in the remainder of this chapter, however, I would like to look at three earlier stories that give a broader picture of the emotional scope and the conceptual possibilities associated with the treatment of children and childhood in Gallant's work.

'Going Ashore' (1954) subtly portrays the strange inversion of a child-parent relationship. The catastrophic implications of this inversion for the child make this story seem like a blueprint for *Green Water, Green Sky*. 'Going Ashore' is certainly more tightly structured than the novel, and in some ways much less risky: as its title makes clear, not the fluid world of madness but rather the dry land of social relationships and appearances lies at the heart of the narrative. And Gallant has certainly made it easier for us to engage with the story of this particular 'abandoned' daughter; where Flor begins and remains an aloof, defensive and curiously unapproachable character, the child Emma Ellenger, 'troubled . . . apprehensive' (OP 77) and on the verge of adolescence, is an immediately poignant creation. The pathos of her situation—social and sexual innocence shading into inescapable knowledge— provides a badly needed foil for the hat-pin wit used to depict her divorcée mother, Lila. As with her treatment of Barbara in 'The Remission', Gallant employs a hypothetical disinterestedness in her presentation of Emma's mother, letting her be seen as she wants to appear—and thus damning her all the more.

Lila Ellenger is on a different sort of threshold from the one her daughter is crossing. Her real voyage is not, of course, the dilatory cruise off the African coast on which she drags Emma, but rather a journeying from the enviable state of being a pretty young woman to the plight of merely being a pretty young woman's impecunious mother, no longer able to make men desire her and pay her bills. Gallant is impeccable in her delineation of the nuances and niceties involved in this downward slide and in Lila's attempts to disguise it. Mrs Ellenger is not yet desperate enough to try and pick up the ship's 'Chink' bartender, Eddy, though she is willing to be the 'friend' of Mr Boyd Oliver, old and fat and rich and—alas—married. A slothful mother (who nevertheless took care to dress her baby daughter all in white), Lila has not bothered to teach Emma the social language that will both protect and advance her, any more than she has packed the appropriate warm clothing for this winter cruise. And so Emma artlessly gushes out the truth of her mother's curious relations with 'Uncle Jimmy Salter' (he has turfed his mistress and her inconvenient child out of his apartment), thereby undoing the appearances Lila has been desperately trying to create. Still a child, Emma is able to tell and intuit the most intractable truths: she has not yet learned, as her mother has, those tricks of memory that will enable her to deceive herself, if no one else.

Emma envisions a new life for her mother and herself, a life 'together, alone, with no man, no Uncle Anyone to interfere' (OP 78)—a life rather like that of Mrs and Miss Munn, another mother and daughter duo on the cruise. But Lila can't manage it, hasn't the intelligence, imagination, or courage for independence—all her plans 'included a man' (OP 72). Incapable of buying winter clothes or mailing a parcel, she expends her energies in fixing her hair, changing her dress, flipping through *Vogue* while sipping brandy-and-water and waiting for a man to come and arrange her life for her. Her most effective act of revenge against 'Uncle' Jimmy Salter is to respond to Emma's confession that she has inadvertently taken away one of his books with 'I didn't know he could read' (OP 74).

Yet the pathos of 'Going Ashore' lies not merely in the impossible situation of Emma Ellenger, forced to soothe, comfort, and console a mother 'adrift on an ocean whose immenseness she could not begin to grasp' (OP 74-5). More importantly, it has to do with the fact that Emma still loves and needs her mother, cannot yet reduce her to the unimportance of the other passengers, 'thin-skinned, elderly people, less concerned with the prospect of travel than with getting through another winter in relative comfort, . . . [lying] in deck chairs, muffled as mummies, looking stricken and deceived' (OP 69). Emma is already beginning to see through Lila's proofs of what a good mother she has been—'teaching' her daughter herself instead of sending her to school; dressing her like a princess. When Lila is consumed with desperation at her helpless drift from being desired to hopeless desiring, Emma comforts her exactly as a mother might a child who wakes up screaming in the night. Yet there is a touch of Linnet Muir in Emma: 'Her pity took the form of exasperation; it made her want to get up and do something crazy and rude—slam a door, say all the forbidden words she could think of' (OP 80). That exasperation derives from the absolute power adults have over their young, insisting that children attest their love for their parents by reassuring them that, in spite of everything, they have indeed done their very best. And Gallant also evokes the exasperation born of the false innocence adults demand from children whom they place in the worldliest situations. Mrs Munn, for example, finds herself unable to use the word 'body' in front of twelve year-old Emma, Emma who has known so many 'Uncles', and who so bravely acknowledges her rootlessness: 'We live all over the place' (OP 71).

Emma, though, is no fool: she will step into experience with her eyes wide open. Unlike Flor, she has taken the measure of her mother, as is evidenced in her private repudiation of her mother's gift—a costly but inauthentic bracelet that leaves greenish stains on her wrist—in favour of a self-evident fake, the tiger statuette she is given as a souvenir of Africa, with its 'Made in Japan' stamp clearly visible. Emma's 'clairvoyance' may disappear in adulthood; certainly it will not make her past experience any less painful, her present less of a dilemma. But if the ability to see things for what they are, to keep one's wits about one, is a prerequisite for independence, then perhaps Emma will break out of the prison of childhood to become another Linnet Muir instead of a Flor.

If 'Going Ashore' presents a familiar pattern of child-parent relations, then 'The Rejection' (1969) features the reversal of these roles from a strikingly different perspective, that of the parent—in this case, the father. 'The Rejection' is a fiction that can be called surreal—a fantasy on the theme of family politics, the power children and parents exercise over one another.

A divorced man is taking his six-and-a-half-year-old daughter, who lives apart from him with her grandmother, on a drive to see a mutual friend. With this Mr Mountford, the child has announced, she has chosen to live: 'He's so much richer,' she tells her father, 'and he has such lovely conversation.' The child's mother, it appears, does not know that her own child exists: the child would seem to be the fantasy of a man who feels intolerable 'pain at the possibility of not being loved' (NY 42). His putative child is 'a small girl, delicate of feature' who habitually wears 'an expression so set and so humorless that her father [feels] weak and dispersed beside her—as if age and authority and second thoughts had, instead of welding his personality, pulled it to shreds' (NY

42). Part of the child's unusual power over her father, her ability to subvert his authority, resides in her terrifying truthfulness: 'she ought', her father complains, 'to have learned a few of the social dishonesties by now' (NY 42). She makes no pretence of loving or even admiring her father—worse still, she does not perform the function parents insistently demand of their children: extending their egos, mirroring their self-image, making them feel authoritative and important to someone, even if that someone is six times smaller than he or she. This daughter, her father reflects, does credit to neither himself nor to her (supposed) mother: 'The child was the bottom of a pool from which both their characters had been drained away. She had nothing, except obstinacy, which he did not admire, and shallow judgement. Of course she was shallow; she had proved it: she did not love her father' (NY 42)

The father's pain at his glimpse of the possibility that he may not be loved by this child whose very existence he has authored does not, however, outweigh his sense of outrage at the dubious and disadvantaged position into which his child has put him: 'He was dealing with a *child*, he suddenly recalled; it was not a father's business to plead for justice but to dispense it' (NY 43). Yet he can do nothing against the child's sudden acquisition of mastery, a power deriving from her newfound knowledge that she can withdraw or offer her love or loyalty just as she chooses. One of the nightmarish aspects of 'The Rejection' is that the six-year-old child is given the confident seductive power of a twenty-six-year-old woman—she has visited Mr Mountford before, it seems; it is her belief that he has offered to have her stay with him. It is on the cranky, miserly Mr Mountford and not on her loving, enlightened father (who wishes her to grow up surrounded by books and flowers and art) that this extraordinary child wishes to depend.

Arriving at Mr Mountford's, the father leaves his child in the car with the grotesque reptilian pet she has brought along ('part lizard or snake, or armadillo, the size of a kitten, and repulsive to see' [NY 42]). He speaks to Mountford, who seems as much a creature of his imagination as is the child, and is delighted to learn that the man has no intention of keeping his daughter—in fact Mountford suggests she should be given to Bertha, the hag-like cook, who seems to come straight out of the Grimms' version of 'Jorinda and Jorindel'.

Wondering how to tell his child—'so confident, so certain she would always be wanted' (NY 44) that the protector on whom she has set her heart professes not to know her and certainly does not want her, the father finds his daughter has disobeyed him, left the car, and entered Mountford's house. As father and child return to the car they hear the cries of the grotesque reptilian pet, 'the frantic note of the creature abandoned . . . the hysteria and terror, the fear that no one would ever come for it again' (NY 44). When the father asks the child to reclaim the pet she has abandoned, she refuses. The father's reproach to his daughter enacts a curious transference, with the pet becoming a metonym for the child, and the child, for the parent:

> 'You can't leave him,' said the man. 'You've taken him out of his own life and made a pet of him. You can't abandon him now. You're responsible for him.' 'I don't want him,' the child said without emphasis.

Recognition of his own child's cruelty produces two responses from the father: to protest that this child can belong neither to him nor to her mother, since 'surely [they] were never guilty of cruelty' (NY 44), and then to decide that his only recourse is to dump his daughter on the mother who is responsible for a child she does not even know exists, 'the result, the product, the thing . . . left' of an abortive union. In the meanwhile, the child sits in the car, 'confident she would never be made to account for anything, that she had another choice, that her chances were eternal'. This fantasy in which a child exerts authority over a helpless parent ends, appropriately enough, with the father stammering about division, destruction, right and wrong, and with the child's calm reproof: '" Who do you think you're shouting at? . . . And why are you bothering me?"' (NY 44).

Childhood, we have said, makes memory possible at all—it does not just give us a past to remember, but creates our very need to remember. In 'Wing's Chips' the narrator, recalling a turning point in her childhood, the summer she spent alone with her curiously negligent father, insists on the unreliability or intractableness of memory: 'some detail is always wrong, or at least fails to fit the picture in my memory' (NY 35). The narrator, also first-person, of the short fiction 'Rose' (1960) begins her inquiry into the past with a question to which the story she relates provides a devastating answer. 'Childhood recollected,' she observes, 'is often hallucination; who is to blame?' (NY 34). It is with the questions posed by 'Rose', a narrative even more surreal than 'The

Rejection', that I will close this chapter on Gallant's 'prison of childhood'.

'Rose' is set on familiar ground—the loveless childhood of the narrator, Irmgard, whose parents do not want and are not interested in her. Her hyperteutonic grandmother, with whom she is sent to spend Christmas, is fond of sitting Irmgard on a high stool for hours at a time, while she reads to the child in German, a foreign language that puts 'a heavy brown veil' between them (NY 35). The grandmother, we are told, educated her own children on the principle of humiliation: one of them, Hans-Thomas, 'had spent whole days of his childhood locked in his room, deprived of food and light and air and voices. Regularly, his head was shaved' (NY 34). Needless to say, he does not become 'good', but grows up to be a financial failure and a bigamist, the father of Irmgard's mysterious cousin Rose.

'Rose' deals not only with the abuses children suffer at their parents' hands but also, most importantly, with the fantasies fostered by a child's experience of familial neglect and indifference. On her visit to her grandmother (an agnostic socialist who permits no Christmas trees or vulgar seasonal paraphernalia in her cheerless home) Irmgard experiences what she describes as an authentic hallucination. She meets her cousin Rose, the exact opposite of all Irmgard has been made to be. Rose is a confection of kitsch 'with long hair that lies in ribbons on a velvet coat' (NY 34). She is allowed, in her grandmother's presence, to utter 'abominations' such as the word 'cute', to listen to sentimental German Christmas music, to eat layer cake decorated with cherries, and saucer-sized sugar cookies instead of the regulation lemon loaf served up to Irmgard. In short, Rose is the adored, indulged, favoured child, permitted to climb onto her grandmother's lap, have her hair stroked, be comforted.

Irmgard, on the other hand, is given a book and a 'diffident kiss' (NY 36) by her grandmother on Christmas morning—no *Tannenbaum* or *Süsser die Glocken* for her. Sent back to her parents, she alludes to whom and what she has seen at her grandmother's house. Her mother pours scorn on Irmgard's account of Rose but nonetheless pumps her for details, showing an excited interest in her brother-in-law's child that she has never shown in her own:

> My circumstances are boring. My mother knows all about my clothes. I wake, I dress, I am taken to school by Germaine, I play with dolls. They would have preferred a boy. Well, it is too late now.

I am here. They should have thought of it sooner. They should have stopped bickering for a moment and come to some decision. Now I am here, and they are here, and we shall just have to put up with one another. Rose needn't put up with anyone; her father is in Mexico, shedding five-dollar bills like leaves. (NY 36)

'I am here'—this is Linnet's cry outside Dr Chauchard's door, 'calling through the letter box every way I could think of, "I, me".' It is the child's imperious and desperate insistence on her right to be heard, to exist, to be loved. Irmgard torments herself, thinking of the unfairness with which she is treated compared to Rose: 'Since Rose is favoured from the start, why is she given things I am told are abomination? . . . Did it amuse our grandmother to give us different glimpses of her world? . . . . Did she see [Rose] often? Did she like her best?' (NY 36). It seems obvious that Rose and her 'Lumpendeutsch' Christmas exist only as fantasies expressing Irmgard's bewilderment, resentment, and curiosity at being as unloved as she is. 'Did she like her best? There is the core of the whole business; and even now the child's puppy ego wakes and shows its teeth: prefer me, if you don't mind' (NY 36). So strong is the force of desire as encoded in—perhaps constitutive of—memory, that the narrative itself cannot decide whether Rose exists or not.

'Perhaps that intuitive knowledge, the piecing together of facts overheard, overcharges the mind' (NY 34), the narrator suggests: perhaps Rose is no more than the product of the eavesdropping that is a child's most efficacious form of education. Yet as Irmgard recalls her 'memory' of that Christmas visit she declares: 'It has the true quality of a hallucination, because I take no part. I can see them, but they cannot see me' (NY 35). This hallucination is like the Christmas drawings that Irmgard's teacher chalks on the blackboard—an image created only to be erased. Yet the memory from which Irmgard's hallucination derives, the memory of her parents' and grandmother's indifference to her, the stringent discipline with which her childhood life was locked and bound, is utterly authentic.

What 'Rose' establishes beyond any doubt is this: if childhood is the seed bed of all memory, some of the flowers it produces are poisonous, best destroyed or left untouched. Some memories gesture toward the persistence of unfulfilled needs so devastating that the line between reason and fantasy no longer holds. This story ends with the narrator's unsatisfied dismissal of Rose, and her drawing of a strict and fearful line between hallucination and reality. 'As though an eraser were coming down on the decorated blackboard, the memory must be rubbed out, or life, and the possibilities of behavior, like my grandmother's heart, will split in two' (NY 37).

*

Gallant's disquieting portrayal of childhood is one of the triumphs of her fiction. In these stories evoking 'the prison of childhood' the reader perceives narrative disinterestedness and detachment as technical devices whereby the painful source of memory itself can be portrayed with neither self-righteousness nor self-indulgence. In fictions as diverse as 'Rose' and 'The Rejection', 'Going Ashore' and 'Jorinda and Jorindel', 'Voices Lost in Snow' and 'The Doctor', Gallant has produced distinctive variations on a common theme: yet for all her insistence on the 'grief and terror' that characterize our experience of childhood, she writes of children in ways that open, rather than shut, the doors of our perception.

Not women and children first, but children first, then women. In the chapter that follows I will examine what Gallant makes of those children who, like Molly in 'The Remission', grow up but do not grow away from our initial condition of captivity—those who remain subject to the need to love, the desire to be preferred above another, the insatiableness of the child's 'puppy ego'. Those who, like Molly, manifest and fall victim to 'women's fidelity . . . women's insecurity . . . women's sense of order' (FFD 114-15).

Notes

[1] Indeed, Gallant's work is rich in allusions to writing for children—those books she devoured in her own childhood, believing they were written by children themselves, so true and telling were their perceptions of the nature of child-parent relations.

[2] 'Meet Johnny: Sturdy and Tow-headed, Johnny Is a City Kid, Wise beyond His Years', *The Standard* (Montreal) 2 Sept. 1944, p. 12.

[3] 'Your Child Looks at You: He Thinks You Yell Too Much, Have Uneven Discipline and Act Silly at Parties. He's Sensitive and Doesn't Like Sitters'. *The Standard Magazine* (Montreal) 18 Dec. 1948, p. 4.

[4] *The Standard Magazine* (Montreal) 29 June 1946, pp. 9, 15.

Chapter 5

The World of Women

> All lives are interesting; no one life is more interesting than another. Its fascination depends on how much is revealed, and in what manner. (PN 142)

With this Tolstoyan dictum Mavis Gallant appears to be conceding a fundamental human equality between classes and sexes, a predisposition to value the 'lives of the obscure' as highly as those of the famous. In the context of feminism one is reminded of Virginia Woolf's declaration in *A Room of One's Own* that she would as soon have 'the true history [of a shopgirl] as the hundred and fiftieth life of Napoleon or seventieth study of Keats . . . which old Professor Z and his like are now inditing'.[1] Certainly Gallant's work bears out her belief that life as women have traditionally been taught to live it—constricted, trivial, structured on niceties essential to economic and social survival—is fit material for fiction. The majority of Gallant's subjects are women: though men figure prominently in her fictive world they are, for the most part, curiously passive and powerless to do much except tyrannize over or live off women. Gallant's male protagonists include veterans good for nothing but subsisting on the shabby side of the Riviera ('In Italy', 'An Unmarried Man's Summer', 'Better Times'), impecunious, much-married painters ('The Circus'), writers who go through women like packets of peanuts ('The Statues Taken Down'), and feckless charmers who end up dependent on cast-off children ('The Prodigal Parent'). Whether psychically maimed, like the fascistic Roy of 'In the Tunnel', moribund, like Alec Webb of 'The Remission', or appalled at the idea of emotional entanglements, like Douglas Ramsay in 'Bonaventure', Gallant's men are also portrayed as the prey of stronger women who are themselves enmeshed in the dubious web of the feminine mystique, women like Olivia in 'Good Deeds', Lydia Cruche of 'Speck's Idea', or the marvellous Carette sisters in 'The Chosen Husband' and 'Florida'.

If equality vis à vis the intrinsic interest of the lives of men and women is a given in Gallant's fiction, then so is moral parity—women are portrayed as victimizers as well as victims, and are given no monopoly on the qualities of tenderness, unselfishness, and loyalty, qualities so rare in this writer's fictive world as to be anomalies. Her female characters, in short, have no special status, except for the privileged, almost aberrant Linnet Muir. As Rosalind Coward has pointed out, fiction that features the lives of girls and women is not necessarily feminist; as Elaine Showalter reminds us, Coward argues that 'it is not their share in the common experiences of womankind, that makes women or texts feminist, . . . but their shared commitment to certain political aims and objectives'.[2] Gallant, in fact, seems to write as if the women's movement had never been, as if feminism had effected no radical changes in the way women perceive themselves and the worlds now open to them. Given that her work can be described as 'woman-centred', and that her vision of human possibility has been largely influenced by her experience of being a woman and of having paid a considerable price to defy the limitations imposed on her by gender, it will be illuminating to look at Gallant's response to one of the most significant social movements of our time—feminism.

*

Asked in 1976 if she would describe herself as a feminist, Gallant replied, 'Well if you mean would I march down the street and throw stones, no, or that I hate men, no. I like men, I like the company of men. . . . Women suffer a lot from women'.[3] When interviewed in June 1987 her response was less evasive: feminism, she insisted, was a 'foreign territory' for her—had become an 'utterly meaningless label'. Although she was sympathetic to, for example, Kate Millett's early writings, she would appear to have rejected the more radical manifestations and theoretical developments of feminism. 'To me,' she asserts, 'the only feminist thing is economic—it's to get the same pay as men.' It goes without saying that Gallant would have no patience with recent feminist valorizations of traditional feminine culture, or with the radical-exclusivist wing of the woman's movement. And as for the impact of feminism on literature and language, she is largely scornful, dismissing the English-speaking devotees of '*l'écriture féminine*'[4] as 'marginal' and, more damning, as having 'no grasp on English' (iJKK).

Why would someone who has succeeded in opposing the conventions and defying the expectations of the patriarchal society in which she grew to womanhood be so recalcitrant about embracing or even accepting more than the rock-bottom economic tenets of feminism? The answer lies, of course, in Gallant's equally fierce desire for independence, in her public views as well as in her personal life. Freedom to occupy a position from which she can observe the ironies and disingenuousness inherent in both the patriarchal and the radical feminist positions is her imperative, a freedom made doubly important by her experience of disenchantment with previous ideologies of liberation. A brief glance at *What Is To Be Done?* makes this abundantly clear.

'World history and sexual politics' could be the subtitle of this play, set in wartime Montreal and first produced on Remembrance Day 1982. Its main characters, the ingenuous, middle-class, starry-eyed Jenny, and the more experienced, flexible, working-class Molly, spend their free time waiting for World War II to end so that men can change the world as they have promised. To fill the time left over from working at jobs the men have left behind, Molly and Jenny 'receive instruction' in Stalinism from a Mrs Bailey as though it were 'Confirmation class' (WTD 14). Jenny works at a ludicrous newspaper job ('Appraisements and Averages'), and Molly spends her evenings writing letters to her husband overseas and telephoning her mother with contradictory instructions about how to treat her baby. Of the two women Molly is the realist. She begins the play by showing to Jenny her most treasured possession—a first-edition pamphlet of Lenin's 'What Is To Be Done?', which her father won in a card game from a Ukrainian merchant seaman. Molly's motive in producing the pamphlet is to win Jenny's admiration and excite her envy (for while her own father was romantically working-class, Jenny's was an inglorious remittance man). Near the play's end, however, Molly speculates on what a first edition of Lenin might be worth to a collector. It is the recently married Molly who declares that love is nothing but 'one foreclosure after another', whereas with friendship 'nothing is owed. . . . You can close the account without publishing a statement. . . . There are no mortgages' (WTD 33). These maxims suggest that Molly will be able to foreclose her own marriage once her husband returns, and to end her friendship with Jenny once it ceases to be useful or attractive to her. Yet Molly is no monster in this play; rather, she is the necessary corrective to Jenny's spendthrift idealism. Molly's mastery of appearances—whether those dependent on 'pancake makeup and sponge' (WTD 94) or those that permit her to pee off stage, talk about abortion and menstruation, and speculate on screwing in doorways ('It must be like being raped in an Egyptian tomb' [WTD 42])—show her to be nothing like the conventional idea of desirable women: fragile 'pastel drawings on which men might leave fingermarks, if allowed too near' (WTD 78). Molly is as independent as and no more unlikeable than any of the men in the play: the ideologue Willie, or Karl-Heinz, the refugee who likens intercourse with a virgin to 'forced labour' (WTD 79).

What Is To Be Done? is a comedy of disillusionment, a satire on aspects of Gallant's own past enthusiasms, the 'intensely left-wing, political romantic' (iGH 39) she was during the first years of her return to wartime Montreal. Gallant still describes herself as *'extremely* interested in politics' (iGH 33): what she has obviously divested herself of is the kind of naïve emotional and intellectual immersion in a cause that promises a simple, straightfoward solution to injustice and exploitation, a solution that cannot tolerate, never mind deal with, the existence of its own inherent contradictions and complexities. It is not her intention in this play to portray in any naturalistic way the experience of political disenchantment. Instead, she insists on the inevitably farcical or burlesque element in her heroines' embrace of left-wing politics, an element that becomes all the stronger as the girls' theoretical knowledge of the liberation promised by Marxist-Leninism develops independently of their practical experience of exploitation as women. At the end of the play Jenny remarks:

> Molly and I never read 'What Is To Be Done?' We never had the right language. I read some other things. In English. Like, 'The Role of Women in Revolution'. Actually, it isn't all that great a role. When he jumps out of the airplane, you hang around in a cornfield waiting to carry the parachute. (WTD 105)

Similarly, Jenny mixes up 'The Death of Minnehaha' and 'Comrade', the trite political poem she has heard Molly recite, remarking that in Longfellow's verse, Hiawatha gets all the best lines while Minnehaha remains silent, even though she is the one who is dying (WTD 106). So intrepid is Jenny's faith in the new world and new order beckoning from the horizon of VE day that she phones her boss, Mr Gillespie, with an idea for a feature story to make sure that 'unfinished matters from the old era' don't get swept under the carpet of peace and new prosperity. The example Gallant gives of gender-based social hypocrisy smacks of burlesque, not pathos:

> There's a place here where they lock girls up and work them to death. . . . It's a laundry. . . . The girls are called 'delinquent Catholics'. . . . A delinquent Catholic is a girl who's been raped by a member of her family. For a Protestant to be delinquent she has to be raped by a total stranger. . . . But with the Catholic girls, well, it's mother's sister's husband, father's nephew's brother, cousin's son's son. That's what counts. These girls . . . they're never seen again, Mr Gillespie. Their heads are shaved. They're starved for food, and starved for sleep, and they have a cruel punishment, and they work in the laundry, and they die. The place is a stone house behind a wall. . . . Your wife sends her tablecloths there? . . . St Ursula and the Thousand Virgin Martyrs embroidered on a tablecloth . . . Done in network? . . . I'm not saying your wife's tablecloth isn't a work of art. A museum piece . . . I'm only saying that I don't see why a girl who's been raped by her sister's husband's father's cousin has to wash, starch and iron St Ursula and the Thousand Virgin Martyrs in order to cleanse society. (WTD 107-8)

It is a typical Gallant ploy. To treat a legitimate subject—the exploitation of the innocent in the name of morality and social harmony—with wildly comic exaggeration is far more disturbing and disruptive of our native habit of accepting whatever is as right, than any 'doleful keening of the righteous' (WTD 52) could ever be. We laugh at Jenny's impassioned naïveté, and at the incrementally parodic touches in her speech—we cannot, however, laugh at her premise that society does not need to be 'cleansed' but only to be made 'a bit more curious' (WTD 108).

What the play brings about is the metamorphosis of Molly from political activist to *Vogue* cover girl, of the Glaswegian Willie, who fought in Spain, into a slick man who does layouts for an advertising company, and, perhaps, of Jenny from an independent to a 'good' girl (WTD 109). The wartime plan for Jenny, Molly, and her husband Duncan to go off together to help make that new world the war against fascism had promised is eclipsed by Molly's vision of what the post-war world will be: 'A big, ugly, ramshackle new house no one had time to finish building. It will be a slum even before the paint dries' (WTD 67). Jenny's response to Molly's increasing disillusionment is revealing: 'What matters is what I felt when I believed. When I thought it was true. I've never been so happy' (WTD 59). It is the same ecstasy of illusion in which marriages begin. Again, Gallant is careful to interweave Molly's cynical awakening vis à vis politics with her discoveries about the cross-purposes on which her marriage is founded. Duncan's letters to her are filled with sexual longing, hers with praxis. He 'has' her in his dreams—she 'has' everyone but him in hers. When he writes to ask her what she is doing with the money she earns, but which he feels himself entitled to control, and when Molly stoically announces her decision to greet Duncan's return by becoming whatever he believed he married (WTD 95) we know this is a marriage that belongs resolutely to the bad 'old era' (WTD 108) and not to any brave new dawn.

What Is To Be Done? is a rarity, a play in which women hold centre stage[5] (even if their interactions and experiences are presented elliptically) and in which men are utterly marginal. The failure of the latter to gratify any of the desires of the former is made eloquently obvious—not only do the ideologues, refugees, and soldiers fail to finish off Franco or change the world in any significant way, but they fail to satisfy women intellectually or sexually. Molly's husband refuses to talk politics in his letters home to Molly; Willie proves a less than dynamic lover to Jenny. Yet if the men are 'omnimpotent',[6] what then are the women? Neither particularly strong nor defiantly loyal to one another. Jenny and Molly are not 'sisters' but friends all too willing to act as sexual rivals for the attentions of the glamorous refugee Karl-Heinz. And while Jenny continues to believe the best of Molly, she accepts her friend's abandonment of her at the play's end with equanimity, even resignation. Yet curiously enough, one of the delights of this play is that the iron bars of closure do not descend on characters or readers/spectators. For the play ends in an ironic ambiguity—the pessimistic as well as cautionary 'It won't happen again', and the 'sweet' singing of that hymn to human liberation, the 'Internationale'. Gallant manages to make the defeat of Molly's and Jenny's political visions resonant rather than merely cynical by gesturing to those ideals that had inspired them. And if she shows her female characters readying themselves to make for the wings as the male conquerors return to centre stage, we're made insistently aware that these women possess the critical intelligence, humour, strength, and spirit to do more than stretch their necks out for the yoke of love and marriage. It is in this openness, this refusal either to project a future full of sisterly and revolutionary bliss or to present her heroines as the helplessly meek and willing victims of a system, whether patriarchal or capitalist or both, that Gallant maintains a fine balance, claiming the vantage point of the disinterested but not incurious observer.

Let's look for a moment at the stance Gallant adopts in her nonfiction—a stance we can describe as feminist in its apprehension of the tacit ways in which women are presumed upon, and by which they have been conditioned to attack each other. In 'The Events in May', for example, we find her reporting on how the mothers of liberation-minded students would take in their children's friends, and sometimes perfect strangers, only to find that 'they would leave dirty water standing in the tub for her to deal with. Slaves at home? The servant mother? Mystifying' (PN 56). Or she notes how, at the 'pigsty' the Société de Géographie has become, only girls are given brooms and told to sweep: 'Girl sweeping says, "C'est aux femmes de balayer", like the wife in the dream in 8 1/2' (PN 61). And Gallant also describes the 'slight stir' that arises from the girls around her when another girl gets up to make a point at a meeting: 'Girls don't like other girls to speak' (PN 87). This occurs, of course, in 1968, two years before the publication of Millett's Sexual Politics, and in a country in which, according to Gallant at least, feminism has not even yet taken hold in more than an intellectual way (iJKK).

The essay in which one would expect such feminist sympathies as Gallant does possess to come to the fore is 'Immortal Gatito: The Gabrielle Russier Case'—her lucid, far-ranging account of the fatal affair between Russier, a divorced lycée teacher and mother of two, and one of her students, a sixteen-year-old boy named Christian. In this introduction to the peculiar labyrinth of the French judicial system, and the quirks and clichés of French cultural life, Gallant succinctly sums up the workings of the double standard à la française, citing the 'prevailing belief that a Don Juan is simply exercising a normal role in society, whereas women have been troublemakers ever since Genesis' (PN 96). Gallant is scrupulous in noting the fatal rigidities and self-deceptions in Russier's own character—the romantic tendency to confuse literature and life, for example, that led her to identify herself 'with Phaedra and Antigone, but [to forget] that the same Greeks who called them heroines admired only heroes in real life, a life in which women had no status—none whatever'(PN 98). Yet Gallant insists that the special harshness of Russier's punishment—imprisonment, loss of job, accumulation of mountainous debts, eventual suicide—derived from the factor of gender: 'It seems to be accepted that a girl of any age is asking for trouble, and should know better, while the man, the seducer, is somehow or other her victim. . . . A man's conduct is considered inevitable and therefore largely innocent, but a woman's thought-out and reprehensible' (PN 109).

French society, Gallant declares from some thirty years' experience, is generally a better place for a woman than English-speaking society: 'A woman's intelligence is respected, her professional status accepted, and as to her personal life, the French are notorious for an indifference to others that is also a form of minding one's business.' But when you step out of private life to become involved with the legal system, 'you discover that women never have the last word. A woman's past as well as something called her "soul" weigh in the balance when she is being judged in court' (PN 109). Not surprisingly, Gallant is also sensitive to the French distaste for divorce: 'if "divorcée" is journalists' shorthand for "floozie" even in America,' she argues, 'what can it be in a country as Catholic and conservative as France?' (PN 133).

In reasoned, measured tones, and thus with all the more scathing effect, Gallant sets out the list of abysmal anachronisms institutionalized in French society until very recently:

Gabrielle Russier was seven before women were allowed to vote, twenty-eight when married women could have bank accounts, and thirty before she could legally get advice from a doctor about contraception. She died before women were allowed to enroll their children in kindergarten without the husband's written consent, or have a say in where the family would live. The shocked protest that followed this last piece of legislation was like something preposterous out of the Victorian era. . . . A woman found guilty of adultery in France can be sent to jail for two years, whereas a man escapes with a fine—and he can only be fined if he was stupid enough to bring his mistress into his home. None of this is to say that if the legal status of women in France were different Gabrielle Russier would have found tolerant magistrates, for Americans do not need to be told at this stage of their social history that you cannot legislate attitudes' (PN 110).

'Immortal Gatito' seems, in part, a feminist '*J'accuse*' in its dramatization of what it means, legally, to be a woman of Gabrielle Russier's generation in France. It is, of course, much more, being a portrait of a society in which culture and politics, the patriarchal code and the legal system, personal life and public pieties are complexly and, to a North American eye, bizarrely enmeshed. And Gallant is as concerned in this essay with the politics of class and race as she is with those of gender. She establishes the fact that Russier was comparatively sheltered and aided by the rigidity of the French class system and the racism of French society as a whole. Had Gabrielle Russier been not a middle-class, university-educated white, but an Algerian street-sweeper, she could have suffered the same miscarriage of justice and no one would have heard of her plight, or expected to. Thus 'Immortal Gatito' is not so much a feminist critique as a general overview of the legal and political structures of a society, and an incisive analysis of some of the more repellent ways and means by which that society perpetuates itself. It is not exclusively the feminist, but rather the comprehensively human implications of the Russier affair that Gallant brings home to us: that unanalyzable 'mystery of what a couple is'; the distinct certainty of human limitation and hypocrisy: 'If every weakness and subterfuge for which infatuation is responsible were punishable by law, no prison in the world would be big enough' (PN 134-5).

Gallant's sympathy for Russier's plight, both as a woman and as an individual, is obvious. So is her puzzlement at why so fine a (female) writer as Marguerite Yourcenar feels compelled to make almost all her male characters mysogynists and to draw her female characters entirely from 'the dismal ranks of scolds, harpies, frigid spouses, sluts, slatterns, humorless fanatics, and avaricious know-nothings . . . who seem to have been created for no other reason than to drive any sane man into close male company' (PN 187). Yet in *Paris Notebooks* she shows herself peculiarly hostile to another of her contemporaries, Simone de Beauvoir. Her remarks about the latter in her reviews of *All Said and Done* and *Hearts and Minds: The Common Journey of Simone de Beauvoir and Jean-Paul Sartre* are theatrically cruel: after a telling criticism ('Why is it that her women have only Christian names and her men only surnames?') Gallant goes on to describe the fifth volume of de Beauvoir's autobiography as providing 'one trifling fact after the other, in a style that has the dazed, ruminative rhythm of a French schoolgirl chewing gum at a concert in time to Bach' (PN 209). And while Gallant's own response to the union between de Beauvoir and Sartre is astute—'Like most systems that try to channel life, theirs had made no allowance for jealousy and pain' (PN 222)—particularly as made by a writer who has, in her own personal life, rejected such a system, there is something unfairly dismissive in her final placing of these long-toothed 'French intellectuals in Majesty': 'Unwilling symbols of a generation once lithe and rebellious, now tamed and fairly thick about the waist, they have survived to become its Darby and Joan, sometimes laughed at but more often respected and, in a way, probably loved. . . . [T]he grandchildren of those vanished, sulky existential adolescents of the 1940s may yet end up playing in sandboxes in an urban landmark called "Square Jean-Paul Sartre, Homme de Lettres et Philosophe"' (PN 224). She does not allude to the possibility of any Square Simone de Beauvoir.

Gallant's sympathies are for the exploited and oppressed, those disadvantaged by the prevailing hypocrisy of those who form an élite—women as well as men—in any given society. She shows little interest in those of her *consoeurs* who are avowed feminists or who have, at times, addressed feminist issues—Margaret Atwood, Doris Lessing, Monique Wittig, for example. But then Gallant has always seemed to stand alone among her sex. Her early success as a writer at a time when women were only rarely admitted into the literary canon, and her ability to establish and maintain her personal independence in the heyday of the Feminine Mystique, stamp Gallant as a unique kind of woman, able to take the full measure of her time and 'place', which she has characterized as being marked by the 'stupid and materialistic . . . Eisenhower mentality'.[7] As the affair of the Montreal Press Club reveals, Gallant was well aware that in the institutionalization of this particular mentality, Mamie played as large a role as Ike:

> I looked forward to the camaraderie [one would have with a Press Club]. . . . But then women were excluded. . . . One of my friends said, 'Look, Mavis, we can't have you because we don't want our wives here.' Then I realized that these men never went home, they got married and left their wives in the suburbs. Once a year, at an office party, they were allowed to come, with their hair done, their little black dress and pearls, all alike, and they were pests—then they'd retire to the suburbs for another year, have another baby

named Ronald or Gary or Nelson. And I thought then, whatever God does with me, that's one thing He's not going to do. I will not be the little woman in the suburbs, waiting at home while he has his fun and his friends and his career. . . . (iKL 18-19)

One immediately remarks that Gallant is as sardonic in her attitude towards 'the little woman' as she is towards the men who have made them into 'pests'. It is, perhaps, the unshakeable attitude of the miraculously reprieved, a woman who was able to get out of the marriage and job and country that were preventing her from pursuing her vocation as a writer. Her plans to live in Europe off her fiction were greeted with ill will by the majority of her colleagues, women and men alike: 'The failure of a woman reassures men just as men,' she explains. 'It reassures the women who have hung onto safe jobs, boring husbands. One's defeat will reassure' (iGH 32). Gallant also recounts the crucial error she made in responding to the news that she had succeeded in her bid for freedom: actually showing people the first cheque she received from *The New Yorker*. She was earning, she recalls, $50 a week when she received that cheque for $600. 'It was a lot of money—I don't think I'd ever had $600 together, ever. . . . I thought it was $60' (iJKK). The response she met from most people was one of resentment, and here again economic issues come onto play. One can imagine how little this revelation—that one of their colleagues, a mere woman, was making so much money—would have 'reassured' the men who hung around the Montreal Press Club. Success for Gallant has always been an economic as well as an aesthetic matter—indeed the two are crucially interdependent, something difficult to register in a society where most writers are dependent on government grants, and not their minimal royalties, to support them. Money, Gallant has declared, can be a direct cause of happiness, since it may set one free to achieve a desired way of life: lack of money is only another form of entrapment (iEB).

'I *am* a Canadian *and* a writer *and* a woman. If the basic facts of my existence created problems for me, I would not be myself but a character in someone else's fiction' (iGH 61). Gallant's pronouncement reveals an astonishing degree of self-reliance deriving from an economic and emotional independence that have been earned, and not inherited. If she has no need for feminism or nationalism or writers' unions, is this proof of arrogance, even ignorance, or rather, of a formidable degree of success that should hearten rather than discountenance us all? The brilliant career of a Mavis Gallant may, in truth, be much harder to handle than the equally remarkable 'failure' of an Elizabeth Smart, for example. Those of us who have not worked ourselves free of the entanglements that preclude or hamper our vocations may perceive a certain incriminatory effect in the famous authority of Gallant's narratives. We may find this authority all the more magisterial because it has emerged out of an intense battle for self-definition, a battle waged not so much for the self as against all those representatives of family and society who would deny or suppress or negate it.

Gallant, then, can be described as a highly individualistic woman, feminist in her insistence on economic equality between the sexes, but a realist—one might even want to say pessimist— in her denial of any possibility for fundamental change in the conflictual relations between men and women, and between women themselves, for that matter. She makes no claims for the moral or behavioural superiority of women: as she remarks in a review of a biography of Colette, 'if an unqualified wife-victim is hard to find, so is an unqualified husband-monster' (PN 229). Her fiction recognizes the various ways in which women have been fated to death-in-life not only by their fathers and husbands, but by their mothers as well. She shows that little help and much hindrance can be expected by women from their sisters and female friends. For feminists one of the most problematic aspects of Gallant's writing may lie in its almost total denial of any romantic ideal of sisterhood. 'The Cost of Living' and 'Its Image on the Mirror', for example, show how actual sisters mingle active resentment and oblique affection in their dealings with one another before finally ceasing to have any communication with each other at all. 'Acceptance of their Ways', 'Good Deed', and the Lena stories collected in *Overhead in a Balloon* show women at daggers drawn with one another, as rivals for mastery in situations ranging from the comically petty (squabbles over yoghurt and mouldy cheese) to the ironically eviscerating (a battle for the legal title of wife, and thus the possibility of having children, that ends only after both women are definitely menopausal).

Linnet Muir, that *non-pareil* in Gallant's work, the self-sustaining, strong, and independent woman, fights her battles entirely alone. The only other ambitious woman she encounters in her working life is the formidable accountant and Ph.D. student Mrs Ireland, described as 'unhappily married' (HT 258)—her husband beats her. Mrs Ireland bitterly advises Linnet not to marry: 'Don't you girls ever know when you're well off? Now you've got no one to lie to you, to belittle you, to make a fool of you, to stab you in the back' (HT 260). Linnet is incapable of taking this advice: 'we were different—different ages, different women, two lines of a graph that could never cross' (HT 260). Yet if Linnet's life does not intersect with Mrs Ireland's, neither does it do so with her own husband's. Of all the opaque spots in Gallant's fiction, the unnamed husband of Linnet Muir is the most conspicuous. What children are to the eponymous heroine of 'Irina'—darling zeros—Linnet's husband is to her, and one is not too sure that the darling part was ever applicable. For whatever reason, Gallant portrays Linnet's coming-of-age and independence quite apart from her actual experience of marriage: the one 'romance' she is permitted is with the idea, not the reality, of the hapless remittance man, Francis Cairns, who ends up in the Killed-in-Action columns of the Montreal newspapers.

It is economics, not erotics, that preoccupies the newly liberated Linnet Muir. What she grasps at the very start of her career is the enormous discrepancy in status, as great as that between master and slave, between men and women: 'I did not think men better than women—only that they did more interesting work and got more money from it. In my journals I called other girls "coolies". I did not know if life made them bearers or if they had been born with a natural gift for giving in. "Coolie" must have been the secret expression of one of my deepest fears'(HT 226).

Instead of meekly joining the female office workers 'parked like third class immigrants' at the far and dark end of the office (HT 255), Linnet insists on a desk and a job that will place her squarely in the ranks of her male co-workers, even if she is being paid significantly less to perform the same meaningless tasks. Linnet comes to realize, however, that there is a worse fate than 'cooliehood'—that of ending up 'a sensitive housewife . . . who listens to Brahms while she does the ironing, and reads all the new books still in their jackets' (HT 278). Linnet's secret name for the shrill, manipulative, and miserable married women of her acquaintance is 'Red Queens', after the frenzied, harrying monster in *Through the Looking Glass*. As for the traditional womanly means of fulfilment and self-expression—the bearing and rearing of children—Linnet's rejection of it is as concise as it is closed: 'The promise of children all stamped with the same face, cast in the same genetic mold, seemed a cruel waste of possibilities' (HT 263); Linnet's possibilities, we might add, not those of her hypothetical children.

But it is not just the laughable status accorded to working women, nor the grotesque delimitations of the roles they later assume, that Linnet Muir rejects. It is also the nature of the relation between the sexes, as defined by those with the power to enforce it—men. Linnet sums up this relation accordingly: 'where women were concerned, men were satisfied with next to nothing. If every woman was a situation, she was somehow the same situation, and what was expected from the woman—the situation—was so limited it was insulting' (HT 262).

As the stories in *Home Truths* make clear, Linnet ranges herself firmly against the angels in her project of independence. In the title story of *From the Fifteenth District* Gallant has one of her characters, a woman consumed by the inexhaustible demands of her husband and children, declare: 'Angels are created, not born. Nowhere in any written testimony will you find a scrap of proof that angels are "good". Some are merely messengers; others have a paramilitary function. All are stupid' (FFD 167). It is not surprising, therefore, to find Gallant setting herself firmly against that stereotype of the woman writer as Angel in the House of Art—a Ruskinian rather than a Red Queen, nurturing and sustaining our tenderest sensibilities, our creative energies and possibilities. Utopian feminisms that predict a brave, free world coming into existence only with the creation of a new, female language, completely independent of the forms and practices of patriarchy, Gallant would no doubt perceive as laughable extensions of the convenient and comparatively recent belief (concocted and reiterated by men) that women are spiritually, morally, even physically superior to (not stronger than) men, and that their role is to sweep and decorate society's spiritual and moral hearths.

Laughter, in fact, is Gallant's *forte*—the kind of subversive laughter practised, for example, by a Jane Austen at the expense of those 'forms of self-expression available to her as an artist and as a woman'.[8] Ridicule of society's accepted conventions and constructs and of those who uncritically endorse them is a practice that can make not only readers but reviewers uneasy. So perhaps it is not surprising to find critics misrepresenting, ignoring, or basically fudging the implications of this laughter. Those who praise Gallant for the 'admirably feminine discretion, tact, humor, self-confidence and kindness' of her writing—as did Eve Auchincloss in her 1964 review of *My Heart Is Broken*—are considerably further off the mark than is a critic like Robert Weaver, describing Gallant's fiction as 'fascinating, irritating, and frighteningly human', and as marked by a characteristically 'bitchy' impatience.[9] Bitchiness, after all, is the corollary of female subversiveness: as feminist critics remind us, 'Feminine propriety, reserve and politeness can give way to bitchiness, since the bitch is what the young lady's role and value imply from the beginning, built [as it is] . . . out of complicity, manipulation, and deceit'.[10] We recall the introductory essay from *Home Truths*, in which Gallant describes how as a young child she was made to call black white if she wanted to be fed her supper; we remember Linnet Muir going in her white suit and gloves to an office Dickensian in its decrepitude, only to have pornographic pictures popped on her desk by a male co-worker; we think of the child Linnet displaying the correct manners on account of which she may be grudgingly included in her parents' parties, all the better to overhear risqué conversations between her elders and betters.

Bitchiness, then, is not a blemish or lapse in Gallant's writing but, as Weaver assumes, a distinctive trait, expressing not malice and spite or mere complaint, but effective opposition to the way things are. And, as we have seen, things are in a fairly bad way according to Gallant: our responses seem limited to a choice between disgust—as voiced by the wife in 'Malcolm and Bea': 'Birth was ugly. Death was another ugly mystery. . . . [M]ost of everything is just dirt and pain' (EW 118)—and bewilderment, as described in 'Irina': 'You looked for clarity . . . and the answer you had was paleness, the flat white cast that a snowy sky throws across a room' (FFD 230). For how much of this are we responsible—how much of it is a metaphysical given? Reading Gallant's work, one finds how complicated is that line between what we can alter and what we cannot; nevertheless, the relentlessly social and political context of her vision forces us to ask these questions again and again.

In this context it is interesting to see what two prestigious male critics make of Gallant's work. Writing of her novels, Robertson Davies seeks to reassure us: 'Mavis Gallant's kind of miserable women stand apart from most writing of the kind because there is no current of anti-masculine grievance in them—no sound of an axe being remorselessly ground without ever achieving an edge....'[11] The implication is that Gallant's bitches may bitch, but not with any cause that could impugn, or effect that could unseat, the patriarchal reader or critic. Second, Davies suggests that the driving force, the central concern of her three novels (*Green Water, Green Sky, A Fairly Good Time,* and *The Pegnitz Junction*—a novella Gallant describes as 'a book about where fascism came from' [iGH 41]) can be summed up in that standard female interest—love. Davies does praise Gallant's work for the aesthetic control and economy that, he claims, have distinguished women rather than male writers (male writers, one presumes, are too busy writing about ideas and transforming the *Weltanschauung* of their age to bother much about form and style, unless, of course, those qualities simply come naturally to them).

Davies leaves us with the notion that Gallant is 'cool' but never tough, a 'classic' writer using 'modern form' to remind us that life always has been and will remain wretched for those whose minds lack 'scope' and 'pause'.[12] He assures us that she blames no one for either inflicting or sustaining this wretchedness. Consolation for aching hearts can be found in her perfect works of art, he reveals; what's more, Gallant does not merely 'enlarge' our understanding of life, she 'cleanses' it as well.[13] (One cannot help summoning up the image, here, of a particularly gritty sort of bathtub cleanser, or else the convent-laundry-redemption service described in *What Is To Be Done?*) What Davies does not concede is that Gallant may be seen as using the immense authority of her language and her mastery of narrative form not to console us, but to disrupt our expectations, to disabuse us of illusions bred by complacency, convenience, or settled privilege.

George Woodcock, on the other hand, offers a serious, extensive, and perceptive look at Gallant's later fiction. While he too compares her work with Austen's—he sees both women as practising a comedy of manners—his comments on the 'impeccable verbal texture and the marvellous painterly surface of the scene imagined through the translucent veil of words'[14] would seem to make Gallant into a latter-day Woolf, not the feminist Virginia of *A Room of One's Own* or *Three Guineas,* but the aesthetically obliging Mrs Woolf of conventional criticism. But when he turns his attention to some of the most challenging and ambitious of Gallant's fictions—*The Pegnitz Junction* and the Linnet Muir sequence in *Home Truths*—he implies that her historical awareness and acute political sense lift these fictions out of the exquisite confines of the comedy of manners, into more profound and ambitious territory. Yet before he can stake any kind of claim for Mavis Gallant as a major writer, Woodcock reneges on his previous observations by retreating to the safety of gender-based categorizations. Her mature work, he concludes, 'is in no way male and ideological; it is feminine and intuitive and the rightness of detail and surface which are so striking come not from intellectual deliberation but a sense of rightness as irrational but true as absolute pitch'.[15]

Davies and Woodcock both attempt to pin Gallant within the conventional category of the woman, even the 'lady' writer, whose penchant for irony or satire is not subversive but rather enlarging and 'cleansing'. It may be argued that because her fiction deals so overwhelmingly with female experience—of society, politics and history, of oppressive family structures and exploitative erotic ties—she is therefore 'a woman's writer'.[16] I would argue that it is what Gallant does with female experience, the things she insists we observe in and about her female characters, that make her fiction important to all readers, regardless of gender. And in all fairness to male, as opposed to 'masculinist', critics, I would like to quote from two particularly apposite responses to the 'feminine' aspect of her work.

In a mixed review of *A Fairly Good Time*, Christopher Lehmann-Haupt follows an intriguing line of inquiry. In spite of what he calls the novel's 'delicious episodes' and 'inexhaustible playfulness', he finds something 'flat and forgettable' about Gallant's second novel; something profoundly lacking in her choice of characters to portray. 'My real suspicion', he concludes, 'is that, for all the richness of detail with which Shirley's character is drawn, Miss Gallant has denied us some deeper understanding. Or denied herself the expression of her true fury at a world that treats its women as children and nincompoops.'[17]

John Ayre, in an article written three years later, is even more insistent on the way in which Gallant traps her characters within a relentlessly trivial 'women's world':

> Gallant's fiction presents a stagnant, woman-crowded world that is hinged on ritual, where the figures display a recurrent impotence in rebelling against a conservative code of feminine behaviour

which is serving only to destroy them. The characters are almost uniformly presented as grown-up orphans . . . roaming Europe. Fragile and powerless, they seem trapped like faded toy ballerinas behind the glass door of an old wooden cabinet. What unifies them all as characters is their central mediocrity and their lack of vitality. Freed from financial worries by small amounts of cash from trust funds or alimony, they are, ironically, tied even more rigidly in their exile to the old North American code of ladylike be-haviour. . . . The only form of rebellion they can manage is to fall apart in the shell of the code that traps them.[18]

Ayre is particularly perceptive in drawing our attention to the economic base of that curio cabinet in which he sees Gallant's female characters imprisoned. And his diagnosis of the *maladie féminine* that afflicts such characters as Flor in *Green Water, Green Sky* is impeccable. But the woman's world that Gallant's early and middle fiction creates is a good deal more varied than Ayre suggests, and in the decade or so since the publication of his essay she has gone on to create new paradigms for female experience, and to transvalue older ones, as we shall shortly see.

*

If he let his thoughts move without restraint into the world of women, he discovered an area dimly lighted and faintly disgust-ing, like a kitchen in a slum. It was a world of migraines, miscar-riage, disorder and tears. (GWGS 114)

'You Fascist!' Why was this always the final shot, the coup de grâce delivered by women? Speck's wife, Henriette, book critic on an un-compromising political weekly, had said it three times last spring— here, in the street, where Speck stood locking the iron screen into place. He had been uneasily conscious of his wellborn neighbors, hanging out their windows, not missing a thing. Henriette had then gone away in a cab to join her lover, leaving Speck, the gal-lery, her job—everything that mattered. (OB 4)

Between these two poles of female experience—a male sponger's arrogant dismissal of the 'kitchen in a slum', and a woman's humiliation of the husband she is walking out on[19]—lies the world of women as observed by Mavis Gallant. Whether pictured as glass cabinet or slum kitchen, office or artist's studio or that chink in a wall through which a naked au pair girl can be glimpsed, this world figures as both labyrinth and thread by which the reader may find her or his way into the labyrinths's often baffling, always constricted heart. The most important feature of this women's world is the way in which, regardless of economic condition or social class, women are bound by personal relationships. Daughters, wives, divorcées, sisters, widows: all are pegged by the roles they assume towards the men in their lives. These roles are encyclopaedic in range—a full list of Gallant's female characters would resemble one of those super-saturated photographs of the aged Victoria surrounded by her prodigally fertile progeny. For our present purposes, a simple list of the various female types that recur in her fiction will suffice.

Let us fix 'husband' as an appropriate dividing line. To one side of it we have an array of daughters, sisters, and working women—teachers, office-workers, servant girls. On the centre line we find the wives, mothers, and grandmothers; on the other side fall the shadows: widows and divorcées. And like an X drawn through the line are the *amoureuses*, a term Gallant coined for Sarah, the determinedly exploited heroine of 'In the Tunnel'. The vocation of the *amoureuse* is to blithely harbour a host of shiftless, worthless, temporary lovers.

Variations in these roles are legion. The daughter can, for example, be the dream-caught, eight-year-old Irmgard of 'Jorinda and Jorindel' or the eightyish Miss Horeham of 'The Moabitess', knit to her dead father's memory by a shared web of fables and dissimulations. She can appear abandoned, as does Rhoda in 'The Prodigal Parent'; orphaned, as does the ill-shod and poorly clad Molly of 'The Remission'; or, like Claudie Maurel, as effectively dead: 'She seemed wax, as if she had died young and been preserved . . . under glass' (AFGT 73). Wives can be doglike *Hausfrauen* who fetch and carry for their husband-masters as do Helga in 'An Alien Flower' or Grete Toeppler in 'The Latehomecomer', or they can be the less servile North American variety, who have taken college courses in love and marriage, like Carol in 'The Other Paris', or who finally leave their errant spouses, as does Doris in *Green Water, Green Sky*. Still others are 'Moslem wives' who permit their husbands to tap their telephones and choose their wardrobes, as does Isobel Duncan in 'Its Image on the Mirror'. Then there are the scatty, beautiful, ambiguously faithless wives—Sheilah in 'The Ice Wagon Going Down the

Street' or Barbara in 'The Remission'.

Mothers can be authentically deranged, like mad Aunt Vera in 'The Moslem Wife'; literally maddening, like Bonnie in *Green Water, Green Sky*; grimly efficient, like Mrs Duncan in 'Its Image'; or consistently batty, like Shirley's mother in *A Fairly Good Time*. And, like Mrs Kennedy in 'A Day Like Any Other', they can ignore the symptoms of panic and fear manifested by their more or less abandoned children in order to submit to the cretinous whims of a tyrannical husband. Only the *amoureuses* seem to be cut out of the same cloth: Sarah of 'In the Tunnel', Louise in 'The Cost of Living', Shirley in *A Fairly Good Time* are perpetual losers, each a Mary Magdalene running up against her lover's *noli me tangere* just at the moment when she is most in need of support. These women's love, pity, and sexual energies are described in terms of emotional capital that cannot be hoarded or invested, but must be recklessly spent on the most fickle of lovers. Even the women whose age saves them from the role of sexual dupe pay a heavy price: the mother who lives off the émigré status of the son she no longer knows ('His Mother'), or the outmanoeuvred manipulator Olivia in 'Good Deed'. Of all Gallant's heroines, none but Linnet Muir is able to avoid the fate of entrapment, and only a rare few give as good as they get—the gorgeously absurd Lydia Cruche in 'Speck's Idea', and Berthe Carette in 'The Chosen Husband'.

As for the situations in which Gallant's female characters are locked, they range from the criminally banal to the routinely violent. Daughters are imprisoned, like their brothers, in 'the prison of childhood' (iHT 225); women enter marriages that infantilize or brutalize them and their husbands—the Reeves of 'In the Tunnel', the Thompsons in 'My Heart Is Broken', the protagonists of 'Malcolm and Bea'. Servant girls are harassed, psychologically if not sexually, by their employers. Mothers cripple their children physically, as in 'The Four Seasons', or mentally, as in *Green Water, Green Sky*. Even the *amoureuses* fall into the trap: they are regularly abandoned, ignored, or betrayed by the lovers they so casually adopt.

Sexual passion as evoked by Gallant seems hardly redemptive or even consolatory: Jean Duncan, having tardily lost her virginity on the dock of her parents' cottage, scrapes away the bloodstains with a knife and is later doubled in two by pain; Flor, woken for conjugal lovemaking from near-perpetual sleep, behaves 'like a prisoner roused for questioning' (GWGS 65). (The only one of

Gallant's female characters who seems to derive any free and spontaneous pleasure from her sexuality is the unlikely chaperone, Miss Baxter, in 'Jeux d'Eté'.) Rape is obliquely treated in 'My Heart Is Broken'; father-daughter incest in *A Fairly Good Time*, and wife-beating in 'Between Zero and One'. And in the Linnet Muir sequence, Gallant presents full-face two standard forms of male aggression: a tramp molests Linnet in a railway station just as she arrives in Montreal to start her new life, and a male colleague at her office shows her photos of a naked woman—his wife—'in a baby carriage with her legs spread over the sides, pretending to drink out of an infant's bottle' (HT 240). 'The unknown that this represented', Linnet observes, 'was infinite.'

In her earliest work Gallant seems to be providing her readers with an unadulterated account of female experience that comes close to being an imaginative correlative and a pessimistic corrective to Friedan's *The Feminine Mystique*. In 'The Burgundy Weekend' she has a peripheral male character sum up a feminine ideal similar to the one Friedan attacks:

> The girls in the nineteen-fifties . . . were made out of butter. They had round faces and dimples and curly hair. Bright lipstick. They smiled. They wore these stiff petticoats. They could have fallen in the Seine and never drowned—they'd have floated downstream on their petticoats. They wore Italian shoes that were a disaster. All those girls have ruined feet now. They looked like children dressed up—too much skirt, mother's shoes. They smiled and smiled and wanted to get married. They were infantile, under-developed. Retarded. (TR 11-12)

Yet Gallant does more than give a *Charm* magazine-cover view of the Mystique: her fiction anatomizes its most pernicious effects: a loss of independent identity and any inherent sense of personal worth; a false concept of female sexuality, which decrees that women's highest, indeed her only legitimate, fulfilment is to be found in sexual intercourse and pregnancy; and finally, a distorted concept of maternity, which imprisons and debilitates both mother and child.

A paradigmatic fiction of this early period is 'The Other Paris', a story first published in 1953. The main characters are Carol, a middle-class American girl primly but earnestly on the track of romantic love in post-war Paris; Odile, a shabby, aristocratic, thirtyish *amoureuse*; and her lover, Felix, a displaced German boy stranded in France without a work permit or visa—the prototype of the rootless and historically dispossessed young Germans who will figure in Gallant's later fiction. Carol has been taught that love is like a geranium: given 'a good climate, enough money, and a pair of good-natured, *intelligent* (her college lectures had stressed this) people, one had only to sit back and watch it grow' (OP 4). Paris, like love, proves refractory: the winter city bestows grippe, not glamour, on Carol's corporation-man fiancé, Howard; it reveals to Carol the same rude people, dull food, and Coca-Cola signs she would have encountered in New York. Gallant's trademark—not so much the reversal as the excoriation of expectation—dominates this fiction:

> No wonder she was not in love. . . . Where was the Paris she had read about? Where were the elegant and expensive-looking women? Where, above all, were the men with their gay good looks and snatches of merry song, the delight of the English lady novelists? Travelling through Paris to and from work, she saw only shabby girls bundled into raincoats hurrying along in the rain, or men who needed a haircut. In the famous parks . . . under the drizzly trees, children whined peevishly and were slapped. (OP 6)

Carol does, against her better judgement, speak to the right person (Felix), turn down an unexpected street (on the down-and-out-and-dirty left bank), open the right door (into a seamy hotel room, the scene of Odile's and Felix's trysts), and, discovering the real Paris, fall in love. After a fitting with her dressmaker to try on her regulation-white wedding gown, Carol accompanies Odile to Felix's room, where she is given coffee and confirmation of the fact that Felix and Odile are lovers. Sickened by the slumminess of their passion, and because she discovers in herself the stirrings of a love that has nothing whatever to do with geraniums, Carol flees back to Howard and consoles herself with visions of the exquisitely-papered apartment in which she will foster marital bliss. The present reality of Paris—'rain and . . . unshared confusion and loneliness' is already being displaced by 'the comforting vision of Paris as she had once imagined it'. 'Happily married, mercifully removed in time, she would remember [Paris] and describe it and finally believe it as it had never been at all' (OP 30).

The duplicity of memory, the ways we use it both to paper-over and to trace reality, is at the perceptual heart of Gallant's fiction. 'The Other Paris' roots the distinction between what is meretriciously accurate and what is true deep within the world of traditional female experience. The untrue is identified with what we might call 'interior decoration'—the psychological reality of American marriage à la mode, circa 1950, while the true finds expression in the illicit and distasteful—whatever romantic convention and sentimental cliché cannot accommodate.

Carol, Odile, and Howard will reappear as Lottie, Vera, and Kevin in 'Virus X' (1965); variations on this theme had also figured in 'Poor Franzi' (1954). The reality of such a marriage as Carol anticipates with Howard is presented in 'Autumn Day' (1955), in which a nineteen-year-old girl, Cissy, finds herself bewildered by her marriage to the twenty-nine-year-old Walt, an American soldier in post-war Austria. Like 'Going Ashore', 'Autumn Day' is a story of transition, from lonely and unsettled girlhood to as lonely and unsettled a marriage. Cissy's helplessness is underscored by her panic at the possibility that she might be pregnant: 'How could I take care of a tiny baby when I wasn't ready to take care of myself, when I couldn't even wear high heels and dress like a grownup?' (OP 48). Marriage, she discovers, doesn't 'settle' anything, but rather, makes life 'untidy and inexplicably frightening'. Walt, described by his new wife as 'this stranger, mute, helpless, fumbling, enclosed' (OP 53) seems to find marriage as alien and difficult as does Cissy. But he has his work, while Cissy has neither child nor friend to distract or console her. Ironically, she misses her one chance of meeting the mysterious opera singer Miss West, the only person who seems to offer her some valuable form of contact and knowledge. The story ends with dubious assurances from the older Cissy that her marriage is a success, that she no longer feels—or at least acknowledges—the sadness of lost hopes and abandoned possibilities evoked by the 'Herbsttag' song she overheard Miss West so perfectly sing.

Marriage at its best is portrayed by Gallant as a Darby and Joan affair, the fate towards which the luckless Peter and Sheilah are headed in 'The Ice Wagon Going Down the Street'. At its worst, as with Malcolm and Bea, it is unadulterated hell. Most often, Gallant presents marriage as inevitable entrapment, permanent enclosure: this is the text of stories like 'The Circus', 'In Italy', and 'Better Times'. And her two novels are primarily concerned with illustrating the utter inadequacy of marriage to create or sustain a satisfactory sense of self and any possibility of happiness or even contentment, particularly for women.

In *Green Water, Green Sky* Bonnie, a witless, pretty, impecunious divorcée, drags her adolescent child Flor across Europe like a handbag on too long a strap. Desperate to marry her off to a suitor with fairy-tale wealth, looks, and social standing, Bonnie has limited success: Flor ends up with Bob, the under-bright son of a moderately wealthy, socially invisible Jewish-American wine merchant. In marriage Flor seeks self-definition through closure—that psychological and physical home ground her enforced peregrinations have denied her. An ingrained symbiosis between mother and daughter, and Flor's latent schizziness, prove stronger than the four walls of marriage: Flor's psyche disintegrates rapidly and she ends up in an expensive asylum while Bonnie, a parody of a clinging vine, winds herself ever more inextricably into her son-in-law's life.

In its depiction of madness, and of the catastrophic possibilities of mother-daughter relationships, *Green Water, Green Sky* seems a regressive sort of fiction compared to Mrs Dalloway or to D.H. Lawrence's short story 'Mother and Daughter'. The novel's closing image—little Flor riding towards her daddy on her very own pony—might even seem a parodic throwback to Rhett and Bonnie Butler of *Gone with the Wind*. Regression, however, is one of the principal motifs of *Green Water, Green Sky*, Flor regressing into sleep, madness, and memories of childhood as the narrative itself regresses from the present into time past. And Flor's malaise is clearly rooted in the childlike dependency demanded by the Feminine Mystique.

That Flor is the very flower of this mystique seems incontestable. 'She looked', we are told, 'like a pale rose model in a fashion magazine, neat, sweet, a porcelain figure, intended to suggest that it suffices to be desirable—that the dream of love is preferable to love in life' (GWGS 77). Flor's husband, trying to to keep her within his own feminine ideal—'some minor Germanic princess, whose nickname might be Mousie, who seems to wear the same costume, and the same air of patient supplication until a husband can be found' (GWGS 105)—cannot prevent her self-destruction. Soon after her marriage she 'joyfully, willingly' destroys those good looks that have made her 'an object as cherished as anything he might buy . . . as if to force him to value her on other terms. The wreckage was futile, a vandalism without cause. He would never understand and he was not sure that he ought to try' (GWGS 37-8). Flor ultimately abdicates her wifely role, refusing any sexual contact with Bob, refusing to accompany him on business-trips or dinners. Bonnie shoulders the responsibilities of 'homemaker', the 'stage business' of trying to create 'an attractive atmosphere for them all' (GWGS 39) while both floor and ceiling of their world crack open.

What is remarkable about Flor's regression into madness is the docility and decorum of it—there is no violence, physical or verbal, just a passive drifting into sleep. The other notable aspect of Flor's predicament is her utter isolation—the two women who try to help her are extraordinarily inept. She dismisses Dr Linneti, her psychoanalyst, as 'a cheat from a known tribe, subject to the same indignities . . . practicing the same essential deceits' (GWGS 32); Doris, a midwestern American girl deserted by her philandering husband, first hides Flor's sleeping pills to prevent any suicide attempt and then, almost gratuitously, gives them back when she decides to take the decisive step of leaving the husband who has already abandoned her. Gallant emphasizes the labyrinthine quality of female entrapment by having Doris proclaim, 'I have made a decision and I have called my father and he is cabling the money and I am going home' (GWGS 83).

Entropic rather than labyrinthine is the word for *A Fairly Good Time*. At first glance Shirley Perrigny seems to have thumbed her nose at the Feminine Mystique. 'Comfortable in chaos', she barely registers the fact that her marriage to the fastidious Philippe is falling apart. She doesn't rebel against the role of *femme du foyer* personified by her mother-in-law, a widow who looks as though she had a 'life's savings sewn up in her corsets' (AFGT 154). Rather, she simply hasn't a clue, thanks to the influence of her own mother's domestic eccentricities. Shirley, it emerges, is really an *amoureuse* with a touch of Lady Bountiful thrown in (she draws a comparison between herself and *Middlemarch*'s Dorothea Brooke). She rescues people who are not worth saving, her insights into experience are arbitrary and evanescent, and in her mystifying attraction to the repellent and manipulative Claudie Maurel she recalls the hapless Louise of 'The Cost of Living'. Shirley sleeps with her next-door neighbour in the same way she would pour a dish of milk for a stray cat, or stroke a lapdog in winter—to get close to something soft and warm.

Yet all the women portrayed in this novel are in their own way as passive as Flor. Claudie, we are told, could have aborted her father's child, but hadn't the wit or energy to ask for the money to do so; the various girlfriends of Shirley's Greek neighbour shuffle in and out of his bed like jokers being discarded from a deck of cards; Renata goes through the motions of a suicide attempt because her boyfriend wasn't around when she wanted him; the devious, husbandless Madame Roux spends her free time at home, disconsolately watching television and sipping tisane. And Shirley, who is described as 'bright, strong, sure' at the beginning of the novel, ends up as a 'beaten dog' whose identity is dependent upon her husband's presence. She refuses to quit the conjugal apartment, not because it had been hers before she even met Philippe, but because, as she says, 'I *live* here. I have a house and furniture and . . . a husband and all that. I'm not a tourist. I'm not somebody who keeps moving on. I'm somebody's wife' (AFGT 199). As the novel ends, however, she is packing to go, having been evicted from her apartment through the connivance of her former confidante, Madame Roux. Her last act in walking out of the building is to post a loving letter to her husband in care of his mother—a letter she immediately realizes to have been an 'irretrievable error' (AFGT 308). Walking off into a wind that 'blew straight from Russia', she expresses her expectation of seeing Philippe again in that evasive realm of dream and recollection in which, as 'The Other Paris' and *Green Water, Green Sky* suggest, truths and fictions coalesce in deceptive and destructive ways. 'The future', we are told, is 'a series of guesses, none of them attached to anything real' (AFGT 257).

Yet there is one of Gallant's fictions that provides a welcome twist to her portraits of silly, spoiled, unenviably innocent or helplessly disillusioned women: 'Thieves and Rascals' (1956) offers an unexpected paradigm of something that can only be called female solidarity. The story details two very different responses to a disruptive incident: the expulsion of Charles and Marian Kimber's daughter from her boarding school, after she has been caught out in a weekend tryst with a young man. Charles Kimber, an amiable, ineffectual lawyer who blithely keeps a mistress, is disturbed at the inconvenience caused by his plain daughter's moral lapse. The reader expects Marian, a beautiful fashion model whose devotion to appearances keeps her in a perpetually hungry and exhausted state, to be even more shallow and selfish than her husband in her response to her disgraced daughter, Joyce. Instead, Marian makes a curious confession to Charles, while lying in bed with an ice pack over her eyes. The reason for the ice pack is her distress not that Joyce spent a weekend with a boy, but that the boy didn't have the courage, wasn't caring enough, to stand by afterwards and refuse to abandon her.

Marian tells the astonished Charles that, though she doesn't hate men, she doesn't like them: they are all '[w]eak, frightened, lying . . . Thieves and rascals. . . . And never any courage, not a scrap. They can't own up. They can't be trusted. They can't face things. Not at that age. Not at any age' (E 86). Her knowledge stems from an experience she had at roughly her daughter's present age, when she ran away with a photographer who did not possess the courage to keep on going and take her with him. Her only profound attachment, she declares, has been to her older sister Margaret, who brought her up after their mother died, the father being 'useless'. It was Margaret who warned her that men were thieves and rascals: Margaret who disappeared after Marian married Charles, breaking Marian's heart and leaving her utterly alone. The story ends with Charles consoling himself with the fiction that the revelations his wife has just uttered are themselves a fiction, something made up so that he won't be too hard on his own daughter: 'At last he fell asleep, undisturbed, leaving his wife to think and to weep alone in the dark, under her mask of ice cubes' (E 86).

More typical of Gallant's conception of relationships between women, however, is 'Careless Talk', a story in which a wealthy, independent single woman, Mary, befriends a young farm wife and 'stray Cockney', Iris, on the basis of a shared language and 'condition in a world they believed intended for men' (IT 123). The two women meet in Burgundy, where Mary has a country house near the farm run by Iris's husband. But the friendship is irremediably skewed by the fact that Iris is tied to her husband, children, and home, while Mary is free to come and go as she pleases: 'Mary was Iris's only friend, and Iris was Mary's when Mary happened to be down at the country place' (IT 126).

Iris is imprisoned but not ignorant: in her view, '[w]omen's lives could be bent like wire in the hands of men. Iris didn't care what was said about modern women in a modern world; she had seen her mother's life and now she was living her own' (IT 125). And she is keenly resentful that her tight-fisted husband will not put in electricity or purchase even a second-hand washer until she bears him a son. Mary, a collector of confidences and giver of none, a perfectly groomed, sophisticated woman whose friendships are described as resembling simultaneous chess games, never completely subordinates the quickly aging Iris, with her two boisterous babies and her decaying teeth. For in spite of everything, Iris appears genuine in her love for her children and in her attraction to her husband—this provides her with the leverage to walk out on a tea party Mary gives for a distinctly unlikeable psychoanalyst-priest and an ancient, eccentric, socially desirable 'Mademoiselle'. Iris and her beautiful children have been summoned to Mary's as though to provide the décor for a fête champêtre. Feeling 'betrayed' by Mary's having discussed her with the house guests, Iris rejects Mary's hospitality and her friendship; the story ends with a conversation at cross-purposes, parallel, not reciprocal, between Mary and Mademoiselle, during which an 'incredible' confidence is vouched by the latter: 'Women float on the surface, but men go down without fear. . . . Men sleep in trust; women float' (IT 140).

What is one to make of this avowal of the relative place of women and men: surface and depths, assurance and anxiety? It is interesting that in all of Gallant's work, women are never presented as possessing abstract intelligence or aesthetic energies: with the notable exception of Linnet Muir there are no musicians, painters, poets, fiction writers, or students of philosophy among her female characters. The role of women vis à vis artistic creation seems to be to hinder and hamper it, or so the male protagonist of 'The Circus' (1964) suggests: women produce children, men produce works of art, and the persistence of the former reduces the efficacy of the latter. In 'The Statues Taken Down' (1965) Gallant gives us the portrait of a poet, George Crawley—feckless, dependent on a succession of all-too exploitable wives, mistresses, daughters, and so open about the deceptions he practises that he seems naïve, not cruel. Crawley's children come to Paris to spend a summer with him: he turns them loose in a public park with nothing whatsoever to do, and it becomes incumbent upon the oldest, Dorothy, to play mother to her brother and, in a curious way, *femme fatale* to her father. In her manoeuvres with him Dorothy is described as 'developing conscious, feminine conceit. Had she been older, she would have asked now for a cigarette and held it just so for the flame' (IT 164). She differentiates herself from the women with whom her father has always been involved, women with 'large breasts and abundant hair, their repeated pregnancies, and their chain-smoking. They had been photographed when the camera was askew or the light bleak, when their hair was lank after rain, when their babies half slipped off their corduroy laps like parcels on a bus. . . . She was from a thinner generation, a generation of stick figures' (IT 168).

Nevertheless, we know that Dorothy too will join the ranks of pliant, serviceable women around her father's altar. George, in fact, teaches her to misread what she knows of her mother's experience, and that of all his other women. Recalling his poem about a swallow that flies too low and is caught in a net, he declares, 'That was your mother'. At first Dorothy takes this to mean that her mother is the swallow, and is puzzled, since she knows her mother isn't at all like that. By the end of the story she realizes that her mother represents the net, her father the swallow—or at least she understands that this is the interpretation George prefers, and desires her to adopt. We are given to understand that Dorothy will take on the role of 'loyal daughter' who, when the time comes, will gladly and gratefully stay by her dying father, exchanging the possibility of an independent life for the honour of bringing him soap and a toothbrush to his hospital bed.

This, Gallant teaches us, is how it is for women without the superhuman courage and single-mindedness to save themselves from the prison of loving, or of needing to be loved. Nine years after 'The Statues Taken Down', she published 'Irina', a story in which an older woman seizes on the opportunity of her writer-husband's death to make a life for herself independent of the needs of her husband's public, her children, or her grandchildren. If, as Molly realizes in 'The Remission', there is no freedom except to cease to love, it is to this freedom that Irina moves in the course of the story. Instead of being 'burned dry and consumed' (FFD 227) after a lifetime spent nurturing a husband and five children, Irina blossoms with 'a sudden April brightness' in her widowhood (FFD 229). The woman her children have always seen as under-educated and reticent countermands her husband's will and becomes his literary executor; grants intelligent interviews and comes to the conclusion that the journals she is editing show her husband's 'moral and political patterns' to be 'fossils of liberalism' that have changed or triumphed over nothing of any importance (FFD 230). She begins to form her own opinions as to what is and is not important in her own life; she, whom her husband had always 'shielded from decisions, [allowing her] to grow in the sun and shade of male protection' (FFD 228) buys herself her own apartment in a small Swiss town, entertains her own friends (including the man who once asked her to desert her husband and children in order to run away with him), and writes to her children that she wishes them to leave her alone, on her own.

Yet Irina is no unmaternal monster: she takes in one of her young grandchildren, Riri, when his mother is due to have a serious operation, but lets everyone concerned know that she will not permit his presence to rob her of her independence. To make this clear she tells Riri an anecdote about a ring given her by her dying mother—something to sell, if ever she had need of money of her own. When Irina had tried to pawn the ring she was told first that she could not sell anything without her husband's consent, and second, that the ring was virtually worthless, since the original stones had been prised out and replaced with paste imitations—most probably by Irina's own father or grandfather. What Irina has learned from this experience she confides to her grandson: 'The women in the family never wondered if the men were lying. . . . They never questioned being dispossessed. They were taught that lies were a joke on the liar. That was why they lost out' (FFD 240).

Instead of offering her homesick grandson a warm bath of emotional support, Irina holds out something immeasurably more important: children, after all, are as dependent and helpless in their prison as wives are in theirs. She tells him that he can be 'independent. No one has to tell you what to do' (FFD 242). Checking on him during the night, she refrains from interfering with even his 'sunken mind, his unconscious movements', and the story ends with an uncharacteristically free and joyous image: the boy's mind, 'in a sunny icicle brightness, was . . . flying' (FFD 243). It is one of the rare instances in Gallant's work in which an adult and a child do not exasperate or betray one another, but co-exist in a beneficent mutual separateness.

If Irina is the most sympathetic and admirable representative of women's new- or tardily-found independence, then Lydia Cruche in 'Speck's Idea' is a purely comic variant of the type, one that does not cancel out an Irina, but in a curious way supports her, since the victories Lydia scores come at the expense of the men who have most desired to exploit her. She is not a writer's but a painter's widow, a type described by the art dealer trying to manipulate her as

suspicious and adamant. She had survived the discomfort and confusion of her marriage; had lived through the artist's drinking, his
avarice, his affairs, his obsession with constipation, his feuds and
quarrels, his cowardice with dealers, his hypocrisy with critics, his
depressions (which always fell at the most joyous seasons, blight-
ing Christmas and spring); and then—oh justice!—she had outlasted him (OB 17-18)

This is not to say that Gallant enshrines this particular female
type—she lavishes a peculiarly satiric attention on the furnishings
of Lydia's house: the TV set 'encrusted with gilt acanthus leaves'
on the sideboard, or the Mickey Mouse napkins with which an appalling supermarket cake is served, but she does this in the same
spirit in which she establishes the petty snobbism of the dealer
Sandor Speck, who forgives the 'spiteful, quarrelsome, and
avaricious' nature of his neighbours 'for the sake of [their] being
the Count of this and the Prince of that' (OB 1). In the end Lydia
Cruche outwits Sandor Speck, but her triumph recedes before the
brilliance of the idea upon which Speck seizes to avert professional disaster at her hands: the story is, after all, entitled
'Speck's', not 'Lydia's', 'Idea'.

*

What then, is Gallant's assessment of the possibilities of women
as explored in her fiction? She has given us a host of captive
daughters, wives, mothers, mistresses, and sisters. She has
sketched the portraits of a handful of free women—Linnet Muir,
Irina, Lydia Cruche—able to hold their own against the men who
try to prey or sit upon them. *Overhead in a Balloon,* her most recent
collection of stories, features not only Lydia Cruche, however, but
also the obnoxious Simone and the flyaway Katia, women who
seem pegged in the conventional roles of wife/mother and
girlfriend as defined by the appallingly lacklustre men in their
lives. And in the Lena stories Gallant gives us a species of déjà vu
in her portrayal of two women engaged in a bitter yet parodic tug-
of-war, not for the affections of the unimpassioned, failed writer
Edouard, but for the legal status of being his wife. Both women
are caricatures—Magdalena of the flighty, naughty, cunning
painted lady with dice instead of brains rattling round in her head;
Juliette of the morose and class-bound 'proper-lady' who cannot

live with Edouard as his wife, since Magdalena will not release him from the marriage of convenience he undertook with her to save her from certain destruction during the war. Magdalena, like Lydia Cruche, does win out over both Juliette and Edouard, and there is certainly an ebullient, indulgent quality to her portrayal, yet the tone of the Lena stories is inevitably soured by the fact of Edouard's narration, his coldly detached, scrupulously self-serving portrait of two radically different marriages. For a sense of alternative possibilities, of Gallant's revisioning of past forms of female experience, we must turn to the recent sequence (which one hopes will figure in her next collection) of 'Carette' stories: 'The Chosen Husband', 'From Cloud to Cloud', and 'Florida'.

In these stories one finds the tempered tone and dream-like nostalgia that figure in the Linnet Muir sequence: in fact, one can only describe Gallant's evocation of mood and period, her detailed observation of such phenomena as the aluminum curlers in which Berthe and Marie Carette sleep, or the chocolate mice presented by one of their suitors, as 'loving'. And this is immensely important in terms of Gallant's conception of women, because the Carette sisters she so affectionately portrays are not exemplary creatures, like Linnet Muir and Irina, but ordinary women whose emotional ties breed a refreshing loyalty to one another, a loyalty that is not destroyed, as happens to the sisters in 'Orphans' Progress', for example, but develops and extends to embrace another woman at the (rather negligible) cost of excluding a son/nephew.

'The Chosen Husband' takes a long look back at that lost Montreal with which the Linnet Muir stories have made us familiar. It is an era of restricted possibilities: the sisters Berthe and Marie 'were Montreal girls, not trained to accompany heroes, or to hold out for dreams, but just to be patient' (NY 49). Accordingly, they live with their widowed mother who has come into just enough money from the death of a male relative to be able to have certain pretensions as to who is worthy of her daughters' hands. Or rather, the hand of her younger daughter, Marie, for Berthe is a knowing, competent, sophisticated, and independent woman, holding down a steady job that allows her to buy her own fur coats, take on married men as lovers, and keep prospective husbands at bay with 'her skill at cards and her quick blue eyes' (NY 49). Marie, on the other hand, is childlike, docile, tractable: we are told she 'could not spell "Fascist" and did not know if it was a kind of landscape or something to eat' (NY 40). Her political ignorance is, in fact, commensurate with her absolute innocence about her own sexuality, never mind that of her fiancé, Louis. What emerges from 'The Chosen Husband' is Marie's adoration of and dependence on her sister; even where her marriage is concerned, Marie will do whatever Berthe wants or feels is good for her, just as when she was a child, she 'always turned to Berthe . . . she had started to walk because she wanted to be with Berthe' (NY 49).

It is Uncle Gildas, an elderly priest who lives in a seminary, tended by a host of devoted nuns, who is given the task of finding Marie a suitor. The boy he chooses, slow-witted Louis, is, however, as reluctant a suitor as Marie is a bride: he proposes marriage only when prompted by the threat of being conscripted for the Korean war. 'The mention of war was a marriage proposal' (NY 48), and so Marie's fate is sealed up with that of this 'stranger who might take [her] away, give her a modern kitchen, children to bring up, a muskrat coat, a charge account at Dupuis Frères department store, a holiday in Maine' (NY 44). At her wedding Marie wears a dead woman's ring, a widow's bridal dress. Yet the dreadful fate promised by these omens fails to materialize. For as the sisters come to realize, Louis 'had not separated them but would be a long incident in their lives. Among the pictures that were taken on the church steps, there is one of Louis with an arm around each sister and the sisters trying to clasp hands behind his back' (NY 49).

'From Cloud to Cloud' makes it clear that the independence promised the Carette sisters by the force of their affection for one another, and the strength of Berthe's character, does in fact continue. Marie's marriage results not in hordes of children begotten in horror, as happens in 'Saturday', but rather in one lacklustre son, Raymond. When the time comes Marie even ignores Louis's inconvenient request to bury him in Moncton—she feels neither guilt nor shame in having him interred in a local cemetery, and then returning to Berthe's flat to kick off her shoes. As for Berthe, her affection for her nephew does not lead her to sacrifice anything for him. Berthe disassociates herself from Raymond once it is clear he is unreliable enough to light out for Vietnam, making off with his mother's car and his father's gold watch. Far from being cramped and unfulfilled, Berthe's independent life is portrayed as literally spacious: 'She lived in a second-story walkup with front and back balconies, a long, cool hall, three bedrooms, on the west side of Parc Lafontaine. She was unmarried and did not need all that space; she enjoyed just walking from room to room' (NY 23).

But it is 'Florida' that comes to the reader as a totally unexpected gift. There is a delicious lightness, as well as appropriate irony, about the device Gallant uses to thread her narrative together—the image of static electricity. When Marie returns from her Florida trips to see her runaway son (he has opened a chronically failing motel business) she is 'riddled' with static: 'When she ate a peppermint she felt it detonating in her mouth'; when she kisses the paperwhite narcissus, it 'absorb[s] the charge and hurl[s] it back', so that Marie has to apply an ice-cube to her lips. 'Berthe couldn't hand her a teaspoon without receiving a shock, like a small silver bullet' (NY 24). The static is, of course, connected to Marie's concern over and dissatisfaction with Raymond.

The sisters are now living together in Berthe's spacious apartment, with Marie still expecting 'what Berthe thought of as husband service: flights met, cabs hailed, doors held, tips attended to' (NY 24). Berthe, however, has established her own conditions in this exemplary ménage. She refuses, for example, to discuss Raymond: 'He had left home young, and caused a lot of grief and trouble' (NY 23) and that is that. Berthe, we are shown, can not only take care of herself, she can also answer back to those who would query her endeavours. The photos she has taken of herself show an attractive woman having a good time; to her employer's comment that if only she had been a man she would have really got somewhere in the business she replies by drawing on her retirement savings and buying herself a lavish mink coat. It is Marie, however, who most beautifully establishes the success of her sister's life with her riposte to the suggestion that Berthe catch herself a widower: 'Berthe doesn't need a widower. . . . She can sit on her front balcony and watch widowers running in Parc Lafontaine any Sunday. There's no room in the flat for a widower. All the closets are full' (NY 26).

We are given a wonderful portrait of Marie as mother and mother-in-law on one of her trips to Florida. No meek and worshipful *maman*, she cramps Raymond's self-created style and irritates his wife, Mimi, who is not only skinny but a Christian fundamentalist instead of a Catholic. Yet when Marie finds out that Mimi is pregnant, she turns around in an astonishing and marvellous instance of that female solidarity we have been accustomed to see as an *ignis fatuus* in Gallant's fiction. Marie dismisses her neglectful son as a 'bad, disobedient boy. He ran away to Vietnam. The last man in our family. He should have been thinking about having sons instead of travelling around' (NY 26). Raymond, she concludes, will always be Raymond, but, as Marie impresses on Mimi: 'This baby has got a grandmother. He's got Berthe. *You've* got Berthe. Never mind Raymond' (NY 27). The silvery electric spark Marie receives in comforting Mimi she interprets as an approving message from Berthe: the embrace in which Marie 'enfold[s] Raymond's wife and Raymond's baby' (NY 27) is a guarantee to the reader as well as to Mimi that the women and their baby will indeed be 'grounded': safe against the shocks that dependence on male protection or affection entails.

It is, by this reader's reckoning at least, the sole instance of an embrace to be found in Gallant's fiction: the one ending that promises a kind of happiness, which is itself 'grounded' by Gallant's portrayal of her characters as distinctively flawed, necessarily limited, but essentially open—characters capable of making choices that permit them the kind of life they wish to lead.

*

What do we make of the way Gallant presents the world of women? We have seen that her pessimism regarding women's roles, status, and possibilities for self-transformation, a pessimism registered most strongly in her fiction of the 1950s and 1960s, is modulated but not renounced in her later writing: we are given a Linnet Muir, an Irina, a Lydia Cruche, and a Berthe and Marie Carette to weigh in the balance against the mass of Flors and Shirleys. This is not, of course, to demand that Gallant's fiction should present us with a panoply of positive feminist role models. Nevertheless, it is impossible not to notice her insistence on the generally closed nature of female experience. Rarely do we see the kind of female friendship shown in a scene in 'Questions and Answers' where Marie and Amalia, peeling vegetables for the evening's soup, take down Amalia's husband Dino several pegs, before he enters the flat and slaps the table with his hand 'to send the two women flying apart, one to put the soup on the stove, and the other to go out and buy the evening paper which he had forgotten' (IT 184). Gallant insists that we read every story in *Home Truths* (and, we may assume, in all her other collections) 'against its own time' (HT xviii): in so doing we will recognize in her an intractable 'memorist' who refuses to allow us to forget what conditions were like for women in the 1940s, 1950s, and 1960s, and how little things have changed for the mass of women despite the progress of feminism. Readers wary of such phenomena as Christian fundamentalism and 'REAL Women' will certainly find Gallant's fiction as much of a cautionary tale on the vulnerability of women's freedom as is Atwood's *The Handmaid's Tale*. And certainly we will read Gallant's delimiting view of female experience against our recognition of the success of her own achievement, as a woman and writer, an achievement that involved the same 'giddy risks and changes, stepping off the edge blind-folded' (HT 226) as those undergone by Linnet Muir. Gallant has insisted that in going off to Europe and living by her pen she was no Doris, underwritten by Daddy's dollops of cash; no Shirley, maintained by a mother-in-law's legacy (iGH 29). In the heyday of the Feminine Mystique she achieved both personal and economic independence on her own terms, by her own efforts, and that in itself is a cause for celebration.

Yet feminists (of both genders) cannot help but read Gallant's fiction against our own time, our own experience and aspirations. We may register the comparative lack of empathy and pathos in Gallant's portraits of trapped women, preferring the compassionate honesty with which a writer like Jean Rhys treats her sorry heroines. Some readers may find that Margaret Laurence's Morag Gunn speaks more directly and compellingly to their experience as women and writers than does Linnet Muir, and that Alice Munro gives a more comprehensive and expansive sense of the lives of 'traditional' girls and women. Yet any conception of female experience, its past, present, and future, will be dangerously incomplete and radically impoverished without the kind of knowledge that a reading of Gallant's fiction so insistently offers to us.

Notes

1 Virginia Woolf, *A Room of One's Own* (Harmondsworth, Middlesex, England: Penguin, 1974), pp. 89-90.

2 Elaine Showalter, 'The Feminist Critical Revolution', Introduction to *The New Feminist Criticism* (New York: Pantheon, 1985), p. 14.

[3]Interview with Karen Lawrence, *Branching Out* Feb.-March 1976, p. 19.

[4]As Showalter summarizes it, *l'écriture féminine* is 'a practice of writing "in the feminine" which undermines the linguistic, syntactical and metaphysical conventions of Western narrative. . . . [T]he most radical French feminist theorists also believe that *écriture féminine* is connected to the rhythms of the female body and to sexual pleasure (*jouissance*), and that women have an advantage in producing this radically disruptive and subversive kind of writing. They urge the woman writer to ally herself with everything in her culture which is muted, silenced or unrepresented, in order to subvert the existing systems that repress feminine difference' ('The Feminist Critical Revolution', p. 9).

[5]The other woman in the cast is, of course, the purely comic, balaclava-knitting, left-wing devotee, Mrs Bailey.

[6]A term used by Constance Brown Kuriyama to describe the psychology of Marlowe's Faustus in *Hammer or Anvil: Psychological Patterns in Christopher Marlowe's Plays* (New Brunswick, N.J.: Rutgers University Press, 1980), pp. 95-135.

[7]Quoted by Martin Knelman, *Saturday Night* 93 (Nov. 1978), p. 29.

[8]Sandra Gilbert and Susan Gubar, *The Madwoman in the Attic: The Woman Writer and the Nineteenth-Century Literary Imagination* (New Haven: Yale University Press, 1979), p. 127.

[9]Robert Weaver, Introduction to *The End of the World and Other Stories* (Toronto: McClelland and Stewart, 1974), p. 13.

[10]Gilbert and Gubar, *Madwoman in the Attic*, p. 174.

[11]Robertson Davies, 'The Novels of Mavis Gallant', *Canadian Fiction Magazine* 28 (*Special Issue on Mavis Gallant*, 1978), p. 69.

[12]Ibid., pp. 70-2.

[13]Ibid., p. 73.

[14]George Woodcock, 'Memory, Imagination, Artifice', *Canadian Fiction* 28, p. 74.

[15]Ibid., p. 82. Woodcock, it would appear, has little acquaintance with Virginia Woolf's 'sketch of the soul', which postulates 'that in each of us two powers preside, one male, one female. . . . The normal and comfortable state of being is that when the two live in harmony together, spiritually cooperating. If one is a man, still the woman part of the brain must have effect; and a woman must also have intercourse with the man in her. Coleridge perhaps meant this when he said that a great mind is androgynous' (*A Room of One's Own*, p. 97).

[16]As it was by one Herbert Leet, in his review of *The Other Paris* (*Library Journal* 1 Apr. 1956, p. 832): 'Enjoyment is limited to feminine special readers in larger public libraries.'

[17]Christopher Lehmann-Haupt, review of *A Fairly Good Time*, *New York Times Book Review* 5 June 1970, p. 33.

[18]John Ayre, 'The Sophisticated World of Mavis Gallant', *Saturday Night* Sept. 1973, p. 33.

[19]Henriette leaves Speck, it's true, but in running off with her lover would appear to abandon her job as well. *Plus ça change. . . .* And yet Henriette is worlds away from the pathetic divorcée Bonnie in *Green Water, Green Sky.*

Chapter 6

The Angel of History

This is how one pictures the angel of history. His face is turned towards the past. Where we perceive a chain of events, he sees one single catastrophe which keeps piling wreckage upon wreckage and hurls it in front of his feet. The angel would like to stay, awaken the dead, and make whole what has been smashed. But a storm is blowing from Paradise; it has got caught in his wings with such violence that the angel can no longer close them. This storm irresistibly propels him into the future to which his back is turned, while the pile of debris before him grows skyward. This storm is what we call progress. (Walter Benjamin, 'Theses on the Philosophy of History')[1]

Here we are together in the fortress. The bodies pile up outside. Don't look at them. ('An Alien Flower' [PJ 188])

. . . what fiction is about—is that something is taking place and that nothing lasts. Against the sustained tick of a watch, fiction takes the measure of a life . . . a look exchanged . . . the grief and terror that after childhood we cease to express. The lie, the look, the grief are without permanence. The watch continues to tick where the story stops. ('What Is Style?' [PN 177])

To shut oneself up in a fortress and turn one's eyes away from the wars raging outside; to take the measure, however temporary, of the damage: these are two profoundly different responses to the demonic 'storm of progress' that both paralyzes and propels Walter Benjamin's angel of history. The 'fortress' mentality is voiced by one of Gallant's characters, Helga, an imprisoned post-war *Hausfrau* whose choice of imagery—a monumental wreck of bodies—is by no means gratuitous: as a child Helga survived the bombing of her city but lost her entire family and thus any effective sense of self that might have helped her to hold her own inside the dubious refuge of marriage. Helga is appealing here to her husband, a stormtrooper of a corporate executive, to make a united front of their dead marriage; her capitulation to his power and authority in the interests of their family's prosperity and very survival entails a refusal of support and compassionate attention to those in the wreckage 'outside'.

The Germans who 'did not know', or rather, who constructed fictions of ignorance about the existence of death camps, were also caught up in the violence of progress: unlike Benjamin's angel, most of them kept their eyes tightly shut against the pile of human debris past which Nazism whirled them. Mavis Gallant, fortunate enough to have been neither perpetrator nor victim of mass murder, found herself its belated witness. As a young journalist working for the *Montreal Standard* she was shown the first photographs of Nazi concentration and forced-labour camps, and was required to write captions and 'a little information of 750 words' for the next day's paper. It would seem to have been the most traumatic and decisive moment of her life.

> One thing you cannot truly imagine was what the first concentration camp pictures were for someone my age. That's something you can't imagine because you've seen them all your life . . . this knowledge is part of your culture. . . . Now, imagine being twenty-two, being the intensely left-wing political romantic I was, passionately anti-fascist, having believed that a new kind of civilization was going to grow out of the ruins of the war—out of victory over fascism—and having to write *the explanation* of something I did not myself understand. I thought, 'There must be no descriptive words in this, no adjectives. Nothing like "horror", "horrifying" because what the pictures are saying is stronger and louder. It must be kept simple.' I remember what I wrote because I kept a copy of it for more than twenty years. I tore it up when I saw that the concentration camp experience, its lesson, its warning, had become kitsch. (iGH 39)

The newspaper, needless to say, did not print the stark text that Gallant kept for so long, a combination of *memento mori* and *aide-mémoire* for civilization itself. It was for Gallant herself to translate that 'little information of 750 words' into her own fiction and the worlds it brings into being, worlds that collide with and rupture our amnesiac own. In *The Pegnitz Junction* she felt she had at last succeeded in articulating the text the editors of the *Montreal Standard* would not run, a text that does not describe what happened, either to the Jews or to the Germans, but rather, deals with the *why*—not the historical causes of fascism—just its small possibilities in people' (iGH 41). Yet even before the publication of the German stories included in *The Pegnitz Junction*, Gallant had been attempting to answer that why, a question 'desperately important to people like myself who were twenty-two and had to live with this shambles' (iGH 40).

The shambles of civilization, of history itself, that supposedly linear progression of intelligible cause and proportionate effect: this is the larger world, the ultimate slum in which Gallant locates the 'kitchen' world of women, and into which she looses so many of her characters, male and female alike. As we have seen, her first published stories had to do with refugees from Hitler's Europe; many of her feature articles in *The Standard* had to do with the post-war plight of displaced persons. She has described how, in her early days as a writer, '. . . the people I met, the refugees I met, seemed to me absolutely charmed, incredible people who came to me out of this extraordinary world that was a literary world, really. I was imposing literature on life' (iBG 23). Later she would force literature to acknowledge life, showing how our conventions of visible order and satisfying pattern, of linear narratives with stable beginnings, middles, and ends, are as much falsifications of experience as is memory itself.

Story and memory are, for Gallant, notoriously duplicitous: ways of knowing, yes, but also ways of unknowing what is too painful or difficult to acknowledge. And this accounts for the problematic qualities of the fictions to be discussed in this chapter, fictions overtly concerned with history and politics as situations in which people are helplessly knotted. In one sense, the fictive worlds Gallant creates can be mapped between the poles of progress—historical time, with its blind, violent forward drive—and the project of memory—the desire to stop and make whole what has been smashed: to make sense out of the shambles. Yet because we so often misuse memory, purposely misreading the past in order to make liveable the present, and because, as Gallant's own comments in 'What Is Style?' make clear, the story-teller's art is an impossible race against time itself, the map that Gallant's fiction creates becomes itself incomplete, a tracing of absence as well as presence. In her constant consciousness of this problem she brings other fiction writers to mind. Joseph Conrad described himself as compelled 'to snatch . . . from the remorseless rush of time, a passing phase of life' so as to 'reveal the substance of the fragment's truth through showing its vibration, colour and form'. Henry James acknowledged that, though the writer's task is to exhibit 'the related state . . . of certain figures and things', he must do so by creating a fiction of shape and structure, cutting off, within an artificial circle, things that 'universally . . . stop nowhere'.[2]

What a work such as the novella 'The Pegnitz Junction' does is to snatch moments from the remorseless rush of time, but obscure their vibration, colour, and form. Such truth as we are vouchsafed is a truth of disconnections and lacunae. If this fiction cuts a circle into the welter of related things, it is not to create the appearance of harmonious shape and manageable ending, but rather to erase portions of the circumference, so that chaos and order leak into one another, creating an 'interference' that prevents the novella's recording consciousness from ever relating any one thing she hears to any other. It is in a piece such as 'The Pegnitz Junction' that Gallant's postmodernist affiliations assert themselves most strongly and, by corollary, most problematically. Discontinuity, obliquity, even opacity—these are not strategies to arrive at or legitimize a meaning that was there all along, either in the text or in the experience it represents. Rather, they are narrative equivalents of Gallant's refusal to put descriptive captions under the pictures of Auschwitz and to write an explanatory text. It is not the artist's task, we may infer, to write the explanation of things she does not understand—things that are, by their very nature, incomprehensible.[3] Such explanations are the seeds not only of kitsch, but also of that process of selective forgetting that is not the opposite of memory, but rather, one of its standard deviations.

Artists like Gallant remind us that because of the duplicity of memory, because of our insistence on and consequent fabrication of explanations, we prevent ourselves from learning lessons from history. Such is the text of Gallant's stories in which children who were victims of the war against fascism grow up to be bit actors playing Nazi officers and Jewish deportees in TV films that bear no relation whatsoever to the fact that 'ninety-eight per cent of the people who stayed in France during the Second World War were neither active collaborators nor active resistants . . . [but] ordinary, uncourageous people'.[4] Gallant's fiction and non-fiction document our human inability to accommodate and be changed by knowledge. Our continuous refusal of history begets our ongoing capacity for committing or condoning atrocity. Gallant does not preach at us or rebuke us for our forgetfulness by urging us to remember the Alamos of Auschwitz and Stalin. Rather, she shows how our own deformation of our collective past, and our children's inability to perceive the reality of the past we have forgotten, make the 'never again' slogan no more than a consoling fiction.

By privileging one particular manifestation of historical consciousness and conscience—Gallant's discovery, as a romantically left-wing radical, of the real legacy of the war against fascism: not freedom, but concentration camps—I do not mean to suggest that her interests as a writer are lodged in the configuration of Nazi Germany and the Jews of Europe, that she is some sort of displaced person within the country of Holocaust literature. Moving to Europe in the 1950s she discovered and wrote about an immediately post-war world. For a long time, traces of the Second World War abound in her stories, rather like the shell fragments Walter keeps finding in his garden in 'An Unmarried Man's Summer', or the burn scars that stud his body. The two volumes of her stories that deal most profoundly with the war and its aftermath are *The Pegnitz Junction* and *From the Fifteenth District*. Yet on becoming a European (in the sense that her primary locus of observation is Europe and not North America) Gallant went on to deal in her fiction with what became the historical and political present of her chosen world—the vulgarization attendant on the Americanization (economic as well as cultural) of Europe, the stupid hypocrisy of the 'One Europe' ideology ('Vacances Pax'), the effects of the Cold War on personal relationships ('His Mother', 'Potter'), the war in Algeria ('One Aspect of a Rainy Day' and 'Sunday Afternoon'), and, in one of her latest volumes, *Overhead in a Balloon*, the ambiance of the New Right in France. Yet in this same collection are found the Lena stories, which zigzag between the Occupation and the Fifth Republic, insisting on the intersection of memory and history, on the uselessness of easy explanations for mysteries that are in no way transcendent but remain stubbornly, unobligingly present.

*

Though, as we have seen, critics such as Robertson Davies and George Woodcock present Gallant as a white-gloved Queen of Fiction unacquainted with those sub-aesthetic thugs, politics and history, a simple look at her work will show that she is anything but the Palace-of-Art recluse some of her critics—and admirers—have made her out to be.[5] Perhaps it is because she has chosen to deal with the experience of history not from a Great-Men-and-Battles perspective, but, rather, in terms of everyday living as experienced by non-combatants—women and children such as Netta in 'The Moslem Wife', for example, or adolescent conscripts such as Thomas Bestermann in 'The Latehomecomer'—that the historical imperative of her fiction has been undervalued or ignored.[6] Or perhaps Gallant's scepticism about the possibility of human liberation through historical progress and political change proves too dispiriting—the closure and constriction of her vision of human possibility hardly bespeak those boundless vistas into which, for example, the allegorical May Day maidens on Russian revolutionary posters effortlessly spring. What seems to me remarkable, however, is the very fact of the continuing development of Gallant's engagement with history; her refusal, in her fiction, to transcend, ignore, or 'wake out of' it, as so many modern writers have attempted to do. It is not just that, in a volume such as *The Pegnitz Junction*, she sets herself the task of tracing the origins of 'the worm that had destroyed the structure' (iGH 40) of German civilization under the Nazis; throughout her work, Gallant's historical sense informs her very language and the concepts it articulates. Thus she has Linnet Muir describe her mother as one who 'smiled, talked, charmed anyone she didn't happen to be related to, swam in scandal like a partisan among the people' (HT 230) and she describes a famous liberal-humanist writer (Richard Notte in 'Irina') as one who 'could on occasion enjoy wine and praise and restaurants and good-looking women', though 'these festive outbreaks were on the rim of his real life, as remote from his children—as strange and as distorted to them— as some other country's colonial wars' (FFD 226).

It is no exaggeration to assert that Gallant's work is permeated by her engagement with history, her commitment to the imaginative exploration of the meaning of historical events, and her perception of history as lived experience, as the property of those outside the conference chamber or battleground, of those bombed or invaded in the streets and houses that have become the main venue for warfare. Gallant's portrayal of history sets her apart from other Canadian writers, most of whose fiction shows them to have been temporary residents or unabashed tourists in Europe. Canadian fiction makes characteristically oblique, ironically allusive use of European history: one thinks of the way in which Margaret Laurence's 'A Bird in the House' points to the Great War to suggest possibilities of love and freedom to Manawaka-bound Vanessa, or of how Alice Munro's 'The Peace of Utrecht' employs the facts of what happened ages ago on another continent to express the narrator's dispossession from her own past, her unrelatedness to the family she has left behind her. Gallant, however, uses recent European history as a kind of filter through whose abrasive metal strands daily life and personal experience are painfully sifted.

Gallant's pervasive historical sense, her awareness of how history and memory both attract and repel one another, has profoundly influenced the very structure of her narratives. Of the story 'Malcolm and Bea', in which the deadly marriages of NATO personnel intersect with their public situation—being forced out of France by De Gaulle—Ronald Hatch has observed, 'The narrative . . . never moves ahead, but always inward and back, the fragmentation capturing the sense of frustration in Malcolm and Bea's relationship'.[7] This lack of forward narrative line and a compensatory backward spiral or 'helical patterning' has been frequently noted in Gallant's fiction.[8] She herself has commented on how her stories 'buil[d] around [their] centre[s], rather like a snail' (iGH 45). A corollary of this, as Hatch has noted, would seem to be that just as Gallant's 'handling of narrative structures takes her well beyond any simplistic notion of realism,' so 'her later sense of character is one in which people seem to "float" in a pond of historical forces' rather than revealing themselves through their personal relationships.[9] And as Graziana Merler has it, Gallant's short fiction eschews the traditional demands of plot and the psychological development of character in order to focus on specific situations, with all their socio-historical resonances.[10]

While these critics correctly identify important characteristics of Gallant's narrative style, they pay inadequate attention to the persistence in her fiction of linearity and progression—plot, if you will—without which the helices and spirals of the stories would lose their tension and uncoil into shapelessness. Gallant's fictive structures are dual: the backward spirals that give her characters access to memory are intersected by the forward hurtle of time. As her fictions repeatedly show, memory can be illuminating and redemptive or falsifying and destructive. If she does indeed try to show how 'the past enforces itself particularly strongly on those who would seek to forget it', that without knowledge of the past one can neither 'enlighten the present nor direct the future',[11] then her fiction must somehow recognize that most problematic human need for plot, or linear progression. As Gallant has remarked on the difficulties of the reporter's lot, 'one of the hardest things in the world is to describe what happened next' (PN 206). A work like 'The Pegnitz Junction' explores precisely this difficulty with its portrayal of how the simple desire to move on, get home, or reach a prosaic destination can be agonizingly thwarted by detours and delays for which memory as well as circumstance is responsible.

Thus if Gallant does develop her various fictions out of their centres rather than from a definite beginning point, it is not to reject but rather to transform her readers' 'sense of an ending', which, as Frank Kermode has reminded us, is inseparable from any concept of linear narrative. The end of any of her stories, Gallant has remarked, has often no direct link to the scene from which it sprang (iGH 47). A work entitled 'The Picnic' (1952) will serve for a model here, dealing as it does entirely with the events leading up to a 'public-relations' picnic staged by American army personnel in France, but never with the picnic itself. Gallant has one of the characters graphically forsee how the picnic arrangements will end in 'failure . . . breakdown . . . fresh misunderstandings and further scandals' (EW 44). Yet all this foreshadowing does not kill our interest in the elaborate preparations for the event; rather, it heightens and accentuates our ironic perception of the characters and their contexts as they pick their ways towards imminent disaster.

*

'The Picnic' deals with the misunderstandings—social, cultural, political—that stem from the dislocation of one society (that of a small French village) by the invasion of another (the American army), which becomes internally displaced in its turn. It is a charmingly comic story with a decidedly *après guerre* flavour, a complete contrast to 'Autumn Day', that other account of life with an occupying army, in which the past war haunts, however elusively, the present peace. Gallant has described the frustration she felt as a young woman on being imprisoned in Montreal during the Second World War—a frustration that is at the fore of the play *What Is To Be Done?* History, in the dramatic, catastrophic shape of a world war, was going on in her own lifetime, and she felt herself shut away from it (iGG). Gallant, one can imagine, was the kind of reporter who would have welcomed the opportunity to be a war correspondant—at any rate, she was determined to get to the Europe from which her nationality and gender had barred her during the war, and to experience it not as a playground, but as the ruin and shambles it still was.[12]

Having written about the refugees she happened to meet in Montreal, Gallant actively sought them out in Europe, shunning the company of North American 'deadbeats' or jumped-up corporation men and their wives (iJKK). While she would write about people privileged enough to holiday in Europe in such stories as 'One Morning in June' (1952), 'By the Sea' (1954), and 'Jeux d'Eté' (1957), about the clash between over-expectant Americans and unaccommodating Europeans in 'The Picnic' (1952) or 'The Other Paris' (1953), or about English couples evading the wintry grimness of post-war Britain by shivering in Riviera villas they can't afford to heat ('In Italy'), she also conjures up the negatives of these people. In 'Better Times' (1960), for example, a story about the disintegrating marriage of a feckless war veteran, Guy, to Susan, his reluctant and much younger wife, we are told that the grounds of the dilapidated Riviera house the couple is 'sitting' are clandestinely used by the 'dispossessed' people of the place: 'wretched men from Italy looking for work in France. The Italians won't let them out and the French won't let them in and so they come as they can' (IT 81). Whereas Susan shows a degree of sympathy towards them, to Guy 'unknown people were ghosts. He could feel neither pity nor fear where they were concerned; they did not expect it. Ghosts have no true feelings; they are mystifying, unreasonable, with no regard for privacy. The whispers in the dark, the footprints on the wet drive, the odd, abandoned clues—one shoe, or a filthy coat—were trappings of chaos. Ghosts and confusion. He was for order, and gaiety, and for dealing with living things' (IT 84-5). In stories such as 'An Autobiography', 'The Four Seasons', and 'Ernst in Civilian Clothes' Gallant turns these ghosts into people we can know, people whose lives make claims upon our attention. Yet even in such early stories as 'Señor Pinedo' (1954), which portrays a tragically undisillusioned Falangist, or 'The Old Place' (1958), with its oblique focus on survivors of a concentration camp,

Gallant uses her art to make 'ghosts and confusion' visible.

The first-person narrator of 'Señor Pinedo' acts primarily as a medium through which certain facts can be registered about life in post-war Madrid: it is as though Gallant were saying, 'I can't tell you everything about these people, there are things that can only be guessed at, implied—never known, especially by the Pinedos themselves'. The precise details with which the narrator provides the reader, descriptions of furnishings, of background noises to the dialogues overheard between the Pinedos (his shouting of 'Silencio' and her reply, 'Viva la tableta Okal!' [a brand of aspirin]) seem not so much to fill as to mark out the gaps in our knowledge of what it is like to be not a tourist-observer, but a permanent resident of a country like Franco's Spain. 'Señor Pinedo' depends for its success not on any surface texture of exotically rendered Hispanic life, but rather on the nuts and bolts of historical reality—Pinedo's having volunteered to fight for the Falange, at age seventeen, and his continuing to believe in and work for Franco's vision of Spain, despite the execrable conditions of day-to-day life in Madrid, both for his own relatively privileged family and for all those much worse off than they.

What is remarkable about this story is the complex deployment of the narrator's sympathies, both to innocent victim (the boy Jaime, who is crippled in an elevator accident) and to victim of innocence—Señor Pinedo, the ever-fervent Falangist. Curiously enough, the narrator of 'Señor Pinedo' does not have the dispassionate, critically calculating voice we encounter in Gallant's other Spanish story, 'When We Were Nearly Young'. The narrator of 'Señor Pinedo' cannot help sharing the lives of her neighbours because of the paper-thin walls of the *pension* she shares with them. In her portrayal of Señor Pinedo Gallant is not out to do a hatchet job on a representative Franco fascist, but to make us see the human reality behind the political label. She has the narrator visit the Pinedos and confront the cruelly ironic collision of dream and reality when Pinedo gives her a book of speeches by the founder of the Falange:

Everything was there, and I read the brave phrases of revolution that had appealed to Señor Pinedo at seventeen. I read of a new Spain, mighty, Spartan, and feared abroad. I read of the need for austerity and sacrifice. I read the promise of land reform, the denunciation of capitalism, and, finally, the Call to Arms. It promised 'one great nation for all, and not for a group of privileged'. (OP 210)

It is the narrator who draws her neighbours' attention to the danger of the weight that counterbalances the elevator in the courtyard of Señorita Elvira's *pension*. When the inevitable occurs, and the weight crushes Jaime, initiating him into a life of 'limping and crutches and pain and expense' (OP 214), the narrator's compassion for the boy and her recognition of the extremity of his plight are deliberately understated. What takes centre stage is the curious deformation of Señor Pinedo's response to the accident: not horror but happiness at being able to score points for the government, extolling its desire to compensate victims of such events. It does not matter whether or not the authorities will give the boy a lifelong disability persion—indeed there is scepticism on the neighbours' part about the possibility of such generosity in poverty-scourged Spain. What does matter, to Señor Pinedo at least, is the fact that at last ideology and ideals theoretically meet. He is able, even if only temporarily, to believe in his political cause as he did earlier, 'convinced, as he must convince others, of the truth and good faith of the movement to which he had devoted his life and in which he must continue to believe' (OP 216).

What one would expect to be the central event of this story— the accident and its repercussions on the victim and his family— becomes decentred by Gallant's focus on the way such criminal events—an accident caused not by random fate but by the sheer negligence of the owners of the *pension*— can be misread, used by interested parties to justify adherence to a questionable code of belief. Señor Pinedo's speech on the accident to the other residents of the *pension*, declaring the goodness and benevolence of his government's promises, is not, however, left to stand as an ironic last word on what has occurred. The last word is an ambiguous silence, of which the narrator reports: ' . . . I could not have said whether the silence was owing to respect, delight, apathy, or a sudden fury of some other emotion so great that only silence could contain it' (OP 216).

That emotion, on the narrator's part at least, is a comprehensive sympathy that refuses to distinguish between the politically 'correct' and 'incorrect'. It is not a question, needless to say, of Gallant's making us feel sympathetic toward the supporters of Franco's cause, but rather of her allowing us to recognize how, under such a regime as Franco's, all are victimized, both supporters and detractors. This extension of sympathetic understanding to those whose political credentials would make them instantly reprehensible can be related to a remark Gallant made in an interview, vis à vis the story 'Ernst in Civilian Clothes'. Its protagonist is a young German who has fought in Hitler's army and then joined the Foreign Legion, only to see the Legion disbanded in the shabbiest of ways. 'I had to take someone basically unsympathetic to me,' remarked Gallant, 'and look for justice. And that is the real justice—it has to be abstract. If you believe in justice your sympathies have to be for even a person whom you'd abhor, if they have been badly, unfairly treated' (iEB). It was such an interest in abstract justice that led her to delineate a special kind of war victim in the story 'Poor Franzi' (1954). Franzi is a young Austrian man who finds himself engaged to be married to a well-meaning, emotionally generous American girl. He, however, is devoid of 'natural feeling' for her or for anyone else. Franzi's 'scandalous' emotional absence is, of course, what enabled him to survive the war at all. The trouble is that he has permanently lost all ability to care or assume responsibility for anyone. We do not, in the course of the story, come to like or admire Franzi in the way we do his grandmother or his fiancée, Elizabeth. But we do understand something of the absence of anything like a moral and emotional core to his character, an understanding that is as unsettling as it is instructive.

It is in a story published four years after 'Señor Pinedo' and 'Poor Franzi' that Gallant broaches—with characteristic obliquity—that most charged of all recent historical grounds: the concentration camps and those who survived them. 'The Old Place' (1958) takes its name from a house in the country, which its American owner, Mrs Arnheim, uses to construct a fiction of the past. Because she remembers the house as sunny and having pretty views, she declares it to have been a haven of happy family life, despite the fact that, as her son Dennis well remembers, she and her husband had quarrelled violently there. Mrs Arnheim has allowed the house to fall into ruins as a means of preserving the past: she 'feared that a stranger might, one day, buy the house and eliminate years of their existence by the simple act of tidying up' (TQ 69). Her perceptions echo those expressed by her second husband, Dr Meyer, a concentration-camp survivor. For Meyer the camps are 'the old place', and the fact that they are beginning to be torn down is for him annihilation of the past. Accordingly, he takes his new wife off to post-war Europe in order to visit the 'old place' and record it with his camera before its traces vanish. To his stepson, Dennis, his photographs are merely 'squares of silence' (TQ 80), pictures of 'fences enclosing silence and space' conveying 'the feeling of silence' (TQ 79). To his daughter, Charlotte, the reality the photographs represent has become a memory she must obliterate if she is to have any present tense at all.

Dennis and Charlotte are typical Gallant creations: the brutally honest young, who refuse the burden of their parents' worlds and claims, and who want only to be left alone. Despite the radical differences in their pasts—Charlotte having survived a concentration camp; Dennis, only a broken but affluent home—they are strangely similar in their rejection of the past and of the futures their parents envision for them. Charlotte is for Dennis a 'mirror image of himself in limbo' (TQ 76); until he meets her, his European tour is a complete blank: 'the whole experience was so out of the ordinary, so removed from anything he would have chosen for himself, that it made no impression at all' (TQ 73). Charlotte commends herself to Dennis by her refusal of his mother's sympathy and guilt. She reproves Mrs Arnheim for expressing regret that she and her son spent the war years in comfort while in Europe people were being deported, tortured, exterminated. 'He was only a little boy,' Charlotte sensibly remarks of Dennis. 'What could he have done? In any case, it had nothing to do with him' (TQ 75). But more impressive by far to Dennis is Charlotte's refusal, on Mrs Arnheim's death, to step in and care for her now twice-widowed father. 'She could not replace his wife. She couldn't fill the role he needed, because it was a lifetime job, and she had her own life to consider. She was sorry about that, too' (TQ 78). If Charlotte rejects the role of Cordelia and sides resolutely with the Gonerils and Regans against her Aged Parent, she cannot be accused of being an 'unnatural' child—for anyone separated from her parents at an early age and 'raised' in an extermination camp, that accusation loses any relevance or meaning whatsoever.

In portraying the claims of the old and memory-riven (Mrs Arnheim, Dr Meyer) against those of the young, blank, and uncaring (Dennis and Charlotte) Gallant shows that in the context of time's disinterested flow, youth take precedence over age. The claims of parents cannot be recognized by their children, the past erases itself as the present takes its place and becomes, in its turn, an unsalvageable and uninteresting past, to which subsequent generations cannot connect. Yet when the claims of the past are not personal but collective, bearing upon our very right to consider ourselves human beings at all, our tendency towards mass amnesia or the fiction of easy explanation (and thus dismissal) becomes critical. Published in the same year as 'The Old Place', Primo Levi's *Se questo è un uomo* (retitled in English *Survival in Auschwitz*)[13] is prefaced by an incantatory exhortation to those 'who live safe in . . . warm houses', to meditate upon, remember, and repeat to their children the what and how, to consider the very why, of Auschwitz. 'Or may your house fall apart,/ May illness impede you,/ May your children turn their faces from you.' It is a curse that describes the inevitable conditions of experience as Gallant conceives and presents it in one of her bleakest stories, 'Malcolm and Bea' (1968).

A detailing of the decomposition of a marriage between a minor English NATO official and his abusive Canadian wife, 'Malcolm and Bea' makes central use of the term 'Pichipoi'. One of Malcolm's colleagues, a badly but decorously married man whose mistress has tried to commit suicide, describes his life as a journey to 'Pichipoi', which, as we have seen, was the word invented by the Jewish children of occupied Paris for the unknown destination to which they were being deported. An innocent word, no different from any of the names invented and passed on in playgrounds and schoolyards, 'Pichipoi' is appropriated by the children's elders to signify an unknown that might not be any worse than where one already was—a consoling fiction. Malcolm rebukes his friend for applying the word to his 'raggle-taggle' history:

> He shouldn't say 'Pichipoi'. It was a word that children invented. That makes it entirely magic. It is a sacred word. . . . He is on sacred ground, with his shoes on. *They were on their way to dying.* If every person thought his life was a deportation, that he had no say in where he was going, or what would happen once he got there, the air would be filled with invisible trains and we would collide in our dreams. (EW 115)

Yet later, facing up to the reality of his own married life ('debris after a crash' [EW 118]); toying with and then abandoning the idea of leaving his wife and daughter, Malcolm makes his own appropriation of 'Pichipoi', one that conflates the historical meaning of the word with Malcolm's attempt to make it fit his own situation with Bea. 'Pichipoi', to Malcolm, comes to mean 'being alone. It means each one of us flung separately . . . into a room without windows. It can't be done. It can't be permitted, I mean. No jumping off the train. I nearly made it. . . . And then what?' (EW 118-19).

The problem with families, Gallant has said, is that 'people simply don't leave each other alone enough' (iGH 24). In this sense, then, 'Pichipoi' is invoked to signify a refuge to which one can jump from the crowding expectations and recriminations of family life. Yet it is also 'a room without windows'. 'Pichipoi' and life as a hellish journey on a deportation train—these become ambivalently clouded images. We participate in the confusion of characters who misuse their own historical inheritance in much the same way one would misuse a book by taking it off a shelf not to read, but to provide a hard surface on which to scribble one's own notes or letters. Gallant, as a writer, faces the dilemma of needing to incorporate catastrophic historical events and terms in her fiction without turning them into kitsch. She uses, and shows her characters using, events such as the deportation of European Jews to death camps, not to drop a penny in the slot of instant poignancy and horror, but to differentiate such history from, yet relate it to, the process of everyday living: to the lives of people safe in their houses.

As Primo Levi's writing shows, imaginative language cannot explain, but it can convincingly evoke the institutionalized inhumanity that governed the extermination and forced labour camps; it can also present the different responses to what Levi, in the subtitle to *Survival in Auschwitz*, called the Nazis' 'assault on humanity'. In so doing, language creates a collective memory for those who are lucky enough to have had no 'history' to remember—history here being synonymous with catastrophe. In reading Levi one finds that this historical past becomes present and inescapably 'ours' rather than 'theirs'. In reading Gallant's *The Pegnitz Junction*, and particularly the novella from which the collection draws its title, one is on very different ground. Her act of 'personal research' into how a people who had 'produced Bach and Goethe, who had been singing "A Mighty Fortress Is Our God" since the Renaissance . . . could . . . drop to zero so quickly and easily' (iGH 40) does not draw readers into or make them part of a horrendously 'other' world, but gives them the role of outsiders granted the mysterious ability to eavesdrop on silent monologues and to pick up disparate, bewildering information that constitutes a very different kind of collective memory.

In 'The Pegnitz Junction' memory swings crazily between past and present, or rather, makes the two collide: it is at the mercy of what Benjamin termed the 'storm of progress' that jerks and hurtles consciousness as though it were a standing passenger in the corridor of an erratic train. This novella is a playfully allusive text, a random survey of the mind of prosperous post-war Germany, a parody of, among other things, Kafka's *The Castle*, and an indecisive love story to boot. It manages to focus all these concerns by using one character, the twenty-one-year-old Christine, as a kind of radio receiver and transmitter for what she calls 'information' and 'interference'—messages sent out by her fellow passengers and by people she observes from the train windows or in railway stations. At the outset of the journey these messages are information—a storm of 'fine silver crystals forming a pattern, dancing, separating, dissolving . . . faster than smoke, more beautiful and less durable than snowflakes' (PJ 23). By the journey's end the crystals have become 'interference', 'dirty cinders' or 'mud' (PJ 85), clogging the girl's thought and preventing her from understanding enough of her world to allow her a definitive word upon anything.

At the novella's start Christine has been 'at one of those turnings in a young life where no one can lead, no one can help, but where someone for the sake of love might follow' (PJ 4). Having gone off to Paris on what she had assumed would be a tryst with her lover, she spends a less than halcyon week with him and his difficult child, and is virtually abandoned on the return journey to Germany, telling a kind of fairy story to her lover's son, little Bert. To complicate matters, her fiancé, an over-analytic theology student, will be waiting for her at the station, if the train ever reaches its destination. The 'emancipation' (PJ 5) for which she had been hoping turns into a species of forced march through the bogs of collective memory and rubbishy consciousness.

Throughout the novella memories of 'the Adolf-time' (PJ 70) are resisted, resented, misinterpreted, and trivialized: among the few characters who do acknowledge the implacable pressure of the past upon the present, shame is substituted for remorse (PJ 80), so that Christine's 'information' uncovers the hypocrisy, shallowness of understanding, and untroubled prejudices that prevail not only among post-war Germans, but also among all those who, having fixed for their consciences a convenient destination, come to believe they are home free when they are only in transit (PJ 54). This revelation, like so many of the events and reflections in the novella, is double-edged, having an immediate application to the mechanics of plot—getting the travellers to the junction from which they can board trains to their respective homes—and to the enormous historical questions about the Germans and Nazism with which Gallant is preoccupied.

Thus it is not only the disjointed 'television screen' narrative that disconcerts the reader but also this sense of doubleness that finds central expression in the extended, inverted parody Gallant creates. For the journey from Paris to an uncertain destination in Germany is an ironic mimesis of the trip to 'Pichipoi'. This train is crowded, unbearably hot and stuffy, without any toilets or wash-basins, food or adequate drink. The windows have been ordered sealed by the authorities—whose dicta no one effectively challenges—because of alleged track-side brush fires, which Christine fantasizes as creating a 'holocaust' (PJ 36) of the train and its passengers. The trains that await them at the various stations along the way 'sounded sad, as though they were used to ferry poor and weary passengers—refugees perhaps' (PJ 15). In a sequence that seems like a flashback *hors du texte*, Christine is ordered into a waiting room by a freightyard, where she joins a horde of women 'grouped by nationality—Polish, French, Greek, Russian, Dutch' and all carrying 'luggage tied with string' (PJ 79). The French-women seem to be sporting wartime fashions, 'hair swept up and forward and frizzed with tongs' and shoes with thick wooden soles, even though Christine is in regulation sixties mini-dress and wears her hair long and straight. These women are described as being 'ill with terror' (PJ 81) at the menacing antics of a railway of-ficial whom Christine, without the least hesitation or introspec-tion—nothing of Kafka's K about her—puts in his place.

Another incident of historical *déja vu*—though decidedly less haunting—concerns an attack launched by a Philistine public against a certain Dr Ischias, a museum curator with a 'funny name' accused of 'sapping morals and contributing to the artistic decline of a race' as well as insulting the purity of German woman-hood (PJ 64). Further references to Nazi aesthetics are conjured up by the leader of an elderly cultural group out for a night at the opera. His listeners are made as 'sad and uncomfortable' by mentions of the Third Reich as is Christine's lover, Herbert, a prosperous engineer. His mother, we learn, had survived a concentration camp only to return with 'bitter stories' about her fellow inmates: 'She had gone into captivity believing in virtue and learned she could steal. Went in loving the poor, came out afraid of them; went in for the hounded, came out a racist; went in generous, came out grudging; went in with God, came out alone' (PJ 13).

Her child absorbs his mother's prejudices and practises a roundabout hypocrisy: he refuses to take little Bert into a station café patronized by foreign 'guest workers' from Turkey and North Africa:

> Though needed for the economy, the guest workers had brought with them new strains of tuberculosis, syphilis, and amebic complaints that resisted antibiotics. Everyone knew this, but the government was hushing it up. . . . Herbert did not want little Bert, young and vulnerable, to drink out of the same glasses as foreign disease-bearers. On the other hand, he must not breathe the slightest whiff of racial animosity. Therefore would Christine please engage the child's attention until they had passed the coffeehouse? (PJ 61)

Herbert's counterpart is a diabetic German widow whose name one can piece together as Frau Joseph Schneider. She eats obsessively, so that the train compartment begins to stink of rotting food, and reminisces to herself (and, unbeknownst to her, the 'telepathic' Christine) about the forty-seven years she spent in America, devotedly preparing gargantuan meals for her husband and relations. The banality of her memories is matched by the triteness of her anti-Semitic clichés: President Roosevelt was really a Dutch Jew from a family of thieves named Roszenfeldt, who had been able to take over the entire USA ten years after emigrating there. Gallant gives an acerbic précis of the historical fantasies this kind of mentality produces:

> There was a plan to save some German cities, those with interesting old monuments. The plan was to put Jews in the attics of all the houses. The Allies would never have dropped a bomb. What a difference it would have made. Later we learned this plan had been sabotaged by the President of the USA. Too bad. It could have saved many famous old statues and quite a few lives. (PJ 53-4)

It need hardly be mentioned that Frau Schneider is not here concerned with Jewish lives.

Herbert was too young to have been a functioning member of the Nazi state; Christine, even younger, comes from 'a small, bombed baroque German city, where all that was worthwhile keeping had been rebuilt and which now looked as pink and golden as a pretty child and as new as morning' (PJ 3). Little Bert, Herbert's 'bratty' son, has been born into a society that refuses to talk or ask questions about its immediate past. The only German in the novella who tries to piece together the fragments of memory is a man who returns every vacation not to the tourist-havens of Majorca or Bulgaria, but to a 'dead landscape' (PJ 60)—the barbed-wire frontier that cuts him off from the village in which he spent his early childhood, and the peasant girl he worshipped there. With an 'expression of infinite sorrow' he remembers not the why but the terrifying how of his family's escape from what had newly become East Germany, on a night he thought to have been the end of the world (PJ 57). But as a counterbalance to this haunting vignette we have a pastiche of Kafka, as Christine looks absently out the train window to observe a family party climbing a hill to what they have been assured is a museum-castle. The whole episode, with its bumbling Uncle Bebo, its gangsterish Uncle Ludwig, and the 'horrible Jürgen', who ends up being knifed by a small boy in a parking lot, has a peculiar air of surrealist kitsch. Taken together with other incidents—a group of revolting school-girls boarding the train at one of its many indeterminate halts, the antics of a fat, spoiled brat, a glimpse of coarse, bedraggled soldiers lounging by a station—the pastiche cements the caricature of the master race sketched by Gallant. The repulsiveness of these Germans seems to be clinched by the attitude of a pregnant, unmarried German girl who passes herself off as an American army wife because she is 'ashamed of being thought German'—not by the foreigners on the train, but by her own countrymen and women. She too is attempting to preserve that myth of German womanhood to which both fat Frau Schneider and the plump-kneed matrons out for an evening's dose of culture with their 'leader' give the lie.

Yet if women—with the exception of Christine—emerge as repellent characters in this novella, they are also portrayed as victims. Christine is exploited and patronized by Herbert, who, when he discovers her reading the essays of Dietrich Bonhoeffer, assumes that her divinity-student fiancé has forced them on her: 'Isn't it a bit of a pose, your reading? . . . What good does it do him if *you* read?' Herbert asks. 'It may do me good, and what is good for me is good for both of you. Isn't that so?' demands Christine, in the classic feminine double-bind, her 'vision . . . shaken by tears' (PJ 45). Even the 'commando' of little girls who board the train are specifically marked out for the general, unenviable fate of 'womanhood': 'The child sitting in Herbert's place had large red hands and the haunted face of a widow. Another was plump and large . . . as if she were already thirty-five and had been eating puddings and drinking beer since her wedding day' (PJ 20). Finally, the cultural scandal having to do with the foreign Dr Ischias has grown out of a photographic display of a model's naked body, and has been trumpeted in the press under the headline: 'ARE GER-MAN WOMEN BABOONS/ AND MUST THEY ALWAYS EXHIBIT THEIR BACKSIDES?' (PJ 65). As if in answer we have the grotesque Frau Schneider who, for an eight-hundred-dollar inheritance, follows up her forty-seven years of marriage by tending the cat-sized grave in which her detested husband's ashes have been deposited. She has purchased another grave for herself, 'nowhere near him' (PJ 86).

Where the men in this novella make announcements respectful of authority or plan to write scathing but discreet letters of complaint to the same authorities, the women sit, muse, and suffer debased or confused recollections. In making the receiver and transmitter of information a young and intelligent woman, and in portraying the German women whose messages Christine transmits as victims as well as perpetrators of 'the myth of German womanhood' (PJ 65), Gallant would seem to be complicating the stereotype of *sales Boches* with which she begins 'The Pegnitz Junction'. She gives us the regulation clichés—the German obsession with eating well and often, with cleanliness, with obedience to orders no matter how ridiculous or insane, and the exaggerated respect for authority—but mediates them according to a perspective from and on female experience, that of the wives, mothers, daughters, and granddaughters of the men who fought for Hitler's Reich.

How does one respond to 'The Pegnitz Junction'? It is an important question, given that this is Gallant's most ambitious fiction and, at least in 1978, was her favourite among her works (iGH 37). Critics are divided—Woodcock, though he ends by applauding the novella, at first found its fragmentation and plotlessness puzzling, and remarked that it was 'bound to give many readers difficulty'.[14] Yet it is not the novella's technical sophistication and surprises that may cause readers the greatest difficulty, but rather the extraordinary sense of decentred detachment that derives from Gallant's choice of narrative strategy—Christine as psychic screen—and the bizarre playfulness that pervades the text. As William Pritchard remarked, Gallant 'seems to evade responsibility for saying or caring very much about her characters and their situation [so that] "The Pegnitz Junction" is too clever, too oblique, too arty, for its own moral and human good'.[15] Perhaps our responses can best be guided by asking a question that shifts ground. What does one make of Gallant's reason for writing about Germany and the Germans as she does in this novella—her assertion that 'the victims [of Nazism], the survivors [of the camps] would probably not be able to tell us anything, except for the description of life at point zero. If we wanted to find out how and why this happened it was the Germans we had to question. . . . The victims, the survivors, that is, could tell us what had happened to them but not why' (iGH 39-40)? One of the refrains of Primo Levi's *Survival in Auschwitz* is 'Ne pas chercher à comprendre'. Yet if to attempt to puzzle out the absurd means and obscene end of camp life would jeopardize one's chances for survival, among those who did survive are some who went on to use their freedom not only to describe life 'at point zero', but also to confront the why with which the young Mavis Gallant was obsessed. Here is Primo Levi:

> As an account of atrocities . . . this book of mine adds nothing to what is already known to readers throughout the world on the disturbing question of the death camps. It has not been written in order to formulate new accusations; it should be able, rather, to furnish documentation for a quiet study of certain aspects of the human mind. Many people—many nations—can find themselves holding, more or less wittingly, that 'every stranger is an enemy'. . . . [W]hen the unspoken dogma becomes the major premise in a syllogism, then, at the end of the chain, there is the Lager. Here is the product of a conception of the world carried rigorously to its logical conclusion; so long as the conception subsists, the conclusion remains to threaten us. The story of the death camps should be understood by everyone as a sinister alarm signal. (SA 5)

It seems unfair to put *The Pegnitz Junction* and *Survival in Auschwitz* side by side: any memoir authored by a survivor is bound to have an authenticity and power that the fiction of an *a posteriori* observer cannot match. And when the survivor is as superb a writer as Primo Levi, the case for the primacy of his narrative seems closed. Yet inevitably one needs to read Gallant's and Levi's texts together, if only for the fact that both aim to give us knowledge not of 'the historical causes of Fascism' but rather, its 'possibilities in people' (iGH 41). Gallant writes with her habitual ironic detachment and a legitimate disinterestedness—she, a non-German, a Canadian insulated and isolated from History with a capital H, is putting the Germans under the lens of her narrative and exposing them, warts and all. Levi, on the other hand, writes not with detachment—how could that be possible for a survivor of Auschwitz?—but with a dispassionate lucidity that makes his observations all the more devastating. There is a gallows, or perhaps one should say a gas-chamber, humour to be found in Levi's book, a humour which can be related to that found in 'The Pegnitz Junction'. Gallant has remarked that 'every situation has an element of farce'—even Auschwitz (iBG 24). Some of the humour of 'The Pegnitz Junction'—for example, Frau Schneider's account of the plan to save historic German buildings by placing Jews in the attics—is not so much black as grey: it leaves not a bitter taste but an undigestible substance in one's mouth. But what of the 'fun' and sheer 'enjoyment' that Gallant describes herself as having had in creating pastiches of classic German texts—how does the clear ludic quality of 'The Pegnitz Junction' affect the reader? Are we disconcerted by the fact that something so ambitious should be so playful as well; that instead of haunting, this narrative bewilders, amuses, disconcerts us? Or do we argue that 'The Pegnitz Junction', an outsider's observation of a representative group of postwar Germans, is more honest, less pretentious than a *Sophie's Choice*, which attempts to integrate the perspectives of an outsider and a survivor?

An answer to these perplexing questions may lie in the possibility that readers of *Survival in Auschwitz* and *The Pegnitz Junction* need not feel compelled to choose between a Primo Levi and a Mavis Gallant—the former demanding that we witness and remember the 'unimaginable' in ways that will allow us to respond to its persistent, 'sinister alarm-signals', the latter insisting that we can never learn from what we refuse, or are unable, to imagine; and that, except for our dreams, we choose to forget what has most hurt us, or misremember that which damns us. We can read these texts 'off' one another as though we were watching 'two screens simultaneously' (PN 15), so that, at the very least, we will be forbidden the luxuries of ignorance or of complacently easy understanding. At the best, we may come to understand the necessity of remembering Levi's Auschwitz and the process by which Gallant's Germans, and many of us as well, have been able to forget the 'Adolf-time'.[16]

As for the jarring playfulness and narrative disruptions of Gallant's novella, one can accommodate these by reading 'The Pegnitz Junction' as a structurally and conceptually necessary prologue to the stories that follow it. The first of these, 'The Old Friends', brings together a survivor, Helena, and a de-Nazified police commissioner who is helplessly enchanted by her. The beautiful Helena toys with the commissioner, letting him pay her infinite loving attentions and then wounding him with references to the camps, to her murdered family. A wonderfully succinct yet poignant passage at the end of 'The Old Friends' is worth quoting in this context. Helena is pondering the response of journalists who interview her on the subject of the camps:

> They want to know that it could not have been worse, but somehow it never seems bad enough. Only her friend, the commissioner, accepts at once that it was beyond his imagination, and that the knowledge can produce nothing more than a pain like the suffering of laughter—like pleurisy, like indigestion. He would like it to have been, somehow, not German. When she says that she was moved through transit camps on the edge of the old Germany, then he can say, 'So, most of it was on foreign soil!'. . . Each time she says a foreign place-name he is forgiven, absolved. What does it matter to her? Reality was confounded long ago. She even invents her dreams. When she says she dreams of a camp exactly reproduced, no one ever says, 'Are you sure?' Her true dream is of purification, of the river never profaned, from which she wakes astonished—for the real error was not that she was sent away but that she is here, in a garden, alive. (PJ 95-6)

Like the journalist, the reader of what has become a flourishing genre, 'Holocaust Literature', is in danger of becoming a voyeur, wanting more and more horrific revelations which are never adequately illustrative of the human absolute of evil that was the logical conclusion of Nazism. The novella with which *The Pegnitz Junction* begins literally throws us off course by giving us the other side of the coin—the Germans, not the victims of their former government—in a narrative of disjunctions and dissociations that yet furnishes infinite variations on the theme of laughter and forgetting, and, intermittently, the terror and grief of remembering. Once our sensibilities and expectations have been utterly disrupted by 'The Pegnitz Junction' we can encounter Gallant's other German stories (including 'The Latehomecomer', which she had wanted to include in *The Pegnitz Junction* but which was published in her subsequent collection, *From the Fifteenth District*) with a degree of freedom from the clichés and kitsch that deform our thinking about Nazism and its attempted annihilation of 'strangers' and 'inferior races'.

As we have seen, the Germans who appear in 'The Pegnitz Junction' are, with few exceptions, a repulsive lot. Yet Gallant's stories dealing with young Germans who were drafted into Hitler's armies in the last days of the Reich extend a rare compassion, the compassion of 'abstract justice', to another sort of survivor. Thomas Bestermann of 'The Latehomecomer', a prisoner-of-war held by the French for an absurdly long time after the war's end, is one of those young Germans whom Gallant has described as suffering from 'inner displacement'. What she has done in this and similar stories is put herself, and her readers, 'in the place of an adolescent who had sworn personal allegiance to Hitler' and who can no more 'tear up [his] personality and begin again than [he] can tear up the history of [his] country' (iGH 51). Ernst, the ex-legionnaire of 'Ernst in Civilian Clothes', epitomizes those deracinated, surviving soldiers who feel not guilt for what they did in the war, but bewilderment at what the war has done to their lives. As Gallant has remarked, 'who can assume guilt for a government? People are more apt to remember what was done to them rather than what was done in their name to others. To wrench your life and beliefs in a new direction you have to be a saint or schizophrenic' (iGH 51).

In a world in which children are orphaned or abandoned before they are old enough to have a sense of self, in that the monuments and records which could identify them have been bombed and burned into thin air, memory is the self's only text. Memory, of course, is notoriously unreliable; we use it to turn our pasts into fictions that console or avenge or absolve us. According to the narrator of 'An Autobiography', the war-refugee Peter 'knew it was no good talking about the past, because we were certain to remember it differently. He daren't be nostalgic about anything, because of his inventions. He would never be certain if the memory he was feeling tender about was true' (PJ 126). While Willi in the story 'Ernst in Civilian Clothes' waits 'for the lucid, the wide-awake, and above all the rational person who will come out of the past and say with authority, "This was true", and "This was not"', his friend Ernst 'makes a new decision. Everyone is lying; he will invent his own truth. . . . He will believe only what *he* knows' (PJ 147). Yet even he is not sure why he has chosen to invent the details he has. He is obsessed with the idea of trying to rescue a child crying for his mother from a collapsed cellar—this is the central clue to who and what he is. Yet only in his dreams, 'where it is no help to him', does Ernst recognize that the victim he attempts to rescue from the cellar is himself.

The narrator of 'An Autobiography' and Helga and Bibi of 'An Alien Flower' are neither saints nor schizophrenics, but representatives of a generation that has been stripped of everything—family, belongings, moral, spiritual, and social roots—and has grown up in a post-war society where life is as corrupt as a mis-translated text. For these women there is no centre, only ambiguous traces of what has been and what cannot mean anything anymore. Hence the disconcerting flatness of tone Gallant gives to these survivors—they have possessed so little, and for so short a time, that the loss of their families and very identities creates no overwhelming anguish or even nostalgia in them. The one exception is Bibi, who commits suicide in response to the ultimate 'personal displacement' in her life—her banishment from Europe to North America, from which she writes 'wounded, homesick letters, one a day' (PJ 185) to the family of her former lover Julius, who was attracted to Bibi in the first place because she was an 'inferior' he could bully and master. Yet Bibi's suicide only points out the emotional paralysis of Julius's wife Helga, who remains loyal not to her husband, but to the house he buys for her and puts in her name: a charm against the ruins and fragments of her bombed-out childhood.

The concept of history we find in *The Pegnitz Junction* is not, of course, 'the history of conquerors', 'that goddess of Hegel and Marx, that incarnation of reason that judges us and arbitrates our fate'.[17] Rather it is, as Milan Kundera might say, the wrong side of this history, a matter of uncertain forward motion lived through inch by inch, day by day, and made visible only through the gaps between forgetting and remembering. In 'The Pegnitz Junction' we receive a sense of the richness and variety of phenomena, but also of closure and delimitation, as we observe how 'information' turns into 'interference', and how the exposed and open consciousness of the young girl Christine is squeezed shut between the competing claims of two men who hardly represent possibilities of emancipation for her. And from all the stories of *The Pegnitz Junction* we derive a sense of how impossibly fragmented life is in the shambles of history, of the impossibility of the fragments ever coming together for the characters, and anything so wilfully and horrifyingly smashed ever being made whole. The Angel of History is both helpless and ruthless, and our relation to him a perplexed one indeed, for he appears as both demon and Doppelgänger. Benjamin's angel comes specifically to mind in a passage from 'The Latehomecomer', in which the tardily repatriated Thomas Bestermann is advised by his future father-in-law to 'look forward, never back, and forget, forget, forget' (FFD 134), the same advice the man has given to a neighbour emigrating to Palestine. (The neighbour is one of the '0.4' proportion of Jews belonging to the post-war population of West Germany [PJ 94]). And yet the very text of 'The Latehomecomer' opposes this advice: the narrative enacts Thomas's remembering of his attempt to come to terms with a past of which he has been dispossessed. This opposition to forgetting, this insistence on remembering the past, even if what one recalls is hopeless confusion, 'useless chaos', and confirmed rather than corrected inhumanity, forms one of the principal texts of Gallant's finest writing.

*

In a recent interview Mavis Gallant declared that after having written *The Pegnitz Junction* she lost her fascination with Germany. 'I lost interest—not in history or anything, but that overwhelming curiosity I had—just deflated' (iJKK). As *From the Fifteenth District* reveals, Gallant's historical sense fastened on other forms and loci of wartime experience and post-war trauma. This stories in this collection are set in convincingly rendered 'foreign parts': Budapest, Paris, Switzerland, the French and Italian Rivieras, as well as post-war Berlin. The locales of Labour-Party England, and Communist Poland, on the other hand, are evoked though her characters' exile and absence from them. If there is a certain opening of physical borders in this 'international' collection, there is a corresponding liberation of possibilities for the characters involved; we witness rare moments of delight and wonder in things that appear beautiful, guiltless, complete—just as the angel wishes to remake them. Recalling Gallant's previous fiction, her depiction, for example, of a blowsy, dirty, vulgar Riviera in *Green Water, Green Sky* or 'Acceptance of Their Ways', we wonder at the fresh, delicate evocation of the natural world in the two southern stories of *Fifteenth District*—the village 'that had grass everywhere' and the sky 'swept clean of storm' that so ravish Carmela in 'The Four Seasons', or the 'light-drenched' and perfumed hotel gardens in 'The Moslem Wife' (FFD 13, 15, 44). In the ashy Berlin of 'The Latehomecomer' Thomas finds the child Gisela 'all light and sheen . . . as whole and innocent as a drop of water' (FFD 127), while a servant girl's first taste of ice cream in 'The Four Seasons' is made into a true taste of heaven. These moments lodge in the minds of Gallant's characters—and of her readers—like slivers of paradise, piercing the grim borders of everyday experience. And though Gallant deals with betrayal, loss, and bewilderment in this collection, she permits us a glimpse of another sort of angel, one from whom a blessing, however tenuous, might be wrestled.

In the opening story of *Fifteenth District*, 'The Four Seasons', we meet Carmela, a young Italian girl working for an outrageously exploitative English family who have settled in Mussolini's Italy. The story begins in the spring before the outbreak of war, and ends a year later, when the indolence of life-by-seasons on the Riviera has given way to war measures—the closing of the frontier between France and Italy and the rounding up, for deportation, of foreign Jews. Among them is the family's physician, Dr Chaffee, who has diagnosed Carmela as anaemic and has also tried to put things to rights in the entropic English household. Near the story's end Carmela, who has kept her prescribed bottle of iron tablets as a treasured personal possession, sees the doctor rounded up with other deportees behind a barbed-wire fence:

> She remembered how she had not taken the pills he had given her—had not so much as unscrewed the metal cap of the bottle. Wondering if he knew, she looked at him with shame and apology before turning her head away. As though he had seen on her face an expression he wanted, he halted, smiled, shook his head. He was saying 'No' to something. Terrified, she peeped again, and this

time he lifted his hand, palm outward, in a curious greeting that
was not a salute. He was pushed on. She never saw him again. (FFD
26)

Ironically, the doctor has mistaken the context of Carmela's expression of shame and apology, and yet this becomes unimpor-
tant. The girl's unfeigned distress at having disregarded the
doctor's instructions becomes an expression of remorse for the
treatment by the Italians of the Jews within their borders. Irony
here becomes the only possible medium of such an expression, one
that keeps the most delicate of balances between poignancy and
sentimentality, possibility and historical reality. It permits the
'bearable lightness of being' with which the story concludes, as
Carmela, having been dismissed by her English employers who
are themselves fleeing back to England, walks back to a home
where she is not wanted. One image dominates her recollection of
the year's varied events: 'Dr Chaffee in his dark suit, stumbling
up the hill. He lifted his hand. What she retained, for the present,
was one smile, one gesture, one man's calm blessing' (FFD 34-5).
In that one, present moment fiction and history come together,
taking the measure of 'a life, a season, a look exchanged' (PN 177);
stopping to awaken the dead and to make whole, however briefly, what has been smashed.

If *From the Fifteenth District* marks a watershed in Gallant's
work, conveying, as Anne Tyler remarked, 'a sense of limitlessness', with each story opening out, like a 'peephole' into 'a
very wide landscape',[18] it is also something of an anomaly. For the
spaciousness, the sense of nascent possibility, the open rather than
constrictive use of irony that characterize both the best stories in
this collection and the Linnet Muir sequence in *Home Truths* are
noticeably absent in Gallant's later volume of stories, *Overhead in
a Balloon*. Her fiction has become preoccupied with the historical
realities of a Europe increasingly forgetful of the traumas of the
'Adolf-time'. In 'Vacances Pax' (1966) she had already exposed not
only the cultural vulgarity of the 'One Europe' concept, but also,
more importantly, the facile political optimism on which it was
based. The concept of an international vacation colony 'dated
from the early nineteen-fifties, when the "One Europe" idea had
enormous emotional appeal, and it was thought that all national
differences would be dispersed, and all prejudices effaced if a few
people believing this could be so were to spend their holidays

together, talking and exchanging ideas and being decent and kind' (IT 192). Gallant's story shows us the idea in practice, with the camp supervisor's 'notions of One Europe all [being] connected with food—everyone eating the same thing, everyone chewing' (IT 196). As for the guests' conversation at table, they

> sounded like the ingenious all-Europe programs in which the best drummer from Denmark performs from a studio in Copenhagen, along with a trumpet from Stuttgart, an electric guitar from Milan, and France's finest clarinet. No musician can hear or see the others, for each is in his home city, but owing to the competence of sound technicians, they can be heard all playing 'Dinah' at the same time. (IT 200-1)

As one character observes, 'Of all the false prophets, those who mixed brotherhood and politics were the worst' (IT 196).

This sardonic assessment of the impact of history's lessons on the European mind informs many of the squibs Gallant has published in *The New Yorker* from 1980 onward, 'From Sunrise to Daybreak (A Year in the Life of an Emigré Review)', 'From Gamut to Yalta', 'Mousse', and 'Leaving the Party', among others. The trivializing and exploitation of the past, the epidemic deafness to history's 'alarm-signals' underscore the opening story of *Overhead in a Balloon*, 'Speck's Idea' (1979), a marvellously funny satire on culture and politics in contemporary France. No decisive pronouncements or overt judgements of the kind voiced in 'Vacances Pax' are made in 'Speck's Idea': the reader must be, *a priori*, sufficiently knowing to be on the correct side of this fiction's telescopic lens. Gallant's account of how an art dealer on the make is first outwitted by the Saskatchewan widow of an obscure French painter, and then triumphs over his rival's attempt to one-up him on the Parisian gallery scene, resembles a minuet through a mine field. If the art world of Paris is portrayed as 'a domain reserved for the winning, collecting, and sharing out of profit', the world of Gallant's story becomes 'a territory where believer and skeptic, dupe and embezzler, the loving and faithless could walk hand in hand' (OB 46).

'Speck's Idea' is a comic fiction, but as we have seen, for Gallant farce is hardly an expression of untrammelled optimism and joie de vivre. What tempers the gaiety of this fiction, breaking out like black spots on an antique mirror, is the political situation it sketches. That the New Age in Paris is firmly allied to the New

Right is suggested by the existence of nostalgia for the fascist days of *Action Française*, the presence of the 'Amandine' bookstore with its window display on *'La France Juive'* and, as another story has it, the 'fashion for having well-behaved Nazi officers shore up Western culture' during the Occupation of Paris (OB 145). Speck, though primarily a businessman who makes no political or moral judgements, is panicked by the possibility of terrorist attacks on his galleries from all sides, not only the right but also the 'determined intellectuals' in their 'costly fake working-class clothes' (OB 12). In the pamphlet that Speck is given near the end of the story there is an idiotic conflation of left and right: 'For the sake of Europe, Fight the Germano-Americano-Israelo-Hegemony . . . Death to the Anti-European Hegemony!' The pamphlet, in fact, gives Speck his clue to constructing a biography of the painter he so cynically 'discovers', a biography that will be politically acceptable to everyone and thus guarantee complete success to his 'Idea' of launching a retrospective exhibition of the paintings of Hubert Cruche. In Speck's catalogue for the exhibition 'Left, Right and Center would unite on a single theme: how the taste of two full generations had been corrupted by foreign speculation, cosmopolitan decadence, and the cultural imperialism of the Anglo-Saxon hegemony' (OB 9).

If, as this story makes clear, French politics is a 'crazy salad', then history is in no less confused a state. As Speck observes, '"Resistance" today meant either a heroic movement sadly undervalued by the young or a minor movement greatly inflated in order to absolve French guilt' (OB 9). The term 'fascist' is used as a term of abuse for husbands by the women who walk out on them, and Speck himself uses it against Lydia Cruche when he realizes that she has, with unsuspected craft and cunning, used him in order to exploit the maximum profit from an Italian dealer who, like Speck, is also onto the Cruche bandwagon. The appropriation of 'fascist' in 'Speck's Idea' is a far cry from the use of 'Pichipoi' in 'Malcolm and Bea'; the sheer comic energy of *Overhead in a Balloon* is almost dizzying, and one comes upon the Lena stories as a necessary respite from this collection's relentless satire and prodigal lampoons.

In 'A Recollection', 'Rue de Lille', 'The Colonel's Child', and 'Lena' we are given a sense of the past without nostalgia, but rather with a selective clarity that serves to delineate, not dispel, the narrator's own obfuscations. An emotional anaesthetizing of the reader takes place, in that we cannot admire, sympathize with, or even mildly like the narrator, Edouard, or his hapless wife, Juliette. As for the dazzling, baffling, impossible Magdalena—she defeats us as she does Edouard. Gallant develops the peculiar relations between the members of this *ménage a trois* not against but through a historical backdrop that emerges as a corrective to the 'politically naïve' idea of wartime France that Gallant had cherished in Montreal:

> The Occupation [of France] was no joke, but it was nothing compared to what the Dutch or the Greeks went through, not to speak of the Poles. The schools and universities were never closed in France. Restaurants, theatres and the opera continued to function, and so did the nightclubs. The upper classes sailed through without much more than inconvenience. The poor, the honest, the conscientious bore the brunt. (iGH 36)

'A Recollection' (August 1983) is an attempt at an honest remembering, not so much of the war as of the personal equations the war drew up between the narrator, Edouard, who, if he seems both glacial and dessicated, at least appears to be honest—'I was lucid and generous and also something of a louse' (OB 158)—and the two women in his life, the earnest Juliette and the arch-frivolous Magdalena. The marvellously 'cosmopolitan' Magdalena, a Jewish convert to Catholicism, a Hungarian transported to *entre deux guerres* Paris, a 'kept woman' who tends her ignorance about politics and history as devotedly as she does her hair and fingernails, is a tour de force. In Magdalena Gallant portrays neither villain nor heroine, nor even an authentic sufferer and survivor—a Fania Fenelon—but rather a *femme moyenne sensuelle*, a woman whose very existence depends on restaurants' and night clubs' staying open through whatever upheavals, and whose cultivated feather-headedness is her best defence against history. Magdalena manages to escape deportation from France to a death camp not so much because of the risks Edouard takes to protect her—marrying her so that she will have French citizenship, escorting her to the south, where she can 'sit the war out in an airy villa—the kind aliens can afford' (OB 158)—but by some miraculous concatenation of flukes. Edouard, in fact, plays a secondary role in this story—the principal character is Magdalena with her red fingernails, her yapping pug dogs with their complicated skin diseases, the silk-stuffed suitcase in which she so casually brings along, like a souvenir theatre program, a coarse yellow star she found discarded on a Parisian pavement. For Magdalena, the mistress of many wealthy and influential men, has become 'a devout, lighthearted, probably wayward Catholic convert, of the sort Dominicans like to have tea with, but she was also Jewish and foreign—to be precise, born in Budapest, in 1904' (OB 151).

How does one read the character of the outrageously blithe and self-centred Magdalena who suffers no deprivations or anxieties when France is defeated and occupied? *Chez elle* 'there was Chanel's Gardenia. There was coffee and sugar, there were polished silver trays and thin coffee cups. There was Raymonde, in black with white organdie, and Magdalena, with her sunny hair, her deep-red nails, to pour' (OB 154). 'On the day when the Jews of Paris stood in long queues outside police stations, without pushing and shoving, and spelled their names and addresses clearly, so that the men coming to arrest them later on would not make a mistake, Magdalena went back to bed and read magazines' (OB 154). Gallant allows Edouard to offer us this information not as a judgement of Magdalena's indifference or stupidity, but as a kind of testimonial to the charmed life she leads, her 'spirit[ed]' (OB 159) rejection of the dictates of history, and her repudiation of human solidarity as well. Readers of Primo Levi will not be able to read about Gallant's Magdalena without picturing those mothers who spent the last night of their lives washing their children's clothes and packing toys to take along to Auschwitz (SA 11). Equal and opposite realities: two screens, watched simultaneously.

'Rue de Lille' (September 1983), brings us abruptly back from occupied France to contemporary Paris. Edouard and his 'second wife', Juliette, respected translator of post-war American literature, daughter of a hero of the Resistance after whom suburban streets have been named, have been living for thirty-odd years in a dark apartment about which Juliette expresses one desire—that she not have to die there. Shortly before her sixtieth birthday Edouard finds her dead of heart failure in one of the dank, dreary rooms: absurdly enough, Juliette has collapsed while searching for a five-franc coin that rolled under a dresser. The knack Gallant has for turning what should be significant and important events—death, for example—into ludicrously small change is shown to full advantage in this story. So is her insistence on demystifying or diminishing romantic expectation. We learn that by the time Magdalena consents to divorce Edouard, Juliette is past child-bearing age: the marriage that finally takes place between Edouard and Juliette seems itself a delayed form of heart failure.

On Juliette's death Edouard (not a writer but an interviewer on radio and TV 'culture' shows) makes the following assessment of his life's partner: 'She was faithful, if "faithful" means avoiding the acknowledged forms of trouble. She was patient. I know she was good. Any devoted male friend, any lover, any husband would have shown up beside her as selfish, irritable, even cruel' (OB 162). The implication is that Juliette was one of those paragons who drive men to vice; that her very virtue absolves Edouard of any selfishness and deceit in his relations with her. Yet so detached is Edouard from Juliette's life and death that what should be a lament becomes no more than a final observation: 'We were together for a duration of time I daren't measure against the expanse of Juliette's life; it would give me the feeling that I had decamped to a height of land, a survivor's eminence, so as to survey the point at which our lives crossed and mingled and began to move in the same direction: a long, narrow reach of time in the Rue de Lille' (OB 163). That historically resonant term 'survivor' seems curiously out of place applied to Edouard's and Juliette's domestic affairs, particularly as the story ends with his memory of her knitting blankets for victims of floods, earthquakes, and political upheaval. 'Those who outlasted jeopardy', he explains, 'had to be covered' (OB 165).

In 'Rue de Lille' Edouard reveals himself in all his imperturbable coldness and callousness—he is, perhaps, the closest equivalent to a Yourcenar character in all Gallant's writing. In 'The Colonel's Child' (October 1983) he provides us with a background to his relationship with Juliette that makes his role in 'Rue de Lille' even more repellent. Edouard, having salved his conscience by taking the invulnerable Magdalena to safety in the south of France, flees to London to join the Free French. A would-be writer with heroic aspirations of making himself indispensable to De Gaulle, he receives multiple fractures on his first training session and concludes, 'I was a cerebral type, who needed the peace of an office job, with no equipment to smash—not even a typewriter' (OB 167). When he recovers, his scars make him look 'amazingly the image of an old soldier' (OB 169); this may be why he attracts the seventeen-year-old, 'virginal, untouched' Juliette, a *fine fleur* of the French Protestant upper class (OB 169). Her father, Edouard learns, is on a secret mission in France; her mother is pursuing an affair in England. Juliette literally offers herself up to Edouard just after learning of her father's arrest and certain death.

It would be the stuff of a TV mini-series, if not for Gallant's flaying of expectation, her pre-empting and distorting of cliché and convention. Instead of a passionate declaration of love, we have Edouard avowing his reluctance to destroy an item 'of French property . . . a colonel's child' (OB 170). 'When for all her shyness she asked if I loved her, I said I would never leave her, and I am sure we both thought it meant the same thing' (OB 172). Juliette forsees Magdalena's gratitude to Edouard for having saved her life: Edouard sees Magdalena gratefully dispensing blessings on the young lovers and granting him a divorce so that he can marry Juliette and give her the five to ten children she requests.[19] As 'Rue de Lille' has made abundantly clear, however, Magdalena will feel no warm glow of gratitude toward Edouard or sympathy for Juliette. She will not, we later learn, grant Edouard a divorce until Juliette is past childbearing age. Life does not imitate kitsch, Gallant shows us; life is a perpetual corrective to desire.

With 'The Colonel's Child' Gallant moves us into a world of tangled, peculiar, personal relations created by a distant war that the elderly narrator well knows will sound more like fantasy than life to his hypothetical listeners. Edouard keeps warning that the past is unimaginable and unconvincing to anyone who has not lived through it—'You have to remember the period, and France occupied, to imagine how one could think and behave. We always say this—'Think of the times we had to live in'—when the past is dragged forward, all the life gone out of it, and left unbreathing at our feet' (OB 167). Yet that same dead past puts a decisive pressure on the present and affects the future in ever more confusing ways. The past, of course, is personified in Magdalena herself. She may seem, with her scarlet fingernails and pug dogs, like a creature out of a forties film, but she never surrenders her star role, larger than life and twice as unfathomable.

In the final story, 'Lena', Edouard and Magdalena are, *mutatis mutandis*, back as they once were before Juliette's intervention in their lives. For all Magdalena's flirtations with neo-Thomism, the world these elderly 'survivors' share is without any metaphysical resonance whatsoever (of Juliette's death we are told, 'From the moment when her heart stopped, there has been nothing but silence' [OB 184]). To Edouard it is thus a world without future or even a credible past: as he confesses, 'Anything to do with the Second World War, particularly its elderly survivors, arouses derision and ribaldry and even hostility in the young' (OB 177). The world has assimilated, trivialized, or forgotten wartime atrocities: Juliette is able to say, with placid faith, 'God knows what he wants'. Edouard's reply—'God wanted Auschwitz?'—is not really a question, but an admission of stalemate (OB 169-70), as is Magdalena's response to his words: a slight pressure on his arm. This allusion to Auschwitz has the same metallic ring—small change, again—as the assiduously observant Edouard's detecting, at Juliette's cremation, the clank of machinery covering the clergyman's voice, or his hearing, during a visit with the bedridden Magdalena, 'the afternoon movie on television in the next room. I recognized the voice of the actor who dubs Robert Redford' (OB 186).

It is thanks to Edouard that Magdalena has a place in a hospital: having once made a grand gesture to save her life, he now goes to no small trouble and expense to ease her inconveniently slow dying. Yet Magdalena, who has triumphantly outlasted Juliette, may well survive Edouard. She gives him, as always, no end of trouble. Edouard explains that elderly inmates of the hospital 'must not seem too capricious, or dissatisfied, or quarrelsome, or give the nurses extra trouble. If they persist in doing so, their belongings are packed and their relatives are sent for. A law obliges close relatives to take them in' (OB 177). For this reason he is at pains to placate Magdalena, visiting her on her birthdays with champagne and reminiscences.

Memory for Magdalena 'is like a brief, blurry, self-centred dream' (OB 178). Under the pressure of his own memories of an increasingly phantom past, Edouard flashes back to Magdalena at the moment when she finally agreed to meet with him and Juliette, ostensibly to discuss divorce, Magdalena 'in a nimbus of some scent—jasmine, or gardenia—that made me think of the opulent, profiteering side of wars' (OB 180). She sailed through the Occupation by refusing to alter her persona an iota, and by 'holding [her] breath' (OB 178), waiting for someone to call her bluff. Just so, she has sailed through any assaults on conscience, any appeals to heart or mind made by the child-hungry Juliette or guilty Edouard. At the death of her rival, Magdalena is consumed with joy:

She at once resumed her place as my only spouse and widow-to-be. . . . The divorce, that wall of pagan darkness, had been torn down and dispersed with the concubine's ashes. She saw me delivered from an adulterous and heretical alliance. It takes a convert to think 'heretical' with a straight face. She could have seen Juliette burned at the stake without losing any sleep. It is another fact about converts that they make casual executioners. (OB 184)

So much for female solidarity, or for Christian virtues of charity and forgiveness. The 'blue, enduring look of pure love' (OB 187) that Magdalena bestows on Edouard is no more than that possessor of unsuspected reserves of coldness and small cruelties deserves, a bewildering benediction from his 'poor, mad, true and only wife' (OB 187) who will no doubt survive him as she has every other danger in her past.

*

The Lena stories are as elegant, comic, and disconcerting as anything to be found in Gallant's work; they would be icily constrictive without the dazzling cipher of Magdalena, a character neither admirable nor despicable, entirely false nor altogether real. The ultimate effect she has on the historical ground to which she is, however bafflingly, tethered, is to obscure and confound it: the extermination of the Jews of France becomes a yellow star found casually on a pavement, 'moved . . . like a wet leaf' with the point of Magdalena's umbrella (OB 155). One can trace the permutations of historical ground throughout Gallant's work: the wartime Europe that the 'politically naive' Gallant imagined in Montreal, the shambles she actually encountered after the war, the tawdry Riviera remnants of a pre-war world, and the slick and seamless surface of Europe's New Age. Do the Lena stories show Gallant to have reached post-historical ground in her fiction, one in which the landmarks and shibboleths that preoccupied her earlier fiction have vanished, leaving only the obscurest, most casual of traces? Or is she merely documenting the transformation of present into past tense, history into the tricks and deceptions of personal memory? One can best approach this question by looking at one of Gallant's latest fictions, 'Kingdom Come' (September 1986).

The almost elegiac tone and mood of 'Kingdom Come' make the piece more symbolic than satiric: it recounts the utter failure of the aged professor Missierna, whose life work has been the study of the language native to a remote 'archipelago of naked islands' named 'The Republic of Saltnatek' (NY 32). 'For twenty-four years the eyes of Saltnatek had appraised him, and had then turned away. He had become to himself large and awkward—a parent without authority, dispossessed, left to stumble around in an airport, as if he were sick or drunk' (NY 34). Not only do the subjects of his linguistic studies reject him, but so do his own children—mention is made of the introduction of a new law whereby children will be asked to acknowledge their parents, and not vice versa. As Missierna observes, 'the new insecurity, the terror of being cast off, was already causing adults to adopt the extreme conservatism that is usually characteristic of the very young' (NY 34). The protagonist of 'Kingdom Come' is, like Edouard in the Lena stories, the aged and declining representative of a past that the young reject or, even worse, simply ignore.

Missierna comes to terms with this reversal of rights and roles, setting himself the task of bearing dispassionate witness to a number of endings:

> He could watch Europe as it declined and sank, with its pettiness and faded cruelty, its crabbed richness and sentimentality. Something might be discovered out of shabbiness—some measure taken of the past and present, now that they were ground and trampled to the same shape and size. But what if he had lost his mixture of duty and curiosity, his professional humility, his ruthlessness? In that case, he could start but he would never finish. (NY 34)

Missierna's project may well be Gallant's own—her readers, however, can be confident that her curiosity and ruthlessness will stand her in good stead as she takes the measure of a past and present 'trampled to the same shape and size'. Her fiction has always been distinguished by a concern to translate History into lived experience, a task she accomplishes in the Lena stories, but with a difference. For here, more clearly than anywhere else in her work, we see this writer's concern to provide a history of History itself, to show us how 'nothing lasts', that the most harrowing public events inevitably turn into personal memories, devalued, ignored, or misinterpreted by succeeding generations caught up in their own creation of the present. Like the angel of history, the writer is caught between the roles of observer and maker, between the desire to bear witness and somehow restore reality to what has been smashed, and the need to rush onward, creating new fictions to observe and take the measure of the storm of time itself. That storm, as Gallant's texts disclose, is the only thing of any permanence reader and writer may know.

Notes

[1] Walter Benjamin, *Illuminations*, ed. Hannah Arendt, trans. Harry Zohn (1970; rpt London: Fontana, 1973), pp. 259-60.

[2] Joseph Conrad, Preface to *The Nigger of the 'Narcissus'*, in *Conrad's Prefaces to His Works* (London: Dent, 1937), p. 51; Henry James, *The Art of the Novel: Critical Prefaces* (New York: Scribner's, 1962), p. 5.

[3] In an interview with Stuart McLean, Gallant speaks again of the shock of seeing the first concentration-camp photos and confirms that, despite her 'success' with *The Pegnitz Junction*, she still doesn't know the why of the camps. It is still a 'mystery', she confesses, a terrifying human possibility that can happen anywhere.

[4] Jane Kramer, 'Letter from Europe', *New Yorker* 12 Oct. 1987, p. 131.

[5] William Pritchard, in his review of *The Pegnitz Junction*, comments that Gallant's narrative evasions prevent her from saying or caring very much about her characters and their situations: 'This is the Palace of Art, and Mavis Gallant is perilously close to residing there . . .' (*New York Times Book Review* 24 June 1973, p. 4). John Hofsess has accused Gallant, along with other 'literary aesthetes', of the 'common laziness' of 'making so little effort to write without shields of irony and masks' ('Citations for Gallantry', *Books in Canada* 7 [Nov. 1978], p. 21).

[6] One critic who has acknowledged and explored Gallant's engagement with history is Ronald Hatch. In his essay 'The Three Stages of Mavis Gallant's Short Fiction' (*Canadian Fiction Magazine* 28 [*Special Issue on Mavis Gallant*, 1978], pp. 92-114), Hatch argues that Gallant moves from a delineation of romantic liberalism as manifested by her various 'exiled' characters in the fiction of the 1950s and '60s, to a description of an entire nation's enervation by and insulation from the history it refuses to acknowledge, in *The Pegnitz Junction*. In the Linnet Muir stories of *Home Truths*, Hatch argues, Gallant achieves a final synthesizing awareness of how individuals inescapably form part of history and are implicated in the common public world which is that history's home ground.

[7] Ibid., p. 99.

[8] George Woodcock, 'Memory, Imagination, Artifice', *Canadian Fiction* 28, p. 75.

[9] Hatch, 'Three Stages', p. 99.

[10] Graziana Merler, *Mavis Gallant: Narrative Patterns and Devices* (Ottawa: Tecumseh Press, 1978), p. 2.

[11] Hatch, 'Three Stages', pp. 110, 102-3.

[12] Gallant chose to go to Spain soon after her arrival in Europe, not only because Madrid was a notoriously cheap place to live, but also because of the whole 'myth' of Spain that she had imbibed via the Spanish Civil War (iJKK).

[13] *Survival in Auschwitz: the Nazi Assault on Humanity* (1961; rpt Collier: New York,1987). Subsequent quotations will be taken from this edition and incorporated in the text under the abbreviation SA.

[14] Woodcock, 'Memory, Imagination, Artifice', p. 101.

[15] William Pritchard, review of *The Pegnitz Junction*, *New York Times Book Review* 4 June 1973, p. 4.

[16] As Jane Kramer points out, 'revisionism' (a term first applied to *Dreyfusards* like Emile Zola, who wanted to 'revise' the accepted opinion that Captain Dreyfus was a German spy and a traitor to France) has now 'been appropriated by French neo-Nazis who maintain that the Holocaust never happened, that there were no camps or crematoriums, that six million dead Jews were a Jewish invention intended to weaken Europe with guilt and doubt'. The 'respectable' German revisionists, Kramer goes on to say, 'contest not the facts of Nazism but the common understanding of Nazism as something morally and historically unique, something that sets Germany apart and gives it special burdens of responsibility' ('Letter', pp. 135-6). Still other 'revisionists' maintain that the Holocaust was no more than a '"relative" unpleasantness in an unpleasant world' (p. 134).

[17] Milan Kundera, 'The Tragedy of Central Europe', *New York Review of Books* 26 April 1984, p. 36.

[18] Anne Tyler, review of *From the Fifteenth District*, *New York Times Book Review* 16 Sept. 1979, p. 13.

[19] When Juliette, an only child, confesses her one overriding desire—to have lots of children—Edouard's response is '"I hate children".... I was amazed that I could say something so definite and so cruel, and that sounded so true. When had I stopped liking them? Perhaps when I adopted the colonel's child, believing she would never grow up' (OB 172). Though he professes amazement at this unpremeditated cruelty, it is not surprising that Edouard has never confessed to Juliette the fact of his marriage to Magdalena—the fact that will make this very correct child of the French Protestant upper class renounce having children, though she blindly puts herself and her future into the hands of 'a man with no

money, no prospects, and no connections. Who wasn't entirely single. Who might be put on a charge for making a false declaration. Who had a broken nose and a permanent limp. Who, so far, had never finished anything he'd started' (OB 174). Juliette, it is clear, is a peculiar sort of *amoureuse*. As for Edouard, all he gives up in taking on Juliette is his novel, which he tears up 'because [he] can't wrench life around to make it fit some fantasy. Because [he doesn't] know how to make life sound worse or better, or how to make it sound true' (OB 174).

Chapter 7

Social Narratives

> Philippe had written a series of three articles on infantile drunkenness in Normandy called 'The Children of Calvados: A Silent Cry', the first of which began, 'It was a silent cry torn from the heart, rending the heavens, searing the universe, and ignored by the middle classes', before going on to say what took place when a baby's formula was half applejack, half watered milk. (AFGT 13-14)

So excellent and so abundant has Mavis Gallant's production of fiction been that one tends to dismiss the six years she spent working for the *Montreal Standard* (from 1944 to 1950) as a no doubt useful but not particularly interesting period in her development as a writer. One expects, from her parody of breast-beating exposé journalism in *A Fairly Good Time*, that the hundred-odd pieces published under her byline in the *Standard* were effectively written, but one's real curiosity is reserved for that famous Edwardian picnic hamper stuffed with juvenilia: poems, stories, plays—the fuel, perhaps, for 'ferocious autos da fé' similar to those lit by Linnet Muir at the end of 'Varieties of Exile' (HT 280). Yet as the publication of *Paris Notebooks* makes clear, Gallant is as fine a writer of non-fiction and what I shall refer to as 'social narrative' as she is of novels and short stories. The sheer length of time she has devoted to her research for a book on the Dreyfus affair—some thirteen years[1]—attests to the interest and importance she accords to a mode of writing that permits the primacy of authorial presence in her texts, giving her the freedom to directly comment, judge, attack, or empathize in her own write, as it were.

This narrative mode, which figures so brilliantly in *Paris Notebooks*, bears a direct relation to the most ambitious and innovative of the pieces that Gallant produced for the *Montreal Standard*. Accordingly, I would like in this last chapter to examine certain salient aspects of Gallant's journalism for the *Standard*, to look in detail at three major essays in *Paris Notebooks*, and to end with a consideration, brief and speculative though it must be, on the Dreyfus book-in-progress. An understanding of the objectives and techniques of these works of non-fiction will provide a more complex and comprehensive portrait of the writer than could be drawn from a study of her fiction alone.

*

Although Gallant soon decided she wanted to earn her living writing fiction, not journalism, she left Canada without slamming the door on the possibility of picking up some sort of newspaper work in Montreal again, should she fail as a writer in Europe. Of her journalist days she remarks, 'I liked the life'—the freedom of travelling alone to strange places and interviewing people she otherwise would never have met (iJKK). She says she left journalism because she saw she was beginning to repeat herself in her writing (iGH 67). The range of Gallant's articles, however, is quite extraordinary; judging from the different beats she covered, and the free hand she was given in approaching her subjects, journalism allowed a woman a life infinitely more open and independent than almost any other to be had at that time.

Gallant's bilingualism gave her the obvious advantage of being able to write incisively and intelligently about aspects of French-Canadian life that her unilingual colleagues on the *Standard* would have been unable to explore. Hers was definitely not a *Two Solitudes* approach to Quebec; she switched from one language and culture to another with an ease and flexibility that can be described as natural, since she learned to feel equally at home in French and English at a very early age. Moreover, Gallant's interests as a journalist were marvellously heterodox. She writes with equal interest about a master jeweller in Montreal, nurses in the Yukon, family allowances, and crimes of passion. A long, detailed analysis of the economic realities of Canada's shipbuilding industry is followed by a piece on the war brides' first impressions of Canada; a hard-hitting attack on the intrinsic dullness of Canadians is followed by an examination of the terroristic devices of fairy tales. She reports on the literary and marital partnership of Hugh MacLennan and Dorothy Duncan, and writes with evident fascination about 'Colette' (Edouardina Lesage), the remarkable woman who was 'French Canada's Dorothy Dix'. Child-rearing, gender differences, infertility, psychoanalysis, Canada's lamentable immigration policy, reviews of radio programs, the price of books and the state of libraries, the incomparable Sarah Binks, the scandalous condition of nursing homes, the plight of displaced persons in Canada, the nature and role of dreams, the manufacture of corsets, the adolescence of the Dionne quintuplets—Gallant tackles them all, sometimes in a few paragraphs designed to accompany a spread of photographs, sometimes in authoritative and impassioned feature articles. Thirteen years after quitting journalism and leaving for Europe, Mavis Gallant was still remembered in Montreal for the excellence and liveliness of her newspaper work in the forties.[2]

One of her coups was a photographic essay on Gabrielle Roy's *Bonheur d'occasion*: it was Gallant's idea to have actors stage scenes from the novel using the same Montreal locales that Roy incorporated into her novel. But perhaps her most striking pieces are accounts of the problems faced by refugees in struggling against all possible odds to make themselves some sort of life in Canada after the war. In her feature articles for the *Standard* Gallant displays the same authority, analytical skills, and stylistic aplomb that characterize her fiction: moreover, there is the same clear-eyed but compassionate understanding in these early articles that we find in her most accomplished social narratives—those dealing with the events of May 1968 or with the Gabrielle Russier affair. Gallant seems always to have had a penchant for looking at things from the perspective of the put-upon and disadvantaged, combining a keen interest in social justice with an ironic eye for social hypocrisy, as shown by her pieces on the 'importation' of Polish refugees to work for minimal wages in Quebec textile mills, and on a Nova Scotia baby-selling racket that made its profits from the shame and fear of unwed mothers.

Gallant's first piece for the *Standard* was a short article to accompany photographs showing a day in the life of a street-wise Montreal child named Johnny. In 'With a Capital T' Gallant has written of the pressures and handicaps under which a journalist works: having to compress a complex body of information into the smallest space and clearest possible language. Describing Johnny she manages to be succinct yet evocative: 'He never cries unless badly hurt, and then it is a brief, watery flurry, lasting until he gets a chance to hit someone else'. Her awareness of the *modus vivendi* forced on city childen is neither sentimental not censorious: 'City children', she states, 'are adaptable and resourceful. . . . That their sense of values suffers is to be expected.'[3] A proportionately large number of Gallant's pieces either deal entirely with children or else make perceptive asides upon their relations with adults: 'Report on a Repat', an account of a newly demobilized soldier's adjustment to civilian life, repeatedly draws attention to the fear and suspicion with which a veteran's young daughter responds to the father she scarcely knows. 'Problem Children' highlights the efforts of psychiatrists in developing post-Victorian attitudes to children's 'naughtiness' and aggression. And the forthrightly titled piece 'Your Child Looks at You: He Thinks You Yell Too Much, Have Uneven Discipline and Act Silly at Parties. He's Sensitive and Doesn't Like Sitters' is an inversion of the standard child-rearing procedure by which children are criticized and parents obeyed—an inversion that shows how longstanding a concern this writer has had with 'the prison of childhood'.[4]

As persistent as Gallant's interest in children is her concern for the refugees and DPs transported to North America both before and after the war. 'Are They Canadians?' is a sustained critique of the Canadian government's outstanding lack of any kind of program to teach Eastern European immigrants the rudiments of English or the fundamentals of Canadian citizenship. Pointing out that the United States offered such classes free of charge during its period of heaviest immigration, Gallant argues that, while Canada's lack of a melting pot may be a positive thing, the resulting survival of violent political opinions rooted in old-country prejudices is actively pernicious. But the onus is not entirely upon the immigrant: Canadians themselves should become aware of the situation and status of immigrants in their country. In this article, written in 1946, Gallant reports that four out of five Canadians polled were ignorant of the fact that Canadian citizens of Chinese origin could not vote in federal elections in British Columbia. Her perception of discrimination against Canadians of non-Anglo-Saxon or non-French extraction is acute, as is her understanding of the implications of such discriminatory practice: 'When you force a Canadian of European parentage to look upon other Canadians as "English" or "French" it is natural for him to cling to his own group, to worry about another country, and the conflicts, hates, and prejudices of the old world.'[5] Gallant's ability to put herself in the position of people from backgrounds utterly different from her own is extraordinary: the generosity of her sympathies and the primacy of her sense of justice are perhaps her chief characteristics as an investigative and analytical journalist.

These characteristics are compellingly expressed in both a general and a particular way in two representative articles—one an exposé, the other a 'human-interest story'. 'Traders in Fear' is a declaration of war on the exploitation of vulnerable young women through the proliferation of baby-farm rackets. Gallant describes how, for a period of nearly twenty years, a Seventh Day Adventist minister/chiropractor and his wife, a trained midwife, drew pregnant single women to the 'Ideal Maternity Home' in East Chester, Nova Scotia. After signing away all rights to their unborn children, the women were made to pay 'Dr' and Mrs Young hefty fees for their room and board and additional fees for the delivery of their babies, whom they never saw again. The owners of the home literally sold the children to couples in Canada and the United States, many of whom would have been turned down as unsuitable parents by legal adoption agencies. Gallant not only lambastes this species of human profiteering— the Nova Scotia Minister of Health and Welfare made numerous attempts to close down the home but was fought tooth and nail by the Chester Board of Trade, avid for the $50,000 a year the home spent in the Chester area—but also the double standard whereby women are made to bear the full blame and fear that pregnancy out of wedlock brings. Most unwed mothers, she reveals, are afraid to go to social agencies, which could help them get free medical help and subsidized lodging, because of a widespread belief that such agencies would report on them to their families.

The picture Gallant sketches of social welfare in Canada in 1946 is a grim one indeed. With a characteristic eye for the hypocritical and grotesque she emphasizes that the kind of no-questions-asked adoption agency run by the Youngs was not unusual for Canada, but just more 'blatant' than usual: 'In fact [the Ideal Home] advertised its wares by means of a huge brass baby sitting on a globe. This emblem, perched on one of the Home's pseudo-Norman towers, could be seen from quite a distance in East Chester.'[6] Perhaps the most disturbing aspect of her article is the fact that, as she acerbically points out, though the 'Ideal Maternity Home' was finally closed by court order, 'the peddling of illegitimate children' continued to flourish in Quebec. And again, the Gallantesque irony shows through: 'It would be wrong', she concludes, 'to say the situation isn't getting any better. Every once in a while the authorities catch up with someone, fine them a stiff $12.50 or so, and give them a good scolding.'[7]

In another representative piece, 'I Don't Cry Anymore',[8] Gallant does a follow-up on an article dealing with Polish DPs who chose to leave the less than hospitable Canada to which they had been shipped after the war, by interviewing Mary Golubeva, a thirty-year-old refugee who came to Canada after losing her entire family and serving harsh terms in German forced labour camps during the war. Gallant spares no pains to make her point that if Mary Golubeva succeeded in making a life for herself in Canada, it was at an enormous cost, and without anything more than minimal help from her new country. Gallant condemns the unfair labour practices applied to newly arrived DPs and shows how ludicrous are the results of making professionals and artists pay off their passage to Canada by working as servants for a year in the households of their sponsors. Gallant's admiration for Mary Golubeva, who spent years in poorly paid domestic service in order to scrape together university tuition fees, is matched by her level-headed condemnation of the tragic waste of human possibility that results from Canada's abysmal treatment of immigrants who have lost their families, homes, countries, and languages, and who are not even given the chance to put their skills and talents to the work they have been trained for.

What of Gallant's own situation as a woman in a male-dominated profession; in what way did sexual politics and gender-differentiation affect her reporting? Certainly she was not relegated to a 'Woman's Page' or proto-Lifestyles section; she seems to have been given the freedom to write about anything she felt would make a good story, whether it was home permanents or mercy killing or the Canadian Senate. And while she appears to be as comfortable writing about men as about women, her pieces on the relations between men and women betray a critical awareness of the devious ways in which the double standard operates. Feminists will applaud the tenor of two of Gallant's articles, one on the role of social conditioning in maintaining stereotyped gender differences, the other a demolition of the romantic myth of marriage—and these in a magazine that carried ads advocating the use of Lysol as a douching agent for women anxious to keep their husbands' love.

'Turning On the Waterworks: Why Is It That Women Use Weeping as a Weapon, While Men Would Sooner Be Found Dead Than Crying?' is a wonderfully subversive piece of journalism. Asserting that 'both sexes are born with the same tear glands, the same nervous system',[9] Gallant argues that not only are women taught as children to cry copiously (and to faint as well), they are also responsible for teaching boy children to be tough. She points out that while women often use tears as a weapon against men, and as a means of getting what they want, women are often 'emotionally stronger and can stand more physical pain. In a family crisis men often go to pieces, whereas women stand up to the strain.'[10] Men, she adds, have been known to cry as passionately as do women—over the deaths of pet dogs, however, not over the loss of their wives or mothers. But Gallant is out not only to flay a few strips off the rhinoceros hide of the male ego: she also makes the point that as each new generation of women becomes more independent and less sheltered, the 'feminine tradition' itself will alter, and for the better. Finally, in 'Is Romance Killing Your Marriage?' Gallant sets out to slam the notion that the sum total of female happiness is to be found at the altar. The article begins with a quote from Don Quixote—'Marriage is a noose'—and ends by likening marriage to 'a besieged fortress. Those who were out were clamouring to get in, and those who were in would give anything to get out.'[11]

To conclude this brief account of Gallant's journalism, one last area of interest needs to be examined: her views on the possibility of an artist's leading any interesting or rewarding kind of life in Canada. Her *cri de coeur* of 1946, 'Why are We Canadians So Dull?', deals primarily with Canadians of Anglo-Saxon extraction, those who had a virtual stranglehold on cultural expression and artistic activity. She mocks the cautiousness of these countrymen and women, the principles of conformity and neutrality governing their style of dress and cast of mind. She broaches the subject of the Brain Drain, asserting that our best and brightest flee south not so much for the money, but in order to be able to try out new ideas. Those who stay behind do not exhibit enthusiasm or voice opinions, she laments, but maintain a 'passive refusal to be jolted by crisis and argument'.[12]

Canada, Gallant decrees, is a granite country, cold and vast—this perhaps explains the chilly and non-committal audiences in Canadian theatres and cinemas, and the flight of creative people to countries where their work will meet with a warmer reception. As for our writing, it shows 'how much we cling to the past, a past which is staid, rugged, and above all, solid'. She quotes Robert Weaver's opinion that because Canadian writers eschewed realism as a literary mode, they 'produced literature without vitality, power or perception'. And she makes a personally prophetic observation of her own: 'Infatuated with their own history, our authors have dabbled in the past and turned out very little with any meaning. Canadian writing, until very recently, never hurt anyone's feelings. It didn't help anyone either.'[13] Certainly the kind of fiction Mavis Gallant abandoned journalism to produce was anything but backward-looking and blandly benign.

*

In a piece on Gabrielle Roy, published in the *Standard* in 1946, Gallant draws attention to two features of Roy's life and work. One, that she went off to Europe five years before war broke out and managed to support herself there by writing, is a fact that can be related to Gallant's own decision to leave journalism and Canada for a writer's life abroad. The other point is that *Bonheur d'Occasion* is 'probably the most authentic picture of the working class to come out of Canada'.[14] Her observation that most critics were 'hurt to discover that poverty is not necessarily an ennobling circumstance' alerts us to an aspect of Gallant's writing that informs not only her journalism and the social narratives collected in *Paris Notebooks*, but her fiction as well: she is, as she has previously described herself, 'extremely interested in politics' and declares her own writing to be 'permeated' with politics (iGH 33).

Gallant's political awareness is complex and keenly responsive to historical developments that have occurred over the last few decades. Asked to identify her present politics as being of the left or right, she replied, 'Those words haven't the meaning they had [in the forties]. Don't forget the war was "Fascism or else!" The situation has so changed now that we'd be hours talking about it' (iGH 33). Yet in a recent interview she showed traces of a 'passionately anti-Fascist' (iGH 34) younger self; commenting on certain right-wing governments, for example, she remarked, 'Every so often it comes over me, something happens—by God, I was right. They really are bastards' (iJKK).

It is true that Gallant's fictions no longer deal with those refugees and displaced persons created by World War II. *Overhead in a Balloon* consists of stories detailing the world-view, the precepts and prejudices of a political, social, and cultural élite, however much Gallant's irony puts that last word into quotation marks. The title story of the collection anatomizes the bizarre clannishness and exploitative greed of a family of *Parisiens* who rent out spare rooms in their deluxe apartment, while in the Lena series Gallant has her fun in delineating the snobbery indigenous to Juliette's particular caste—the clannish French Protestant gentry, with their softly clicking consonants. As David O'Rourke has pointed out in an essay on *My Heart is Broken*, Gallant has always been interested in 'problems of the status quo':

> The sterility of an old order, frequently manifested by a pseudo-aristocratic gentility and symbolized by the season of winter, is contrasted with a vitality traditionally assigned to the working-classes and youth. Characters suffer 'revolutions' in which they come close to losing 'control' or lead 'double lives' in order to conform to societal expectations and, at the same time, retain what is essentially human and true.[15]

Stories such as 'Bernadette', 'The Four Seasons', and 'An Unmarried Man's Summer' do not romanticize the servants who emerge as the most worthwhile and likeable characters, but make the point that while the 'upper class' can sail through the most difficult circumstances 'without much more than inconvenience' it is 'the poor, the honest, the conscientious' who bear the brunt of whatever responsibility and suffering circumstances demand (iGH 36). Rather like Henry James in such stories as 'Brooksmith', 'The Real Thing', and 'In the Cage', Gallant excels at the ironic inversion of class-based definitions of 'inferior' and 'superior'. One thinks, for example, of the story 'One Morning in June', in which she allows a particularly silly snob to convict herself out of her own mouth. 'Stay away from the public beach,' this wealthy American lady counsels her niece. 'It is nothing but tents, and diapers, and hairy people in shorts. Wherever possible in France, one prefers private property' (OP 181).

That Gallant's fiction includes within its scope observations of the economically privileged as well as of the deprived does not, it need hardly be said, mean that her politics have swung from ultra left to extreme right, or that she has no political or class identity of her own. She declares herself to have led a 'normal bourgeois life' since settling in Paris (iJKK), and in her introduction to *Home Truths* she mentions with approval the 'old-fashioned, liberal and humanist' idea that artists owe no more to their own countrymen and women than they do to anyone else. Presumably, then, an artist owes no more allegiance to the class and political party she or he happens to be born into, or to embrace in early adulthood, than she does to any other. For Gallant, as *What Is To Be Done?* makes clear, to have been passionately anti-Fascist in the forties meant to have been decisively left-wing. Having left the 'stupid Eisenhower mentality' behind her in North America when she came to Europe in 1950, Gallant suffered an inevitable disillusionment about the war against Fascism and the French resistance movement. By the time she settled permanently in Paris she was looking for a bourgeois rather than a 'marginal' existence (iJKK). If writing involves a certain way of life, then for Gallant bourgeois stability and comfort are more favourable to the production of fiction than the kind of abject poverty and insecurity known by the narrator of 'When We Were Nearly Young'—particularly when the writer has no loyal and hard-working spouse to keep the wolves at bay.

Gallant has revealed that when in the process of re-reading certain of her essays for publication in *Paris Notebooks* she was 'struck with how much to the right everyone had moved. And that shift to the right one finds constantly in life; that's why young people are left, I suppose—because they'll go to the right. People who were kids then are now married with children and are very much more conservative than they were. Hardly anyone has stayed as they were. . . . Even I sound somewhat unrecognizable to myself— so *passionnée* '(iJKK). Gallant's very awareness of the slippages in one's political fixations, of the way in which the conventional course of human life re-aligns one's concerns from the general to the particular, from others to self, or at least, to those others intimately connected with oneself, is an integral part of her interest in people as political beings. She has recalled how she met, recently, two officials from the Canadian embassy who had been students at ENA (the school of National Administration in Paris) in May 1968. 'They were completely scornful of the '68 thing, but then they had been living in the *seizième arrondissement*. They said they used to stroll out and look at this nonsense and then they'd stroll back to the safety of the *seizième* where things weren't on strike—of course they weren't, the *seizième* [never is]. And I said to myself, "How funny", because my whole world was in it, and all of my friends, even in the chic *seizième*, because their children were in it' (iJKK).

Gallant's intense involvement in the events of May 1968, as recorded in *Paris Notebooks*, gives the lie to any contention that because she is an exile and expatriate she must preserve a necessary distance and detachment from the life around her, and from the responses of those who hail from her country of origin. Her ironic appraisal of the way in which two Canadians officials misremembered the past, or at least refused to concede any alternative version of the events of 1968, recalls her indignant response to the 'official' Canadians she encountered in poverty-stricken Madrid after the war. 'Do you know that these people—honest to God—came from small towns [in Ontario] and sat talking about the servants. I was furious, because with the poverty of Spain at that time, you'd be ashamed to have a servant' (iJKK).

Gallant's decision, once she came to Europe, to choose her friends not from the 'deadbeat' or highly salaried North Americans working or holidaying there, but rather from among native Europeans and the refugees in their midst, is all of a piece with the interest in the plight of strangers, refugees, and DPs that characterizes so much of her journalism for the *Standard*. She was attracted to Spain partly because of the mythical status that country had attained through the civil war; once living in Madrid, however, she discovered that what she and fellow leftists had apotheosized as myth was, in fact, the grinding everyday life of real people. 'I had the same shock in Italy,' she adds. 'It was the time of the Vittorio de Sica films. . . . And when you saw the reality it was so much more sad. God knows the films were sad, but the reality was worse, more humdrum. . . . I realized how much one is cheated in art. . . . There's nothing pretty about [reality]. You know, there's pretty-sad and ugly-sad. Art is essentially a cheat . . . being a displacement. I don't mean that Rossellini or de Sica prettied up reality, my God they didn't. But you left the theatre, and when you saw the reality outside . . .' (iJKK).

The reality outside is the stuff of Gallant's long essays in *Paris Notebooks*, a reality she treats from the vantage point of what we might call participatory observation. These social narratives, which appear in the first part of the volume, are 'The Events in May: A Paris Notebook, I and II', 'Immortal Gatito: The Gabrielle Russier Case', and 'Paris: The Taste of a New Age'.[16] In their conception and articulation, their organization and pacing, these narratives are fully as fine as any of her fictions. As with the other texts in *Paris Notebooks*—particularly the longer essays on such literary figures as Léautaud, Yourcenar, and Céline—they are both highly instructive and immensely pleasurable. One receives no impression of haste or high seriousness in Gallant's narration: she lingers when she wishes to tease out the implications of certain phenomena, and she sets up her arguments with the skill of a master builder. Most importantly, she takes her readers with her, so that we share the vantage point from which she makes her ironic assessments and oblique attacks. As we have seen, this is not always the case in Gallant's fiction.

Readers of *Paris Notebooks* will receive the same literary rewards that Gallant's fiction provides: the effortless fluency that forty years of writing for her living have assured, the elegant, epigrammatic style—'All emigration is based on misapprehension; so is every welcome' (PN 157) or, 'Analyzing Giraudoux is like plucking a hummingbird and sorting out the feathers for color and size' (PN 197)—and the wickedly incisive 'signature' detail: 'Some churches in Paris now look like post offices and somehow smell like them' (PN 162). But it is in her social narratives more than anywhere else that Gallant directly reveals the compassionate clarity of her vision, extending sympathetic understanding to the exploited and oppressed without a trace of Chadbandian ooze. Her prose is characterized by the lucidity that comes of disinterestedness, and by the *passe-partout* of imagination, her ability to get inside the skull and skin of other people, whether a brilliant lycée teacher or a Parisian cleaning-woman. What is particularly notable in *Paris Notebooks* is the way Gallant's own beliefs emerge, undeflected by ironic or elliptical constructions. Though she admits, à propos of 'The Events in May', that 'eighteen years after the events, even the "I" of the journals seems like a stranger' (PN 4), the 'I' of the preface can still remark: 'The collective hallucination was that life can change, quite suddenly, and for the better. It still strikes me as a noble desire, and the answer I heard when I asked one woman what she had expected to emerge out of all the disorder (*"Quelque chose de propre "*—something clean, decent), still seems to me poignant' (PN 2-3). Closer analysis of Gallant's social narratives will uncover precisely this kind of conviction.

*

'The Events in May: A Paris Notebook' was, for reasons of length, published in two instalments in *The New Yorker*, and this arbitrary division has been reproduced in *Paris Notebooks* (though Gallant herself is puzzled as to why the publisher chose to do so [iJKK]). She has taken care to state that she was not commissioned by *The New Yorker* to write anything on the student uprising. William Maxwell had telephoned her in the spring of 1968 to ask if she had any fiction to send to the magazine, and she replied that she hadn't: she was preoccupied with noting the happenings in Paris in her journal. Maxwell immediately asked her to send the relevant portions of the journal to *The New Yorker* (iJKK). Hence the unusual form of 'The Events in May', a fluid, unsystematic, entirely compelling record of immediate impressions and emotions. That this text is not an essay but a 'notebook' narrative perfectly suits the character and outcome of these particular events, and this, of course, is why Gallant's work is invaluable. As her journals reveal, it was impossible for anyone actually living in the midst of such occurrences to dispassionately record, analyze, and neatly sum things up. That the printed text of 'The Events in May' did not tidy away the confusion, fear, and excitement felt by all Parisians living outside the safe and chic *seizième*, or whose children were at the barricades, guarantees to Gallant's text an authenticity and validity that later, all-said-and-done accounts can never possess. Her narrative is alive with fluctuations of mood and response that manifest the texture and conditions of life under the disruptive rule of rumour and radical uncertainty. And this is the matchless quality of 'The Events in May': its being a spontaneous, articulate, involved response on the part of a resident, not just an observer of Paris, to extraordinary, unpredictable and uncontrollable events—politics and history on the *qui vive*.

Again and again Gallant returns in her journal to the notions of 'dream' (PN 23), 'collective hallucination' (PN 5), and 'siege psychosis' (PN 49) to distinguish the fictions created by participants and bystanders from the events actually taking place in Paris (fictions ranging from the supposedly impending marriage of the revolutionary student leader, Cohn-Bendit, to an aristocrat, or his being summoned to Peking for 'instruction', to 'ludicrous' allegations of repeated rape in crowded police vans [PN 67]). 'Seems to me,' she writes, 'the reality of the revolution is in people's minds. (That is, the revolution they are imagining—nothing has taken place)' (PN 57). Part of the *cinéma-vérité* effect of her narrative stems from the concrete examples of 'siege psychosis' she is able to produce:

Butcher's dark, gloomy, everyone nervous, curious atmosphere in the sense that everyone seemed to be trying to be nice to the butcher, in case of a shortage, and he, usually so pleasant, was being a little dictator, sneering. Yet there is *no* shortage of meat! They were all acting in an imaginary situation! (PN 40)

Throughout 'The Events in May' Gallant reveals the quickness and completeness with which one becomes 'installed in the abnormal' (PN 29). The resultant dream-state in which events occur or are reported through the media breeds an infectious confusion and uncertainty: did one really witness what one thought one did? Exacerbating the general relativity of impressions is the media manipulation of events, with journalists refusing to report some, and distorting others: it is at this point that Gallant's journalist's training comes to the fore. Listening to an interview with a member of the student's union who claimed there had been six deaths after the *grande manifestation*, she applauds the reporter's response:'I am a newsman and until you give me the names of the dead there are none' (PN 19). It is this insistence on backing up allegations with fact, as well as Gallant's refusal to tidy up or make spuriously objective the presentation of incidents in her journal, that makes 'The Events in May' such a sensitive and accurate record of one of the major political occurrences of the 1960s, that hallucinatory decade which Gallant herself calls 'our tatty era', with its folklore comprised of 'China, Cuba, Godard's films' (PN 22).

Yet for all that the impending revolution is a product of imagination, not accomplished action, Gallant insists upon the reality of crisis that envelops Paris: 'We are quite literally waiting to see if there will be a civil war' (PN 73), she notes, as the entire city appears to go on strike, massive hoarding begins, and the siege mentality descends. The concerns she registers are both public and personal; she remarks on the difficulties doctors will have in getting to their patients, once petrol supplies vanish; on the suspicion with which people treat her when she walks into a pharmacy and asks for a kind of eye drop that will neutralize the effects of tear gas. And, when she is mistaken for an Algerian by a woman anxious to prove her lack of racist feeling, she describes how loathsome it feels to be 'on the receiving end of liberal kindness. The awful sugar' (PN 19).

Gallant's narrative stance throughout her journal entries is a disinterested but not dispassionate one. She refuses to dramatize her situation: she is not, after all, a Frenchwoman whose children and status quo are at risk, but an adoptive *Parisienne* whose city is undergoing extraordinary turmoil, as fascinating to a writer's observant eye as it is distressing to a resident's. Gallant avows that her 'North American upbringing' has made her much less conscious of class divisions than a European upbringing would have done (PN 89); this gives her an enviable mobility as an observer and recorder. And the voluntary nature of her residence in France allows her a critical, independent edge. On the rare occasions when she does feel a foreigner in France, marked out by the difference of her responses to things, she can remark, 'Thank God I am not a refugee; I can pack up and leave whenever I like' (PN 90).

The fact of being a Canadian and not a *Française* gives Gallant a vantage point from which to observe, for example, striking 'mutations' in French national character: from selfishness to generosity, from xenophobia to an openness that finds voluble expression in the students' chant *'On s'en fout des frontières'* (PN 34). She maintains her own integrity in a bewildering and compromising situation by persistently resisting the hysteria of 'siege psychosis', refusing to hoard food, to indulge in either noncommital cageyness or the kind of panic manifested by those *bourgeois* who refuse to trouble themselves with questions of the legitimacy of the students' demands, and the abstract questions of justice that their actions have raised.

Gallant shows herself impassioned enough to actually intervene in certain fraught situations: shouting out to a young man ripping a French flag from its pole, *'Ce n'est pas élégant!'*; performing ambulatory mourning—'stunned, grieved' (PN 44)—over the sheer wreck and ruin of the city, its smashed cars, charred trees, garbage-strewn and rat-infested streets. Yet politically she is disengaged enough to manifest an impartial admiration for courage, whether exhibited by the left or the right: she is profoundly moved by the 'great dignity' that characterizes the tone of the grand march of 13 May (PN 16); she is equally impressed by the action of two right-wingers from *l'Action Française* demonstrating against the flying of red flags at the Sorbonne: 'That is brave of them,' she comments. 'They are only two' (PN 33). Her revulsion is reserved for those who keep to themselves about the events, waiting to see which way the wind blows, thus giving the students the dangerous conviction that everyone is on their side. And, while not sharing her views, Gallant can still voice admiration for a 'tough, outspoken, honest' friend who had the courage and integrity to speak out against the revolution before De Gaulle made it safe to do so (PN 93).

Gallant's journal recognizes the legitimacy of student demands for reform of an educational system that has obviously become mismanaged and decayed—sabotaged, really—by Byzantine bureaucratization. Astutely, she assigns blame to those who merit at least a substantial part of it—the elderly professors suddenly on the side of their students:

> If they thought these reforms were essential, why the hell didn't they do something about it before the kids were driven to using paving stones? Maurice Duverger, professor of political science—gray crewcut on TV, romanticism of barricades. Wanted to say, 'Come off it, *vieux père.*' (PN 13)

Yet if Gallant pits the 'secret hostility and jealousy of the entrenched' against the impatient idealism of the young (PN 38) pointing out the culpability of the students' elders in letting a revolutionary situation develop in the first place, she also underscores the narcissism of the young, the inexperience and historical ignorance on which their courage is founded—an ignorance that leads them, for example, to put up posters of Stalin in the forecourt of the Sorbonne. At one point she talks with a young girl who complains that the German students are being deported: '"We need them here—they are organized, they can tell us what to do. *Oui, nous avons besoin des Allemands"*.' Gallant then remarks on the silence of the girl's mother, who spent the war years in a concentration camp, and observes, 'I feel as if I were watching two screens simultaneously' (PN 15). This dual vision, the ability to see the present from the perspective of the past, and vice versa, is, of course, the distinguishing mark of Gallant's historical sense. The events of May 1968 she perceives through a screen of analogy: to the post-Occupation period and, as the *contestations* lose momentum and 'authority' re-emerges to 'normalize' things, to the collective trauma of Algeria, so that she can say, 'we have somehow come full circle back to 1958' (PN 91). In a more directly critical way she can compare 'screens' to make trenchant observations on a *manifestation* launched by the parents or elders of the striking students:

> When I heard the students last week shouting *'Nous sommes tous des Juifs allemands!'* I thought they were speaking to their parents. Today the parents answer: *'La France aux Français.'* . . . I liked those kids. They were generous and they were very brave. And when they shouted a slogan they were always asking for some sort of justice, usually for someone else. What is generous about *'La police avec nous'*? . . . I think (but don't say) that if the police had fought the Germans as they now fight these children, there might not have been a 1940. (PN 76, 79-80)

Gallant's sympathy for the generosity and idealism of the students in no way blinds her to those realities of class that hopelessly skewed the events in May. Not only does she underline the workers' recognition of the striking students not as liberators but as future *patrons*, she also reveals the 'guarantees' afforded by entrenched class privilege and loyalties to the wild children of the bourgeoisie. Exploding at the idiocy of the students' attitudes towards the workers they presume to lead, she observes that'the police have been beating people up for years, without the romanticism of the barricades. . . . If the Night of the Barricades had taken place in a working-class suburb like Saint-Denis we would have known no more about it' (PN 67). Yet ultimately Gallant judges that the very ignorance of the young, their nourishment on imagination, make them better than their elders. Because 'they have never been frightened. Frightened in theory but not in fact' (PN 34), they are capable of a nobility of vision, a generosity of act, impossible to those who have lived through the War and Occupation. The implications of this observation are profound, suggesting as they do that the wisdom experience brings is, except for rare, isolated cases, a matter of *sauve qui peut* and *'la police avec nous'*; that—as Molly and Jenny illustrate in *What Is To Be Done?*—commitment to justice, liberty, truth is for the cloistered or inexperienced who have nothing to fear because they don't yet know they have everything to lose.

Gallant's own political wisdom stems from her ability to put herself in the minds and, as importantly, the shoes of others. She ultimately condemns the student leader, Cohn-Bendit, for lacking this quality: 'He has the ruthlessness of someone unable to put himself in another's place' (PN 20). Yet she also shows herself infected by the sheer confusion and wish-fulfilment bred by the events: in response to the mindless racism and savage rumours fuelled by Cohn-Bendit's actions, she declares herself 'acutely unhappy over all this and wish[ing] C.-B. would just vanish forever' (PN 66). Gallant shows herself equally *'passionnée'* in her distress over Paris itself, the defacement the city endures at the hands of the *manifestants* and their opponents. Lamenting the destruction of the trees, the spreading chaos—'so many holes in the ground, and so many stray wood, stone and iron *things*. Nothing has a shape or name' (PN 41)—she draws analogies between political confusion, social chaos, and the disruption of the natural world itself. Yet her apprehension of the wreckage and waste is given its proper ironic borders: for example, what she initially interprets as signs of emotional instability—weeping in the Métro—is revealed as an automatic reaction to the pervasive spraying of tear gas; later she records, 'Radio, after news of two deaths, one in Lyon, gives us "Douce France"' (PN 44).

'The Events in May' is a subjective chronicling of chaotic events and disturbances by a writer renowned for her objectivity and detachment: it is the mix of public and personal, impassioned and reflective statement that gives this narrative its characteristic urgency and ultimate staying power. Cheek by jowl with her sardonic observations on the 'sinister' Writers' Union—'Incredible that anyone should want it, with the writers' trials in Russia still fresh in everyone's mind. Whenever a new society seems imminent, everyone wants to be Minister of Culture' (PN 55)—comes the play of Gallant's typically deflationary wit: 'Am told that writer neighbor has lavish interior life, which always sounds to me like stomach lined with Moroccan leatherwork' (PN 59-60). Such mobility of emphasis and mood does not, needless to say, imperil the 'truth value' of this narrative of the events of May 1968, but rather corroborates it. Moreover, the astuteness with which Gallant registers and records permutations in the political climate of Paris during the 'events' is enormously revealing of the way in which open and spontaneous desire for significant change, radical reform, disintegrates towards the end into the sparring of right and left: 'Like grade-school science experiment—the positive and negative poles and the iron filings' (PN 88).

Especially impressive, then, is Gallant's summation of the 'events', a summation that avoids the either/or of polarizations by using the 'simultaneous screens' technique. Thus she records a friend's hostility to the students' *contestation*, and her own, differing view:

> Suzanne B. opposed in every possible way to student movement: the disorder, the violence, the mud stirred up from the very bottom. I tell her that the core of it is *pur*, that they are bewildered at how political parties have taken over, and disgusted that it turned into an interminable wrangle about wages and hours. That they were innocent enough to want a change without realizing what 'change' means or the forms it takes. That this sordid *cuisine* is not what they fought for. Suzanne says bitterly, 'Do you think that those who died in the Resistance died for the life we have had since 1944?' (PN 82)

Gallant's narrative is a *tour de force* in its elucidation of precisely that confusion of motive, that muddle of emotions in which 'street politics' are conceived and carried out. 'What exactly did we want?' she asks herself, as De Gaulle upstages and out-manoeuvres the students and things return to normal in Paris. 'A revolution with nothing broken and no one hurt?' (PN 82) ' Hopeless, impossible to describe what took place. Will be classed as "collective folly", "contagious hysteria". Can already imagine all the books and articles I shall most certainly not read. What they wanted at the beginning, at the Sorbonne, was pure delirium, and all sorts of cynical people are already delighted it could not have happened' (PN 91). As for those caught in the middle, people like Gallant and those of her friends who found themselves hoping for 'something marvellous such as never has taken place', they greet the end of the events with 'relief, bewilderment, disappointment, fatigue. It is like the feeling after a miscarriage—instant thanksgiving that the pain has ceased, plus the feeling of zero because it was all for nothing' (PN 82). Familiar psychic territory-- this is the world as so many of Gallant's characters experience it in her fictions: life, in this peculiar instance, imitates art.

At the end of her narrative Gallant declares that though the laudable desire for sudden, positive changes in people and institutions was betrayed by the political turn events were made to take, what happened in Paris in May 1968 will leave some trace on the mind and spirit, will make the young question and judge their world and its givens (PN 95). Yet in her introduction to *Paris Notebooks* she remarks of May 1968, 'Nothing was left but a confused collective memory, the stuff of kitsch' (PN 3). What is left in the reader's mind after encountering 'The Events in May', however, is something quite different: a lasting account of how extraordinary disturbances in the social and political field look and feel to one caught up in their midst, with no foreknowledge of events, but only the lived experience of and necessary attention to history to guide her responses. As importantly, Gallant's social narrative leaves us with the sense that a desire for justice, abstract and concrete, need not be exhausted, however much it is sabotaged by politics. This is perhaps why one particular image remains in the mind long after one has read 'The Events in May', a paradigmatic image for Gallant's readers. It concerns the way what she sees as an ordinary, post-May gathering of students, who happen to have a red flag, frightens the wife of a shopkeeper so that she is unable to cross the street to where the students are standing:

> What was sad was the matter of vision. Where my mind would have registered something like 'students, intellectuals, readers of *Combat* and *Le Monde*', *her* mind said to her, 'Dangerous, brutal, will hurt you'. . . . Funny thing is that she is a brave little person, with a passionate sense of justice. She says that she dreams about 'the events'—that she is with the Minister of Social Affairs or the Minister of the Interior, and that they go on and on talking about the situation, and that *in her dream* it keeps her from sleeping: 'I wake up as if I hadn't slept at all.' 'Do you tell the Ministers what you think?' 'Oh, no. *Je suis beaucoup trop petite.*' (PN 94)

The matter of vision and the matter of speech. The writer's ability to 'get inside the skin' of the shopkeeper's wife; the writer's responsibility to tell her readers—be they neutral North Americans or 'the Ministers' themselves—what she thinks. The preeminent values of courage and a 'passionate sense of justice': these are the things summoned up by the image of the writer taking the arm of the shopkeeper's wife and walking her across the street into a group of students who, 'of course', take no notice of them.

*

Gallant's 'Immortal Gatito: The Gabrielle Russier Case' is a 'translation' (PN 96), into American idiom, of the impact of a love affair between a lycée teacher and her student, on French society and on the French legal system. As with 'The Events in May', it is not so much a closely reasoned essay as a narration of paradigmatic forms of loss and bewilderment, detailing an intensely complex and problematic situation for which no definitive or conciliatory solution can be found. The reader of 'Immortal Gatito' cannot conveniently assign Gallant to any well-defined 'side', whether that of convention as opposed to romantic freedom, or of youth against age. The very title of this piece indicates the poles that Gallant's observations and explanations will touch: 'Immortal Gatito' recalls the poignancy of Russier's adoring students—who gave her the nickname of 'little cat'—chalking the door of her vacant apartment with 'Z' after her death, while the use of the word 'case' underlines the inescapably public, legal repercussions of this curious love affair. Gallant's article on the Russier affair shows us that the desire for freedom and hope of change expressed by the striking students of 'The Events in May' persist among the very young, and also among those adults who retain a passionate, dangerous commitment to life as it is lived in literature. Yet the old order continues to frustrate such desires and hopes, as Gallant suggests by her scepticism as to whether new laws will actually improve the situation that led to Russier's taking her own life after her release from a particularly harrowing detention in prison.

One further preliminary should be noted: Gallant's choice of epigraph: 'If she had been a hairdresser, or if she had slept with a young apprentice, it would have been different.' This pronouncement by the Deputy Public Prosecutor makes absolutely unavoidable one of the key aspects of the Russier affair, as Gallant understands it: the class basis of social reality thanks to which Russier was both privileged and victimized. 'There is absolutely no doubt', Gallant tells us, 'that if she had been obscure and "humble" she would never have been heard of and there would never have been an editorial about her on the front page of *Le Figaro*' (PN 124). To establish her point, Gallant mentions the virtual silence surrounding the riot of Algerian prisoners in the Santé prison in Paris: 'It was just simply not interesting. . . . Unless a middle-class public can see its own image reflected in someone like Gabrielle Russier, nobody—nobody in the middle-class, that is—cares' (PN 124). As Gallant reveals, it was Russier's perceived *lèse-majesté* in abandoning the conventions and betraying the niceties of middle-class life that made inevitable the prosecution's fatal appeal 'to a higher court' than the one that had let her off with a suspended sentence. The appeal called 'for a stiffer sentence . . . to make certain that the teacher will have a prison record, thus making it impossible for her to earn her living anywhere' (PN 97). It was after learning of this appeal that Russier took her own life.

Gallant's communicative strategy at the beginning of her narrative is to translate certain public forms of the French mindset into North American terms. But as 'Immortal Gatito' quickly establishes, 'this is not an American tragedy. It needs its own context, which is custom-bound, authoritarian, with laws established under Napoleon and a Mediterranean tradition of paterfamilias; it needs a sheltered academic atmosphere where literature is taught as a way of life, almost as a substitute for experience' (PN 98). That context she authoritatively and deftly supplies in the course of making her report on the salient events (which also belong to the watershed year, 1968) following Russier's involvement with her student, Christian Rossi.

Gallant's narrative interests itself only briefly in the love story, the teacher-student romance that occupied so little space in the whole affair. Its main focus is the self-deception governing Russier's actions, the catastrophic ineptitude with which Christian's parents handled his involvement with Gabrielle, and, finally, the legal and social repercussions of the 'affair' once it left the realm of private and personal relations. She charts the collision course between Russier's interpretation of events and vision of possibilities, and those of her society: she counts the ways in which immersion in literature can derange our sense of reality, leading us to look for self-images in other people's stories (PN 124). She also establishes the role that gender, as well as class, played in damning Gabrielle Russier, and here we find echoes of the journalist who reported on how women are invariably the victims in those crimes of passion society treats so lightly.[17]

Gallant is equally unsparing when she reveals how brutally authoritarian parental relations with children can be in France, both in describing Christian's suffering at his parents' hands and in suggesting how terrorized Russier's own children must have been by their mother's repressive methods of child-rearing. Much of the narrative is given over to the appalling treatment of Christian—how his parents were able to force him to undergo the notoriously painful and dubiously effective 'sleep cure', and to incarcerate him in a private psychiatric clinic—actions that are perfectly acceptable in France: 'The guardian of a minor has not only the law but the full weight of public opinion behind him' (PN 117). Not surprisingly, Christian's treatment at his parents' hands led him to total repudiation of his family, a voluntary self-orphaning, after Russier's death. Gallant does not inform us of the fate of Russier's own children, the nine-year-old twins virtually locked into separate rooms by their mother, who would forbid them 'to leave their rooms without permission, or interrupt adults . . . or help themselves to food when they were hungry' (PN 100).

Gallant also moves from a brief consideration of the peculiarities of the French educational system—Russier's uniqueness in inspiring worship from her pupils, her astonishing abilities as a teacher, despite the absolute lack of instruction in pedagogic methods customary for those, like Russier, of the *agrégé* caste[18]— to a consideration of the French system of preventive detention. In France, if you are *presumed* dangerous to society, she explains, you can be held in jail as long as the magistrate deems necessary. If you are innocent, and lose your job because of preventive detention, you have no recourse against the law. If you are middle-class and respectable, you can be set free pending your trial; if you are 'penniless and shabby, [or] of a race considered inferior' (PN 112) then *tant pis*.

Gallant is particularly lucid in demonstrating how different the French legal system is from the American—a difference crucial to understanding the ins and outs of the Russier affair. 'In French law', she remarks,

> there is no such thing as a plea of 'not guilty'. It does not exist. What the prisoner has to prove is that the examining magistrate had no right to indict him—in other words, that the state has no case. He can only protest his innocence, and attempt to prove that he was arrested without reason. . . . For all its failings, French law is more lenient and elastic than Anglo-American law on the question of guilt and intention, precisely because of the subtle but distinct separation of the fact from the circumstances. (PN 130-1)

Thus you can cause the victim's death, but still not be guilty of the crime the state has charged you with if the jury finds evidence of extenuating circumstances.

Gallant's narrative is not just a guided tour through the legal and social labyrinths of contemporary France, nor is it a mere

recording of the facts and explication of the contexts of the Russier affair. One of Gallant's objectives is to unmake our expectations, and to confer upon her readers her own special gift—the
ability to 'get inside' the minds of people who seem utterly different, other, foreign—not only the lovers in the Russier affair, but
also their opponents: Christian's parents, for example. She takes
care to disabuse us of any clichéd preconception of what the
relationship between the thirty-year-old Russier and the sixteen-
year-old Christian entailed:

> She was thirty, but looked eighteen. She was tiny, just over five feet
> tall, and weighed about a hundred pounds. Her hair was cropped
> short, as boys' hair used to be. More than one person shown a pic-
> ture of her after her love affair became public property thought it
> was the boy in the case they were seeing, not the woman. . . . She
> was not pretty; her nose was too long and she had the intellectual
> sheep's profile that for some reason abounds in academic circles.
> (PN 98)

Christian, on the other hand, 'was tall, heavy, "almost stout", and
had longish hair and a beard, which inevitably caused him to be
compared with every bearded figure in history from Christ to
Castro. . . . At fifteen and a half—his age when Gabrielle Russier
met him—he could easily have been mistaken for a man of twenty-four' (PN 102).

Having deftly corrected our original notion of the older woman
and her vulnerable prey, Gallant shows us the less attractive side
of the disinterested and generous Russier:'there is a lack of humor,
an absence of humorous grace, even in love. Could anyone but a
humorless woman have signed letters "Phèdre" and "Antigone",
or compared herself to the nymph Chloë?' (PN 102). And yet
Gallant is able to give us a comprehensive, convincing, and compassionate account of Gabrielle Russier, one that does not explain
her away, absolve her of or condemn her for her self-delusions, but
that recognizes and reinforces the ultimate mystery of human
behaviour. This, the only mystery that, according to Shirley Perrigny in *A Fairly Good Time*, is worth bothering with at all, is the
mystery enveloping the objects, motives, and effects of love.

Gallant ends her consideration of the Russier affair with the
Eluard poem that President Pompidou, 'an *agrégé* in French litera-

ture (as Gabrielle Russier had been)' (PN 139) recited when questioned about Russier during a televised press conference. The poem is about

> a girl whose hair was cut off after the Liberation, probably because she had slept with Germans, and who was punished to divert attention from real collaborators, the truly guilty. The poet—and the President, apparently—felt 'remorse' only for the victim who lay on the pavement 'with the look of a lost child', who resembled 'the dead' who perished 'because they were loved'. (PN 139)

What seems to interest Gallant is not that the poem 'explains' the Russier affair, but rather, that Pompidou's 'turning to literature in order to explain himself' (PN 140) seems peculiarly significant, a mirror of Russier's characteristic mode of behaviour. And the last two paragraphs of Gallant's narrative draw us further into the mystery of human behaviour by contrasting the immediate effects of Gabrielle Russier's death upon the lives of others: the passing of a law supposed (with some scepticism) to make preventive detention the exception rather than the rule, and the poignant tribute of her students, chalking the door of their dead teacher's apartment with '"Z", meaning "She lives", and "Immortal Gatito"' (PN 141).

*

'Paris: The Taste of a New Age' begins with a moral fable in which Gallant evokes two utterly disparate figures connected with that part of Paris near which she makes her home—the stretch between Rue de Sèvres and Rue du Cherche Midi. Both the Christian pessimist Joris Karl Huysmans (who spent much time trying to conjure up the spirits of the dead) and St Vincent de Paul (whose mortal remains, plus a wax face and hands, are cached in a Lazarist chapel of 'gentle ugliness' [PN 161] on the Rue de Sèvres) are in similar danger, Gallant implies: danger of eviction from tangible memory. For the streets with which both men are associated are falling prey to the 'arbitrary projects' of a process of urban change that, she stresses, has nothing to do with urban needs (PN 163). Previously, passers-by might have perceived in the appearance and ambiance of a particular street a trace of the different kinds of life that once animated it; now, however, the pressures of property development have effectively erased such traces. 'In the 1970s, when the value of property in Paris began its heady ascent, the Lazarists sold nearly all that was left of their land [stretching from Rue du Cherche Midi to Rue de Sèvres]. The sale resulted in the construction of an undistinguished apartment block, a supermarket, and a shopping arcade', a 'bleak tunnel of storefronts' that have proved unrentable because unnecessary (PN 163).

The moral of Gallant's opening illustration is clear: much recent alteration of the streetscape of Paris has served 'to drain the street of its vitality rather than to infuse it with new energy' (PN 163). An unexpected phenomenon of 'architectural anemia' is afflicting Paris, and its repercussions, as the rest of this narrative make clear, take their human as well as aesthetic toll. The task of the narrator of 'Paris, the Taste of a New Age' is to give the reader a guided tour of different kinds of damage and, by means of a monologue that is elegant, witty, and distinctly *engagé*, to indelibly impress upon us the absurdity and enormity of the ill-judged transformations of the Parisian scene.

Readers of Gallant's fiction will be familiar with the themes on which 'Paris, the Taste of a New Age' is structured: the unreliability of memory, the relentlessness of time's onward rush—which our fictions can interrupt but not arrest—and the erasure of the past through the delusive suasions of the present. Gallant makes explicit reference to the corruptions induced by memory, or our preference for fiction over reality. And she lays special emphasis on the way in which current development practices in Paris assist the practice of unremembering: 'The nature of a neighborhood has been so fundamentally altered by a single *unnecessary* structure that collective memory is wiped clean' (PN 168). 'The mind's eye is unreliable,' she warns. It lingers 'in Place Saint-Sulpice under enormous chestnut trees cut down years ago when the underground parking space was built' (PN 163). Just so the mind's eye can be comfortable with the *clochards* 'curled up on the sidewalk in an effluvium of urine and spilled wine' (PN 164)—*clochards* are a Parisian institution: moreover, they are indisputably French. What the mind's eye does not accommodate are the 'resident aliens' of Paris, as recent a feature of the city as xenophobia is a time-honoured one.

Gallant's strategy is to shut the mind's eye by opening the more exigent eyes of present observation. Through anecdotes she focuses on the pervasive racism that afflicts French society the way 'architectural anemia' saps the streets of Paris. With the creation of the Common Market and the consequent mobility of the European work force, France has found itself host to large numbers of Spanish and Portuguese workers and their families. 'The blame for the decline of spoken French, particularly in Paris—its slurring and sloppiness, the intrusion into the language of alien words, nearly always given the wrong meanings—is placed on the number of foreign children now in the lower grades' (PN 164), Gallant dispassionately announces. Just as dispassionately, she informs us that the native-born French have a 'debatable' grasp on their own language; that French 'has certainly been affected by a prime minister who did not pronounce his *t*'s and a garrulous Communist party leader unable to utter a *v*' (PN 164). Anecdote after anecdote upholds Gallant's point about the inherent xenophobia of the French and its unavoidable corollary, racism—features of the French psyche that make it quite clear why, as she has pointed out in her fiction, articles, and interviews, the bulk of the French did not suffer overmuch at the Nazi occupation of their country, and why, when the celebrated, viciously anti-Semitic writer Céline 'died peacefully at Meudon 16 years after the end of the war, there were fewer than 200,000 Jews in all of France' (PN 220).

A digression to Gallant's exemplary review essay on Céline may be useful at this point, since it will establish the pertinence of the issues broached in 'New Age'. After acknowledging the superbness of Céline's prose, the greatness and uniqueness of his contribution to French literature, Gallant deals with the question of his present readership:

> Nowadays Céline is read by the young. Occupation arguments bore them. His anti-Semitic writings are suppressed, and only the most diligent and curious readers are likely to pry them out of the Bibliothèque Nationale, an institution not open to everyone. This means that his new wave of admirers do not know exactly what he was charged with or why he and his cronies thought it prudent to flee to Germany when the army and government protecting them pulled out. Young persons are apt to look upon him as a heroic rebel harassed by stuffy authority or 'le système', as if all systems are one. The explanation that he was openly racist at a time when Jews were being murdered on his doorstep will quite often draw a blank. The respectability of French anti-Semitism is its longest

taproot. The educated and intelligent Robert Brasilach wrote, with pride, 'Anti-Semitism is not a German invention, it is a French tradition'. (PN 218)

About Céline's anti-Semitism, Gallant decides, no conclusion can be reached. Only a question can be asked: 'Do we refuse the novels because we disapprove of their author, as Jean-Paul Sartre decided we must, or do we . . . thin[k] that everything Céline wrote should be in print?' 'Rejection', she goes on to observe, 'is always emotional and capricious. Some people will not listen to Wagner because he disliked Jews, but do the same people shut their eyes when they go by a Degas in a museum? Turning away from the novels of Céline is shutting one's eyes in the museum' (PN 219).

Gallant's essay on the taste of contemporary Paris accomplishes two important tasks: it draws our attention to the continuing French tradition of racism, a tradition whose butts, now, are the conspicuously foreign among the working class whatever their race or religion, and it prevents us from shutting our eyes. It is not good enough, she implies, simply to ignore the new Paris, or the nastier forms of French xenophobia. One must register these phenomena and consider their implications. Thus the fact that '*Bonne* ("maid") and *Espagnole* hang together, like *J'suis Français* and *J'suis pas idiot . . .*', that when '[w]omen say "*mon Espagnole*", "*ma Portuguaise*" ; no one asks, "Your Spanish what?"' (PN 166), bespeaks the same disturbing tendency to reification, to treating people as disposable objects rather than as fellow human beings, which is part and parcel of the Fascist response to 'undesirable elements' in any given society. This underlining of Gallant's awareness of the pernicious quality of French racism is neither exaggerated nor idiosyncratic, as recent developments in that country's coming to terms with—or deliberate forgetting of—its past have made clear. For example, in July 1987, during the final days of the Klaus Barbie trial, a government minister publically proposed that unwanted foreigners in France be deported on 'special trains'. The resurgence of the extreme right, the attention paid to Jean-Marie Le Pen, who has staged political rallies at which portraits of Maréchal Pétain have been prominently displayed, suggest the daunting ease with which 'collective memory' can be erased or written-over.

As one would expect, Gallant presents the plight of Spanish and Portuguese immigrants in Paris sympathetically. Not for their children the permissive and indulgent childrearing fashionable among the middle and upper classes. Such consolations as thumbsucking or the clutching of security blankets, she reveals, 'are absolutely forbidden to immigrant children, who get soundly whacked for putting their thumbs in their mouths'. Yet Gallant is quick to point out that the immigrant mothers who strike their children are suffering from psychological as well as physical displacement: these women 'are tired and bewildered, lonely and lost' (PN 169)—conditions that also 'hang together' with the words 'Espagnole' and 'Portuguaise'.

In the last part of 'New Age' Gallant addresses what the physical removal of the past means for its inheritors, the young who will know Paris only in its present anaemic guise. She protests against the 'pricing' of the authentic parts of the city beyond the means of the majority of its citizens. 'Art means culture, culture means the past, the past means our cultural patrimony, which is bound to include some of the stuff in the attic. For an intangible something it comes pretty high' (PN 169). With the sharpest, most incisive of lines she underscores the hypocrisy, charlatanry, commercialism, and plain bad faith involved in the current transformation of Paris, as 'irreplaceable buildings [are] allowed to crumble for obscure commercial reasons' while 'fake and gimcrack restoration' flourishes (PN 170).

Gallant's prognosis is not a reassuring one: in many ways the Paris of 'New Age' is as brutal to our entrenched romantic expectations as is the post-war, 'other' Paris that Carol Frazier encounters on her first trip abroad. Yet what was scarred and begrimed in 1953 has become a permanent absence—demolished—in 1981. 'Nothing can be done', Gallant wryly laments, 'against a combination of political influence, private corporations, and state-controlled banks' (PN 170). 'The past belongs to those who can afford to turn it into an urban fairy tale. The present is for the dispossessed, eased out of the city to the concrete ring to the treeless suburbs' (PN 172).

The Beaubourg art centre is Paris for these young dispossessed, their 'urban initiation', as Gallant terms it. 'They come out of . . . a world where, for the young, there is absolutely nothing to do, nothing to see, nothing to think about. There are no playgrounds; small children play at setting fires in garbage cans. Tell some of the older ones that here there were trees, houses with breathing space, and watch the look you get: puzzled, then wondering, then doubting, then indifferent' (PN 173). 'Paris: The Taste of a New Age' is, for all the wit and flair with which it is narrated, a lament—for the waste of this 'youth and strength and vivacity' in the concrete suburbs (PN 173); for the loss of historical perspective and continuity, for the lack of shared knowledge. The young, she concludes, will not know what they have been cheated of. Nor will future *Parisiens*, since contemporary novelists and film makers refuse to tackle so challenging a subject, preferring to 'stick to minute bourgeois cheese-parings, the mouse-view' of present-day society (PN 173).

*

Gallant's collection of her most recent fiction, *Overhead in a Balloon*, certainly does not attempt to deal with French society's stupid waste of 'youth and strength and vivacity'. Perhaps it is a subject that only a native of France, or someone who has spent her or his whole life in Paris and has children growing up there now, could adequately tackle. What Gallant has directed her efforts to is a breathtakingly extensive and formidably detailed view of a society that has completely vanished—the Paris of the Dreyfus era. 'The Dreyfus story is so dense, so dramatic, that while I was investigating it, contemporary French life seemed pale by comparison' (iGH 66). Yet she is quick to point out that she began her research not out of any personal compulsion, but at the request of her publisher, having previously turned down demands to write on Dreyfus because she could not spare the time from her fiction (iJKK).

Like her account of the Russier affair, Gallant's book on Dreyfus will be a study of context and of character (principally, that of Dreyfus and the villain of the piece, Esterhazy). 'The first part is a long, long essay which just sets the thing in its time, Paris of that period, and the early life of Dreyfus and Esterhazy, back to back. Their childhoods and their marriage contracts . . . and [back-grounds]. It's all very well to say [Dreyfus] was an Alsatian Jew, but what was an Alsatian, what was a Jew, at that time? Then I take it year by year from 1904 till he comes back from Devil's Island in 1909; every one of those years is a chapter. [The narrative] is what happened, as far as I know, and when I don't know, I say. . . . It's all from books and from what people told me—I was lucky enough to [interview] the children of these people' (iJKK).

The heart of the work, at least so far, would appear to be this introductory essay, in which Gallant records and interprets the minutiae of ordinary life for one segment of late nineteenth-century French society: 'what people ate for breakfast in Paris at the time. . . . The literature, the paintings' (iJKK). Yet she is also concerned to combat the stereotypes about Dreyfus, and to avoid the polarizations that characterize most discussions of the affair. 'He was just a man, he had all sorts of flaws and failings. One hardly dares [to discuss these] because of the stereotype. . . . But he became very sympathetic to me' (iJKK). So sympathetic that for Gallant the boundaries between history and memory, fact and imagination, became curiously and productively fluid: 'I lived it so completely that it was in my dreams' (iJKK). As she relates in the introduction to *Home Truths*, the Linnet Muir stories grew out of her research on Dreyfus: 'I had thought of [this book] sometimes as a river where I was drifting farther and farther from shore. At the same time . . . there began to be restored in some underground river of the mind a lost Montréal' (HT xxii).

As for when Gallant will complete the Dreyfus manuscript, and how many more 'lost cities' and 'underground rivers' it will uncover, one can only wait and see. From her mastery of the social narrative as displayed in *Paris Notebooks* one can anticipate a work that will be well worth the wait: this *recherche du temps perdu* may even prove to be, in its reconstruction of the past through the truth of the imagination and the fiction writer's art of observation, Gallant's finest, most significant and compelling text.

Notes

[1] In her 1978 interview with Geoff Hancock for *Canadian Fiction Magazine*, Gallant remarks: 'I never dreamed, when I began, that I would spend four years doing research alone' (iGH 65). When I interviewed her in Paris in June 1987, she declared that all the groundwork had been completed for the Dreyfus book; that only the writing-up of the chapters remained to be done.

[2] Dusty Vineburg, 'Mavis Gallant's New Novel has Quebec Setting', *Montreal Star* 9 Nov. 1963, p. 12.

[3] 'Meet Johnny: Sturdy and Tow-headed, Johnny Is a City Kid, Wise Beyond His Years', *The Standard* (Montreal) 2 Sept. 1944, p. 12.

[4] 'Report on a Repat: Canadian Army Private Makes an Easy Transition to Civilian Life', *The Standard* (Montreal) 28 July 1945, pp. 2, 4-5; 'Problem

Children: Psychiatry Examines Root of Behavior Difficulties', *The Standard* (Montreal) 25 Oct. 1947, pp. 16-17; 'Your Child Looks at You: He Thinks You Yell Too Much, Have Uneven Discipline and Act Silly at Parties. He's Sensitive and Doesn't Like Sitters', *The Standard Magazine* (Montreal) 18 Dec. 1948, pp. 3-4.

[5]'Are They Canadians?' *The Standard Magazine* (Montreal) 11 Oct. 1947, pp. 6-7.

[6]'Traders in Fear', *The Standard Magazine* (Montreal) 24 Aug. 1946, p. 10.

[7] Ibid., p. 10.

[8]'"I don't cry any more": Mary Golubeva Is One DP Who Is Adjusted To Her New Life. But Among Her 40,000 Fellow Immigrants Are Many Who Are Confused, Maladjusted and Unhappy'. *The Standard Magazine* (Montreal) 22 April 1950, pp. 5, 14, 28.

[9]'Turning On the Waterworks: Why Is It That Women Use Weeping as a Weapon, While Men Would Sooner Be Found Dead Than Crying?' *The Standard Magazine* (Montreal) 25 Jan. 1947, p. 3.

[10]Ibid., p. 8.

[11]'Is Romance Killing Your Marriage? A Phoney Myth About Love Is Responsible For Today's Staggering Divorce Rate', *The Standard* (Montreal) 6 Sept, 1947, p. 22.

[12]'Why Are We Canadians So Dull?' *The Standard Magazine* (Montreal) 30 March 1946, p. 2.

[13]Ibid., p. 3.

[14]'Canadian Story: Gabrielle Roy's First Novel, *Bonheur d'occasion*, Deals With the War and a Working-Class District', *The Standard* (Montreal) 2 March 1946, p. 3.

[15]David O'Rourke, 'Exiles in Time: Gallant's *My Heart is Broken*', *Canadian Literature* 93 (Summer 1982), pp. 106-7.

[16]The first two appeared originally in *The New Yorker*, and the third in *The Atlantic*.

[17]'Love is a Motive for Murder: Crimes of Passion Have Been Making Fantastic News of Late and Most of the Victims Have Been Women', *The Standard Magazine* (Montreal) 29 Oct. 1949, pp. 5-6.

[18]The *agrégés* are those who, after their university studies, and initial examinations, pass the highly competitive state exams that will allow them to take up more lucrative teaching posts in lycées and universities.

Index